Sustainability

Sustainability

SECOND EDITION

A BEDFORD SPOTLIGHT READER

Christian R. Weisser
Penn State Berks

bedford/st.martin's
Macmillan Learning
Boston | New York

For Bedford/St. Martin's
Vice President, Editorial, Macmillan Learning Humanities: Edwin Hill
Senior Program Director for English: Leasa Burton
Program Manager: John E. Sullivan III
Executive Marketing Manager: Joy Fisher Williams
Director of Content Development: Jane Knetzger
Developmental Editor: Lexi DeConti
Content Project Manager: Louis C. Bruno Jr.
Senior Workflow Project Manager: Lisa McDowell
Production Supervisor: Robert Cherry
Media Project Manager: Rand Thomas
Manager of Publishing Services: Andrea Cava
Project Management: Lumina Datamatics, Inc.
Composition: Lumina Datamatics, Inc.
Text Permissions Manager: Kalina Ingham
Text Permissions Researcher: Arthur Johnson/Lumina Datamatics, Inc.
Photo Permissions Editor: Angela Boehler
Photo Researchers: Candice Cheesman and Lenny Behnke/
  Lumina Datamatics, Inc.
Text Design: Castle Design; Janis Owens, Books by Design, Inc.;
  Claire Seng-Niemoeller
Cover Design: William Boardman
Cover Photo: Thomas Goeppert/EyeEM/Getty Images
Printing and Binding: LSC Communications

Manufactured in the United States of America.
1   2   3   4   5   6   23 22 21 20 19 18

For information, write: Bedford/St. Martin's, 75 Arlington Street, Boston,
  MA 02116

ISBN 978-1-319-05661-2

Acknowledgments
*Text acknowledgments and copyrights appear at the back of the book on pages
325–327, which constitute an extension of the copyright page. Art acknowledgments and copyrights appear on the same page as the art selections they
cover.*

The Bedford Spotlight Reader Series is a growing line of single-theme readers, each featuring Bedford's trademark care and quality. The readers in the series collect thoughtfully chosen readings sufficient for an entire writing course—about thirty-five selections—to allow instructors to provide carefully developed, high-quality instruction at an affordable price. Bedford Spotlight Readers are designed to help students make inquiries from multiple perspectives, opening up topics such as borders, food, gender, happiness, humor, money, monsters, and sustainability to critical analysis. An editorial board of a dozen compositionists whose programs focus on specific themes have assisted in the development of the series.

Bedford Spotlight Readers offer plenty of material for a composition course while keeping the price low. Each volume in the series offers multiple perspectives on the topic and its effects on individuals and society. Chapters are built around central questions such as "How Is Sustainability a Political Issue?" and "How Is Sustainability Connected to Local and Urban Environments?" and so offer numerous entry points for inquiry and discussion. High-interest readings, chosen for their suitability in the classroom, represent a mix of genres and disciplines as well as a choice of accessible and challenging selections to allow instructors to tailor their approach. Each chapter thus brings to light related—even surprising—questions and ideas.

A rich editorial apparatus provides a sound pedagogical foundation. A general introduction, chapter introductions, and headnotes provide context. Following each selection, writing prompts provide avenues of inquiry tuned to different levels of engagement, from reading comprehension ("Understanding the Text"), to critical analysis ("Reflection and Response"), to the kind of integrative analysis appropriate to the research paper ("Making Connections"). An appendix, "Sentence Guides for Academic Writers," helps students with the most basic academic scenario: having to understand and respond to the ideas of others. This is a practical module that helps students develop an academic writing voice by giving them sentence guides, or templates, to follow in a variety of rhetorical situations and types of research conversations. A website for the series offers support for teaching, with a sample syllabus, additional readings, video links, and more; visit **macmillanlearning.com/spotlight.**

Preface for Instructors

In many ways, sustainability is the ideal subject for college courses focusing on writing and critical thinking. Its importance is obvious, since sustainability focuses on life itself and humanity's future on planet Earth. Its relevance is clear, because debates and conversations about sustainability surround us every day in media, politics, and other public and private venues. Sustainability is personal, and students are quick to recognize that their lifestyles, consumer habits, food preferences, modes of transportation, careers, and countless other aspects of their lives are shaped by sustainable (or unsustainable) choices. Its complexity is both a challenge and an attribute; grappling with the diverse and sophisticated issues surrounding sustainability can help students develop critical thinking skills in ways that an easy or simple subject (with clear answers) might not allow. And sustainability is comprehensive and inherently interdisciplinary — nearly every social, academic, and professional arena contributes to the sustainability conversation.

Most important, though, sustainability is discursive and rhetorical. College writing courses are fundamentally about analyzing and creating texts, and sustainability is a concept that is shaped and molded through texts of many types. Each text in this book can be seen as a different rhetorical act that seeks to change the ways we consider or define sustainability. These texts all contribute, in some way, to our understandings of sustainability, and they all hope to influence our thoughts and actions. Students will develop their own rhetorical abilities as a result of the reading, writing, and thinking they will do in a course using this book, and those persuasive skills will carry over to other aspects of their personal, professional, and civic lives. In that way, *Sustainability* is more about helping students think and communicate than it is about any particular subject.

This book is informed by my ongoing interest in environments, ecologies, networks, and the ways in which writing shapes and is shaped through discursive systems. One of the things I've learned about systems over the years is that they are healthiest when they are most diverse. A thriving, sustainable system relies upon variety, openness, interaction, and diversity; systems fail when they are closed, isolated, or dominated by any one thing, activity, or approach. When I first started thinking about a textbook about sustainability nearly ten years ago, the principle of diversity was a guiding concept. My goal was to create a book that would contain a diverse and comprehensive range of subjects, genres, opinions, perspectives, and voices on sustainability. Rather than trying to advance any particular position or subject, I wanted to present as much of the conversation about sustainability as possible. I wanted my students (and other readers of this book) to encounter and engage with the diversity that makes sustainability such a promising yet challenging topic.

Of course, the book I originally envisioned would not fit on any bookshelf. It was necessary to choose representative texts about sustainability rather than including everything that's been said and written on the subject. However, I think this book does a pretty good job of capturing the essence of the conversation—I hope you will agree. The collection begins with several landmark historical texts about nature and the environment that have influenced our conceptions of sustainability. Understanding how our contemporary discussions of sustainability are informed by preceding texts is important, and I believe students benefit from the contextual readings in environmental writing that appear early in this book. Most of the readings that follow are current, and they cover a wide range of questions and perspectives. The selections in Chapter 2, in particular, are intended to demonstrate the diversity of opinion on sustainability. It is likely that you will disagree with some of the perspectives in this collection—I certainly do—but it is vital to expose students to the wide-ranging viewpoints surrounding sustainability, allowing them to situate their own beliefs in the process. Similarly, the readings in Chapters 4 and 5 reveal the ways in which sustainability is at once an inherently local issue, requiring local solutions, while at the same time a transnational issue, in that solutions to the big problems of resource use, equity, and humanity's future must be conceived and addressed on a global scale. Collectively, the readings in this book cover a wide range of subjects and viewpoints regarding sustainability.

Sustainability includes literary texts, government reports, journalistic accounts, scholarly and scientific articles, personal narratives, blog entries, web-based texts, and arguments of various sorts; these texts reveal the diversity of genres, styles, and voices in the sustainability conversation. The book also includes images of some iconic people, places, and events influencing our notions of sustainability—I encourage you to discuss the impact of these images with your students. Each chapter is grouped to highlight the interaction and negotiation between voices and perspectives on sustainability, and the introductions, headnotes, and inquiry-based questions are intended to spark productive discussion and critical engagement.

The alternative tables of contents (grouped by discipline and theme) may help you create a syllabus or reading list that engages with the subject in new and unique ways. The disciplinary table of contents reveals the genre, perspective, or viewpoint of each piece and may be useful for instructors who wish to discuss how different disciplines approach a complex topic. A thematic table of contents is also included. In short, this book is designed to provide real opportunities for students to think and write about the complex issues surrounding sustainability, while giving instructors many choices in how they approach those goals.

It is worth noting that this printed book is a static text about a dynamic, constantly evolving subject; the conversation develops every day, while a printed text is rooted in time. Likewise, a print publication like this one is (currently) unable to include the many multimedia texts that increasingly influence the sustainability conversation. For that reason, I encourage you to visit **macmillanlearning.com/spotlight** for materials that will enhance your class and your students' currency and engagement with sustainability, including a variety of links to multimedia, such as videos and websites, that you may find useful. In addition, you'll find syllabi and assignments that you can use as you prepare your own classes on sustainability and writing. I encourage you to send me your recommendations for related material, since the site will be updated with new and important texts about the subject.

As a final note: sustainability is more than just the subject of this book—it is also a guiding principle in the production and distribution of the text itself. I commend Bedford/St. Martin's and Macmillan for their efforts to produce this book in sustainable ways. Please see page xiii for more information on sustainability at Macmillan.

New to the Second Edition

New and Diverse Reading Selections

Because the conversation about sustainability is constantly evolving, this second edition adds many new readings from which you can choose. Approximately half of the readings in this book are new to this edition, and of those readings, the majority were published within just the past few years. Consequently, students reading this textbook will be exposed to the most current debates and issues concerning sustainability. Notable new readings include JR Thorpe's "What Exactly Is Ecofeminism?," Elizabeth Kolbert's "The Sixth Extinction," and Jack Hanna's "What Zoo Critics Don't Understand."

Increased Coverage of Fossil Fuels and Climate Change

Because the relationship between fossil fuels and climate change is such an important, complex, and controversial topic, this edition expands its coverage. Bill McKibben's "A Moral Atmosphere" adds one of the most prominent voices on the topic, which pairs effectively with Al Gore's "Climate of Denial" article. At the same time, the topic of climate change is more fully addressed from a conservative perspective with the inclusion of Manzi and Wehner's "Conservatives and Climate Change" as well as Roger Scruton's "How to Think Seriously about the Planet: A Case for an Environmental Conservativism." Collectively, these new pieces and others in the book provide a more comprehensive look at the debates surrounding fossil fuels and climate change.

Updated Treatment of Crises and Disasters

Five years ago when the first edition of *Sustainability* was being conceived and edited, crises and disasters like Hurricane Katrina, Hurricane Sandy, the BP oil spill, and the Fukushima nuclear disaster were relatively recent. Many of the articles in the first edition that discussed those events were written during or in the immediate aftermath of the crises, and the long-term consequences were still unknown. This edition provides an updated and more current treatment of some of those crises through pieces such as Lindsay Abrams's "Hurricane Katrina's Unheeded Lesson" and Mark Hay's "Five Years after Fukushima." This second edition also provides articles addressing other crises that have come to the forefront since that time, including Alison Singer's "Fracking: The Solution? Or the Problem?," Heather Brady's "Four Key Impacts of the Keystone XL and Dakota Access Pipelines," and Christine Evans-Pughe's "Cleaning Up the Great Pacific Garbage Patch."

Expanded Attention to Technology and Sustainability

Technology is inextricably tied to sustainability, since it is both a cause of and a potential solution to the challenges facing planet Earth. Several new articles in this edition focus specifically on the connection between technology and sustainability, such as Jeff Sutton's "Why Social Media and Sustainability Should Go Hand in Hand" and Kendra Smith's "The Cities of the Future Will Be Efficient, Sustainable, and Smart." Other new articles in this edition reference the growth of computer networks, new recycling technologies, emerging alternative energy sources, and other technological innovations, demonstrating the ways in which technology permeates nearly every aspect of contemporary society.

New Visuals

Our students live in a visual culture, and this second edition provides more visuals to better engage students with the readings. These new visuals include tables, charts, graphs, and photographs—all of which will help students grasp the key concepts in each reading. Furthermore, many of the new articles provide more headings and section breaks to help readers digest complex information. One of the goals of this edition was to present a user-friendly and accessible text for students at various levels of development, and we hope we've accomplished that goal. Updated instructor resources include suggestions for films, YouTube videos, websites, blogs, podcasts, and other forms of multimedia to supplement the course. The instructor resources still include an introductory video entitled "What is Sustainability?" that may be useful in the early weeks of the semester.

Acknowledgments

Many people helped in the creation and development of this book. First, I'd like to acknowledge the students who helped me understand why sustainability and writing are important to them. Numerous students at Penn State Berks offered insights and ideas about the readings, questions, and other materials through courses on sustainability, writing, and rhetoric. I am grateful for the assistance of Penn State students who helped with various stages of research for this book, including my current editorial assistant Rachel Hayes; video editor Erik Lewis; and former editorial assistants Kara Kennedy, Lydia Conrad, and Ashley Offenback. I also continue to benefit from ongoing feedback from the amazing students in my Sustainability and Rhetoric seminar at Middlebury College, who served as the "test pilots" of this book when I taught a winter seminar there in 2014 and who continue to provide feedback to this day.

I deeply appreciate the many generous scholars and colleagues who have contributed to my thinking about sustainability, writing, and rhetoric. My biggest debt is to my friend and ongoing collaborator Sid Dobrin. Our work together through *Natural Discourse: Toward Ecocomposition*, *Ecocomposition: Theoretical and Pedagogical Approaches* and other scholarly projects has had a fundamental influence on my thinking and on this textbook. Equally important, Sid has been a model for how to take the work very seriously without taking yourself too seriously in the process. Also important to me were the conversations about sustainability, writing, rhetoric, discourse, ecocomposition, and ecology I have had with colleagues and friends including Jimmie Killingsworth, Marilyn Cooper, Steve Brown, Derek Owens, Jon Isham, Bill McKibben, Julie Drew, Joe Hardin, Chris Keller, Michelle Ballif, Anis Bawarshi, Bradley Dilger, Mary

Jo Reiff, Raul Sanchez, Gary Olson, Peter Goggin, John Ackerman, Byron Hawk, Peter Vandenberg, Paul Heilker, Holly Ryan, and too many others to mention. In their own ways, each of these people has helped shape the direction and focus of this book.

I would like to acknowledge the staff, faculty, and administrators at Penn State Berks for their support of my research and writing endeavors. I am particularly appreciative of the Research Development Grant I received from Penn State in 2016, which gave me time and resources to get started on the second edition of this book.

I am grateful to all the reviewers who provided thoughtful and detailed feedback during the book's development process: Marilyn M. Cooper, Michigan Tech; Sid Dobrin, University of Florida; Darrel Elmore, Florida International University; Peter N. Goggin, Arizona State University; Brad Monsma, California State University, Channel Islands; Amy Patrick Mossman, Western Illinois University; and Heidi Stevenson, Northern Michigan University.

I owe a massive thank you to the wonderful people I have worked with at Bedford/St. Martin's. First and foremost are associate editors Lexi DeConti and Stephanie Thomas, who patiently guided me through the second edition of this book. I also thank executive editor John Sullivan, who supported me through the first edition of this book and continues to support it in many ways. I thank Leasa Burton and Sophia Snyder for encouraging me to take on this project in the first place, and for their open-mindedness in considering what it could become through various editions and incarnations. I recognize the many other people at Bedford/St. Martin's who contributed to the development, editing, and marketing of this book, including Edwin Hill, Joy Fisher Williams, Louis Bruno, Kalina Ingham, Angela Boehler, and Hilary Newman.

I couldn't write a book like *Sustainability* without the support of my family. They have willingly accompanied me on countless hikes; snowboarding and scuba trips; adventures in rivers, lakes, and oceans; and other outdoor expeditions while I subconsciously considered, planned, and wrote (in my mind) this book. They have also patiently and sometimes quietly tolerated the many hours I spent in front of a computer screen making this book a reality. I do it all for them and couldn't do it without them.

I dedicate this book to my father-in-law Don Kasun. He gave me some excellent advice in the early stages of this book: include as many perspectives and viewpoints as possible and allow people to make up their own minds about the issues. That advice became a guiding principle for the book, and it has resulted in a more comprehensive and inclusive collection. I continue to benefit from Don's advice on this and on so many things in my life, and I am grateful for his influence.

Contribution

A portion of my proceeds from this book will go to Surfrider Founda-tion USA, a grassroots nonprofit environmental organization that works to protect the world's oceans, beaches, and waterways. Surfrider was my first contact with sustainability issues more than three decades ago, and the foundation's efforts still inspire and motivate me to stay involved. Check them out: www.surfrider.org.

Christian R. Weisser

At Macmillan, Sustainability Is More Than an Aspiration — It's Part of Our Mission

At Macmillan, we take great pride in the work we do. We believe that in partnering with authors to publish their great books, we are changing millions of lives for the better through education, stirring the imagination, and providing satisfying reading experiences. We view our role not only as a corporate contributor but also as a global citizen.

Corporate Sustainability as Mission at Macmillan

We strongly believe that creating a sustainable future is necessary not only in our business but also for our world. Sustainability has become part of our everyday discussion and a key factor in our business decisions. It is as important as our company growth, as important as our profitability. Every business will need to address sustainability issues sooner rather than later if they hope to *stay* in business. It's more than "doing well by doing good"; it's the basic allegiance that any global citizen should pledge to society at large.

As Publishers We Have Certain Responsibilities to Society

In 2009 we took a year to conduct a comprehensive investigation of our practices and to determine our carbon footprint. Next, we established employee-led committees to look at all aspects of our business and to make ongoing recommendations on how we can reduce carbon emissions.

The biggest area of environmental impact for a book publisher remains paper consumption. Paper, combined with transportation, printing, and distribution of books accounts for over 80 percent of Macmillan's carbon footprint. Because of this, our initial effort has been dedicated to looking at every possible way we can reduce the carbon emissions resulting from our paper usage while maintaining our books' quality specifications.

Making Great Strides

In 2016, for the third year in a row, Macmillan USA was carbon neutral. This was achieved with a 38 percent reduction in carbon emissions, over our 2009 baseline, combined with the purchase of carbon offsets that subsidized renewable energy projects along with reforestation initiatives, efficient cookstove projects, and landfill gas-to-energy projects.

Macmillan Learning has made impressive progress in significantly reducing the carbon **intensity** (like-for-like) of the paper we purchase directly: we achieved a 70 percent decline in 2017 compared to 2010. Of course, with the declining number of ink-on-paper textbooks that we've produced in recent years, the **absolute** (total consumption) reduction is significantly higher. Additionally, the increasing percentage of digitally printed texts—and the higher efficiency of paper yield—has likewise increased our performance in this area.

Our continuing migration to cloud-based computing—versus data center–based servers—has yielded significant reductions in the carbon emissions associated with this aspect of our business.

Bedford/St. Martin's is as passionately committed to the discipline of English as ever, working hard to provide support and services that make it easier for you to teach your course your way.

Find **community support** at the Bedford/St. Martin's English Community (**community.macmillan.com**), where you can follow our *Bits* blog for new teaching ideas, download titles from our professional resource series, and review projects in the pipeline. Also learn more there about our commitment to becoming a carbon-neutral publisher, as part of Macmillan Learning.

Choose **curriculum solutions** that offer flexible custom options, combining our carefully developed print and digital resources, acclaimed works from Macmillan's trade imprints, and your own course or program materials to provide the exact resources your students need.

Rely on **outstanding service** from your Bedford/St. Martin's sales representative and editorial team. Contact us or visit macmillanlearning.com to learn more about any of the options below.

Choose from Alternative Formats of *Sustainability*

Bedford/St. Martin's offers a range of formats. Choose what works best for you and your students.

- *Popular e-Book formats* For details of our e-Book partners, visit **macmillanlearning.com/ebooks**.

Select Value Packages

Add value to your text by packaging one of the following resources with *Sustainability*.

LaunchPad Solo for Readers and Writers allows students to work on what they need help with the most. At home or in class, students learn at their own pace, with instruction tailored to each student's unique needs. *LaunchPad Solo for Readers and Writers* features:

- **Pre-built units that support a learning arc.** Each easy-to-assign unit comprises a pre-test check, multimedia instruction and assessment, and a post-test that assesses what students have learned about critical reading, writing process, using sources, grammar, style, and mechanics. Dedicated units also offer help for multilingual writers.

- **Diagnostics that help establish a baseline for instruction.** Assign diagnostics to identify areas of strength and for improvement and to help students plan a course of study. Use visual reports to track performance by topic, class, and student as well as improvement over time.

- **A video introduction to many topics.** Introductions offer an overview of the unit's topic, and many include a brief, accessible video to illustrate the concepts at hand.

- **Twenty-five reading selections with comprehension quizzes.** Assign a range of classic and contemporary essays each of which includes a label indicating Lexile level to help you scaffold instruction in critical reading.

- **Adaptive quizzing for targeted learning.** Most units include LearningCurve, game-like adaptive quizzing that focuses on the areas in which each student needs the most help.

Order ISBN 978-1-319-05661-2 to package *LaunchPad Solo for Readers and Writers* with *Sustainability* at a significant discount. Students who rent or buy a used book can purchase access and instructors may request free access at **macmillanlearning.com/readwrite**.

Instructor Resources

You have a lot to do in your course. We want to make it easy for you to find the support you need—and to get it quickly.

Visit the instructor resources tab for *Sustainability* at **macmillanlearning .com**. In addition to sample syllabi, you will find suggestions for films, YouTube videos, websites, blogs, podcasts, and other forms of multimedia to supplement your course.

Contents

Introduction for Students   1

Chapter 1   What Are the Foundations of Sustainability?   19

Chapter 3   How Do Crises and Disasters Create Challenges for Sustainability?   121

Chapter 4   How Is Sustainability Connected to Local and Urban Environments?   163

Chapter 5 How Is Sustainability a Transnational Issue? 225

Contents by Discipline

Culture and Society

Economics

History

Journalism

Literature

Philosophy and Ethics

Politics and Policy

Science

Contents by Theme

Active Lifestyle

Activism

Agriculture and Food

Animals

Conservation

Culture

Destruction and Disasters

Ecology and Pollution

History

Natural Resources

Personal Narrative

Philosophy

Politics and Policy

Public Spaces

Technology

Introduction for Students

Sustainability: A Bedford Spotlight Reader is a textbook that can serve a variety of purposes. First and foremost, it is designed to help college students become better readers, writers, and critical thinkers. As you can see by surveying the table of contents, all of the articles and essays included in this book are focused on one particular theme: sustainability and humanity's impact on planet Earth. You may be wondering why a college writing textbook would be "about" something so specific; there is a good explanation for this, having to do with what college writing — and thinking — is. This introduction will explain what it means to be a college writer, provide a brief overview of sustainability and why it is an appropriate subject for a college writing course, and describe the organization and apparatus of this book.

What Is College Writing?

College writing represents a conjunction of skills that includes not just writing but also critical reading and critical thinking. *Critical reading* means being able to comprehend complex texts by reading closely, working to understand terms and theories, applying your own knowledge to them, cross-referencing other sources, asking questions of the text, and using strategies like note-taking and journal-keeping that result in enhanced understanding of a piece of writing. *Critical thinking* means being able to evaluate the merit of what you are studying by reflecting on and judging the information and arguments you are engaged with by thinking about them from multiple perspectives, probing their claims, recognizing biases, and questioning assumptions made by the authors. This conjunction of critical reading, critical thinking, and writing are part of the intellectual framework you will need to be successful in your academic and professional life — no matter what you choose to do.

Some students might say to themselves, "I am going to college to become a dentist, so when am I ever going to need to write a paper

1

about sustainability?" Or, "I am majoring in criminal justice, so why do I need to learn about environmental issues?" These are understandable questions, but there are answers to them most educated people would agree with. First, the intellectual processes involved in comprehending complex ideas, applying those ideas to your own observations and experiences, formulating rational questions (and provisional answers to the dilemmas posed by your questions), and producing negotiated responses all constitute a basic structure inherent in every academic field and professional environment. The abilities you develop as a college writer in this course, and through this subject, will help you in all of your other classes as well as in your personal and professional life because nearly every facet of life requires effective reasoning and communicating. Second, it is vital to your college studies to cultivate curiosity about subjects that may seem initially uninteresting to you or unrelated to your future career. Developing skills as a critical thinker, reader, and writer will allow you to engage with new ideas and subjects in potentially exciting and challenging ways. This is one of the fundamental lessons of college studies: not all themes will immediately engage you or seem directly relevant, but all of your studies will contribute to your development as a critical thinker, an effective writer and communicator, and a valuable member of society.

As you advance in college, and eventually graduate — and perhaps move on to graduate or professional school or your first "real" job — you will transform in many ways. One of the major aspects of this transformation involves moving from student to professional, a turn from being a receiver of knowledge to being a producer of knowledge. To be a producer of knowledge means simply that you will be shaping the world by contributing your ideas and practices to it, and overwhelmingly you will do this through language: listening, reading, speaking, thinking, and writing. To be able to contribute to professional organizations and social institutions capably, responsibly, intelligently, and sensitively is a long-term goal that college writing can help you achieve.

What Is Sustainability?

You've probably heard the term "sustainability" in some context. It is likely that you've used some product or service that was labeled as sustainable, or perhaps you are aware of a campus or civic organization that focuses on sustainability. You may even recognize that sustainability has to do with preserving or maintaining resources; we often associate sustainability with things like recycling, using renewable energy sources like solar and wind power, and preserving natural spaces like rainforests and coral reefs. However, unless you have an inherent interest in sustainability, you probably haven't thought much about what the term actually means. In fact, many people do not have a clear sense of what sustainability is or why it is so important. The following description will provide a starting point for your investigations of sustainability, but your own ideas and perspectives will emerge as you get further into the subject through this book and through your class discussions and activities.

Simply put, sustainability is the capacity to endure or continue. If a thing or an activity is sustainable, it can be reused, recycled, or repeated in some way because it has not exhausted all of the resources or energy required to create it. Sustainability can be broadly defined as the ability of something to maintain itself, and biological systems such as wetlands or forests are good examples of sustainability because they remain diverse and productive over long periods of time. Seen in this way, sustainability has to do with preserving resources and energy over the long term rather than exhausting them quickly to meet short-term needs or goals.

Many current discussions about sustainability focus on the ways in which human activity — and human life itself — can be maintained in the future without exhausting all of our current resources. Historically, there has been a close correlation between the growth of human society and environmental degradation — as communities grow, the environment often declines. Sustainability seeks new ways of addressing that relationship, which would allow human societies and economies to grow without destroying or overexploiting the environment or ecosystems in which those societies exist. The most widely quoted definition of sustainability comes from the Brundtland Report by the World Commission on Environment and Development in 1987, which defined sustainability as meeting "the needs of the present without compromising the ability of future generations to meet their own needs."

In other words, sustainability is based on the idea that human society should use industrial and biological processes that can be sustained indefinitely or at least for a very long time and that those processes should be cyclical rather than linear. The idea of "waste" is important here; a truly sustainable civilization would have little or no waste, and each turn of the industrial cycle would become the material for the next cycle. A basic premise of sustainability, then, is that many of our current practices are unsustainable and that human society will need to change to ensure that people in the future live in a world that is virtually no worse than the one we inherited.

As a quick example of sustainability, think about aluminum soda cans. In the past, many soda cans were used and thrown away without a whole lot of thought. Their creation, use, and disposal was a linear process, and lots of soda cans wound up in landfills and trash dumps. The practice of throwing them away was unsustainable because ready sources of aluminum are limited, and landfills and trash dumps were filling with wasted cans. Consequently, governments and private corporations began to recycle aluminum soda cans, and today more than 100,000 soda cans are recycled each minute in the United States. In fact, today's typical used soda can returns as a new can in just sixty days. A billion-dollar recycling industry has emerged, creating jobs and profits for the workers and businesses employed in that enterprise, while at the same time using limited resources more thoughtfully and reducing the impact on the environment. The process has become cyclical, resulting in the continued use of materials, rather than linear, in which a soda can is used once and then becomes waste. Many questions remain about the actual benefits of recycling — some of which you can read about in this book — but most people agree that recycling is a more sustainable solution than pitching our used soda cans into the trash.

But sustainability is about more than just the economic benefits of recycling materials and resources. Although the economic factors are important, sustainability also accounts for the social and environmental consequences

kaisphoto/Getty Images

of human activity. This concept, referred to as the "three pillars of sustainability," asserts that true sustainability depends on three interlocking factors: social equity, environmental preservation, and economic viability. Some describe this three-part model as People, Planet, Profit. First, people and communities must be treated fairly and equally — particularly with regard to eradicating global poverty and ending the environmental exploitation of poor countries and communities. Second, sustainable human activities must protect the earth's environment. And, third, sustainability must be economically feasible — human development depends on the long-term production, use, and management of resources as part of a global economy. Only when all three of these pillars are incorporated can an activity or enterprise be described as sustainable. The following diagram illustrates the ways in which these three components intersect:

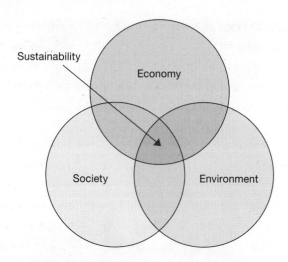

As this model should make clear, sustainability must consider the environment, society, and the economy to be successful. In fact, the earliest definitions of sustainability account for this relationship. The term *sustainability* first appeared in forestry studies in Germany in the 1800s, when forest overseers began to manage timber harvesting for continued use as a resource. In 1804, German forestry researcher Georg Hartig described sustainability as "utilizing forests to the greatest possible extent, but still in a way that future generations will have as much benefit as the living generation" (Schmutzenhofer, 1992). Although our current definitions are quite different and much expanded from Hartig's, sustainability still accounts for the need to preserve natural spaces, to use resources wisely, and to maintain them in an equitable manner for all human beings, both now and in the future.

Our current definitions of sustainability — particularly in the United States — are deeply influenced by our historical and cultural relationship with nature. Many American thinkers, writers, and philosophers have focused on the value of natural spaces, and they have contributed to our collective understanding about the relationship between humans and the environment. Some of their writing is featured early in this book, and their ideas contributed to the environmentalist movement that emerged in the second half of the twentieth century. Environmentalism advocates for the protection and restoration of nature, and grassroots environmental organizations lobby for changes in public policy and individual behavior to preserve the natural world. The Sierra Club, for example, is one of the oldest, largest, and most influential environmental organizations in the United States; you can read an essay by its founder, John Muir, in Chapter 1.

Environmentalism and sustainability have a lot in common. In fact, some people think that our current conversations about sustainability are the next development or evolution of environmentalism. However, earlier environmental debates often pitted the environment against the economy — nature vs. jobs — and this dichotomy created a rift between those supporting one side of the debate against the other. The battle between the "tree huggers" and the "greedy industrialists" left a lot of people out of the conversation. Many current discussions involving sustainability hope to bridge that gap by looking for possibilities that balance a full range of perspectives and interests — a win-win solution rather than a win-lose scenario. Sustainability encourages and provides incentives for change rather than mandating change, and the three pillars of sustainability emphasize this incorporation. Many sustainability advocates imagine new technologies as mechanisms to protect the planet while also creating economic opportunities and growth; other sustainable approaches simply endorse new ways of thinking and acting. In essence, sustainability looks for coordinated innovation to create a future that merges environmental, economic, and social interests rather than setting them in opposition.

As you read the essays and articles in this book, all of which focus in one way or another on sustainability, you should think about how each of the authors operates from a different perspective, how the readings might influence your own definition of sustainability and, perhaps most important, what you should do to create a more sustainable world. It is likely that your views and perspectives on sustainability will change as you make your way through this textbook, and your critical reading and thinking skills will certainly develop as you become a more analytical writer.

Why Should I Study Sustainability in a College Writing Course?

In short, "sustainability" is a topic that will allow you to practice and hone your critical reading, thinking, and writing skills. You might ask, then, "Why sustainability? Why not something else?" This is a fair question. Sustainability is among the best single themes for a college writing course for the reasons outlined in this section.

Sustainability Is Important

In some ways, sustainability is the most important conversation taking place in our society today. The earth is our home, and it provides all of the things we need for our survival and nourishment. However, that home has limited resources, and our collective future will depend on the successful management and use of those resources. We are living in a critical time, in which global supply of natural resources and ecosystem services is declining dramatically, while demand for these resources is escalating. From pollution, to resource depletion, to loss of biodiversity, to climate change, a growing human footprint is evident. This is not sustainable. We need to act differently if the world and its human and nonhuman inhabitants are to thrive in the future. Sustainability is about how we can preserve the earth and ensure the continued survival and nourishment of future generations. You and everyone you know will be affected in some way by the choices our society makes in the future regarding the earth and its resources. In fact, your very life may well depend on those choices.

Sustainability Is Relevant

Sustainability impacts nearly all human endeavors, and it is tied to nearly every social, academic, and professional arena. When you consider sustainability in relation to science, business, economics, political science, art, music, literature, history — or indeed any field of study — you will no doubt see that ideas and assumptions about sustainability are important both to the shape of those fields and to the work done within them. Further, the readings in this collection are particularly relevant to American readers and writers because debates and conversations about sustainability can be found all around us — in the news, on television, in film, and perhaps even among people in your own family or social circles. Therefore, understanding sustainability will help you understand an important facet of your future life and work. This relevancy will allow you to respond to these readings in a way that wouldn't be possible with a less accessible or less timely theme. Because sustainability spans many fields of study, it offers a convenient research topic that accommodates diverse interests and many different kinds of writing (including personal, analytical, and argumentative).

Sustainability Is Complex

Sustainability is a complex subject that involves many different topics, conversations, and perspectives. Much of what we think and do concerning sustainability emerges from "expert" opinions on scientific, economic, and political issues, and it may seem daunting to try to form your own opinions based on your limited knowledge. Even the experts often disagree, and it can be confusing and difficult to sort through the complexity of the issues involved in the sustainability conversation. In fact, you may feel as if the subject is better left to those experts to address. However, you should recognize that it is that very complexity that makes the subject of sustainability worth addressing. Sustainability is a broad and diverse subject with no clear answer or set of answers. Consequently, it will allow you to form your own opinions; use research, reasoning, and evidence to support your claims; and contribute to the conversation in your own way. As you engage with the issues surrounding sustainability, you will develop your critical thinking skills in ways that an easy or simple subject (with clear answers) might not allow. Addressing the complex subject of sustainability will help prepare you to address other complex issues and subjects in your professional, personal, and social life.

Sustainability Is Interdisciplinary

Along with its complexity, sustainability is also an interdisciplinary subject. This means that it can be addressed or analyzed from many different academic perspectives and that various "disciplines" can be combined in its understanding. Interdisciplinary thinking is about crossing the boundaries of specific, traditional fields of study to look at a problem or subject in more holistic, comprehensive ways. In this respect, sustainability combines a variety of disciplines, including science, economics, politics, humanities, and others. In fact, it is hard to think of an academic discipline that could not contribute to the sustainability conversation. Your academic program or major — whatever it may be — can be a useful perspective on sustainability, and you can learn a great deal about the subject by exploring it through a range of disciplines and perspectives.

Sustainability Is a "Discourse"

All intellectual endeavors involve participation in an ongoing conversation called a "discourse." This is not the same type of conversation you might have with a roommate or with a group of friends; it is the type of conversation that takes place among many people over many years in various methods of expression: books, essays, articles, speeches, and other kinds of articulations. All university students are expected to develop skills to absorb, assimilate, and synthesize information gathered from various sources within various discourses and to find their own voice within them. This is a basic pattern in the creation of knowledge. Sustainability is an emerging conversation or "discourse" in our society — its definition is still developing, and the reading, writing, thinking, and talking that you do can contribute to that definition. This book offers a range of interrelated readings focusing on the discourse of sustainability; learning how to evaluate and analyze that discourse and how to shape your own voice and perspective within that discourse is an important skill.

Sustainability Is Political

Because sustainability is concerned with how we use limited resources on the earth, it is essentially a political issue. All of the debates surrounding sustainability are political, since they seek to change the ways people think and act, often with the goal of influencing public policy and law. The essays and articles in this book emerge from a wide variety of political perspectives, ranging from liberal to conservative, and one goal of this book is to expose student readers to these varying perspectives so that they can develop their

own opinions and beliefs. This book is intentionally designed to offer varying perspectives, even when these perspectives seem to be in opposition.
As you read this book, think about the political perspective of each of the
authors and the ways in which their politics inform their message.

Sustainability Is Rhetorical

Simply defined, rhetoric is about the ways in which speakers or writers
attempt to persuade or motivate an audience. An effective writer will make
careful choices in the language, delivery, timing, and other factors involved
in a piece of writing because he or she wants those words to be understood, accepted, and acted on. Each selection in this book can be seen
as a different rhetorical act that seeks to change the ways we consider or
define sustainability. They all contribute, in some way, to our understanding
of sustainability, and they all hope to influence our thoughts and actions.
Because sustainability is such an important, complex, and political issue, it
is vital to analyze the words and images that are used to define it. You will
develop your abilities to understand rhetoric as you read further into this
collection, and you will certainly develop your own rhetorical abilities as a
result of the reading, writing, and thinking you will do. These persuasive
abilities will carry over to other aspects of your personal, professional, and
civic life.

Sustainability Is Personal

Sustainability affects each of us on a personal level. The communities
we live in, the foods we eat, our modes of transportation, the jobs we
pursue — each of these aspects of our lives and countless others are
shaped by sustainable (or unsustainable) choices. By learning more about
sustainability, you will learn more about the world you live in and the
influence it has on your own personal well-being. Furthermore, each of us
has the ability to choose sustainable behaviors to improve our own lives
and the lives of those around us. Your own perspective on sustainability
will likely evolve as you consider the essays and articles in this book, and
that will shape your values and decision-making, enabling you to create a
healthier, happier, and more sustainable lifestyle for yourself.

The Units in This Book

Sustainability is a vast subject, and many experts devote themselves to just one small aspect of it. Scientists, politicians, businesspeople, writers, journalists, and others are involved in the sustainability conversation, and, as noted earlier in this introduction, they often speak different "discourses" focused on their own specialization and expertise regarding sustainability. In fact, even the experts in sustainability can be uninformed about certain aspects of this complex and expansive topic. For instance, a climate change researcher may understand the science behind global weather patterns, but she may not fully understand how political leaders might respond to environmental changes. Likewise, an economist may be able to predict the financial impact of an increasing population on a third-world country, but he may not be able to account for the ways in which new technologies might alleviate some of that impact. Writers and journalists, in particular, struggle with the vast amount of information they encounter when researching sustainability issues, and they often seek input and advice from trusted experts as they report on sustainability issues to the public at large.

It is impossible to know everything about sustainability, and this book certainly does not aim to make you an expert on every facet of sustainability. However, the collection does provide a broad overview of many key questions relating to sustainability in the world today. Most of the pieces you will read are current, and many are selected from popular media sources like newspapers, websites, and blogs. As a result, they should be easy to digest and understand — and I hope you find them interesting and informative. A few pieces are selected from expert sources, but even those are relatively short and accessible for general readers. The goal is to expose you to the general conversations taking place regarding sustainability and prepare you to contribute to the ongoing discourse about how we will manage our planet's resources in the future. You will certainly play a role in this discussion one way or another, and this book may help you to contribute in a more effective and active way as a student, citizen, or employee — or perhaps even as an expert on some sustainability-related topic in your own right.

This book is designed around the following six key questions relating to sustainability, each with a corresponding chapter.

Chapter 1: What Are the Foundations of Sustainability?

This chapter's goal is to establish a "sustainability literacy" by exposing you to many classic or landmark texts in sustainability and environmentalism. The chapter reflects on and establishes definitions of key terms, such as "sustainability," "environmentalism," "ecology," "conservation," and so on. The reading selections lay the groundwork for the other chapters and conversations in this book by providing necessary background for sustainability readings and discussions.

Chapter 2: How Is Sustainability a Political Issue?

This chapter highlights the important texts involving sustainability and environment as political and social topics. It focuses on human relationships with and in environments and the ways in which persuasive discourse shapes our public perceptions of those places. The central purpose of this chapter is to provide a range of perspectives from liberal to conservative, comparing and contrasting the ways they use language to shape public understanding about sustainability. It highlights major media outlets on different ends of the political spectrum as key participants in debates concerning sustainability and environmentalism.

Chapter 3: How Do Crises and Disasters Create Challenges for Sustainability?

This chapter addresses several recent environmental disasters, with a focus on those in the United States. Drawing on media, governmental, and scientific publications, the chapter describes the ways in which disasters create challenges and opportunities for sustainability. The reading selections cover some of the more recent environmental disasters, like Hurricane Katrina and the BP oil spill in the Gulf of Mexico, as well as other important issues connected to crises and disasters, such as fracking, oil pipelines, and species extinction.

Chapter 4: How Is Sustainability Connected to Local and Urban Environments?

This chapter looks at sustainability efforts in cities, suburbs, and other urban areas. The chapter's goal is to erase the dichotomy of environmentalism as a focus on preserving "natural" places, while highlighting the ways in which sustainability has been discussed as a personal and social activity. The reading selections address food and consumption, the pros and cons of recycling, the growth of "green jobs," the future of sustainable foods, campus sustainability efforts, the impact of social media on sustainability, and other related topics.

Chapter 5: How Is Sustainability a Transnational Issue?

This chapter highlights sustainability and environmental preservation as global, transnational issues. The chapter examines worldwide issues of population, resource use, global climate change, and the limits of global food production. To correspond with Chapter 3 (recent environmental disasters), this chapter also includes reading selections focusing on global environmental challenges, including the environmental effects of a major tsunami in Japan, dangers to coral reefs, the expansion of the Pacific garbage patch, and the challenges of sustainability on the African continent.

Chapter 6: How Are Tourism and Recreation Connected to Sustainability?

This chapter examines the role of tourism, leisure activities, and recreation in creating a more sustainably minded public. It begins by focusing on the ways ecotourism can both harm and help protect environments through sustainable planning and development. Other reading selections address high-interest activities (including surfing, skiing, and hunting) and the ways in which these activities shape sustainability. The chapter also addresses the role of zoos and public aquariums in educating people about sustainability.

● ● ●

By concentrating on these key questions relating to sustainability, you will develop a broad understanding of the conversation today. In fact, I believe that by the end of your course, you will know much more about sustainability than most people in our society. You will be a sustainability expert as a result of the reading, research, writing, discussing, and exploring that you will do. Each chapter is designed to add a new dimension to understanding sustainability — how it developed, how it is political, how disasters have shaped sustainability, how it affects local and global communities, and how it relates to tourism and recreation. Each reading in the chapters is intended to be put into conversation with the others, so as you read, note where intersections and discrepancies appear. Part of critical thinking and reading involves integrating sources, allowing them to "speak to" one another by noting where they agree and disagree, where they help clarify and expand one another, and where one sheds new light on another.

Across all the chapters, you will see many opportunities to share your experiences and personal perspectives about sustainability; to add your observations about the current state of the earth and what the future might look like; to place the readings in relation to one another; to engage with scientific, political, ethical, and economic issues related to sustainability; and in general to work within the discourse of sustainability to challenge the readings as much as they will challenge you. Most of all, I hope you will see that the intellectual processes you will engage in by reading, thinking, and writing within this discourse will translate to the kind of applications of critical reading, thinking, and writing you will perform throughout college and into your personal and professional life.

A Note on the Questions

At the end of each essay or article, you will find three sets of questions to help you think about the readings. The first set, "Understanding the Text," is designed to help you comprehend the reading on its own terms. These questions ask for clarification of the main point or theme in the articles, interpretations of the meaning of unique claims, and extrapolations of the examples and illustrations the author uses to support his or her overall positions. These are "reading comprehension" questions that can help you read the pieces closely and understand the author. Consider them as author-centered questions because they focus on understanding the author's main point or perspective.

The second set of questions, "Reflection and Response," asks for your contributions of examples, gathered through your experiences and observations, and your opinions or ideas about the articles as a whole or about their specific claims. These questions are intended to bring you into the conversation. Consider them as reader-centered questions because they focus on your own perspective and responses to the readings.

The third set of questions, "Making Connections," is designed to help you think of the readings as parts of larger conversations rather than as individual perspectives. These are often more complex writing prompts that ask you to consider reading in clusters, to look for correlations between different writers, and to examine sources outside this book. These questions also ask you to think further, to include your own claims and examples, or to offer counterclaims and counterexamples. Because each question calls for understanding various texts, positioning yourself within the conversation, and combining and cross-referencing other texts, you can think of these as discourse-centered questions.

I cannot predict how your instructor will use this text — and I would not want to suggest one way of using it that would be better than another. Each instructor will use it in his or her own way, based on the objectives of the class. Some teachers may select a few of the chapters in this book and investigate them exhaustively. Others may use all of the chapters in this book but perhaps in a different order than they appear. Your instructor's goals will also determine the types of assignments and questions you will draw from the book. One instructor may prefer to focus on the "Reflection and Response" questions, for instance, in a writing class that favors expressive essay writing or writing from experience. Another may value research-based writing and stay in the "Making Connections" section more often than not. Still another may prefer to modify these questions, combine them, or even ignore them and invent his or her own writing assignments. No matter how these readings are used, however, two things are certain: (1) this subject matter opens multiple ways to learn college writing; and (2) the readings elicit an important thread running through all good writing: *relevancy*. The relevancy of sustainability provides an undeniable immediacy and importance to whatever kind of work you produce about it. After all, these readings address the fundamental role of human beings and our future on earth. What could be more relevant and important than that?

On a personal note, I want you to know that this is one of the first writing textbooks devoted to this emerging and progressive topic. Sustainability is a cutting-edge subject for a writing class, and I think you are lucky to be taking a course that addresses it. I am deeply interested in your questions, ideas, and perspectives on sustainability and on this book. Please feel free to e-mail me at crw17@psu.edu.

Good luck with your writing and research!

Christian R. Weisser
Penn State Berks
Courtesy Christian R. Weisser

1

What Are the Foundations of Sustainability?

Sustainability is an important subject in our world today, but few people have a clear sense of what sustainability means or where the term came from. You probably recognize that sustainability is somehow tied to preserving resources and protecting the environment, but it is likely that your definitions do not extend much further. That's okay — you will know far more about the foundations of sustainability after you've read, discussed, and written about the selections in Chapter 1.

The goal of this chapter is to help you establish a *sustainability literacy* — a basic understanding of what sustainability is all about and how the term and its related concepts have evolved. To develop this understanding, you will read and consider some of the primary texts that are central to the sustainability conversation. These readings will serve as a background to other selections in this book — in fact, many of the authors in Chapter 1 are referenced throughout the rest of the collection. In a way, you can consider some of the authors in this chapter as the forerunners of contemporary sustainability because what they said and did has had a big impact on our current views. This background will be tremendously useful as you begin to understand and participate in your own conversations about sustainability.

The first piece in this chapter is entitled "Sustainability: A History." This piece is designed to give you an overview of the term *sustainability* while also describing some of the criticisms associated with that term. This is a good place to begin learning about this complex idea of sustainability, especially when coupled with the "Introduction for Students" at the beginning of the book.

You may notice that the next few selections in this chapter — written by Thoreau, Muir, Carson, and Leopold — do not reference or use the word *sustainability* directly. For those writers, the term was not yet a part of their vocabulary. What these authors offer, however, are fundamental perspectives on human relationships to the world. This chapter is loosely chronological, and the early authors included here are pioneers. Many of

photo: Thomas Goeppert/EyeEm/Getty Images

them explored the natural world while also writing about it, giving us valuable insights on places, ecologies, and environments. Thoreau and Muir are among the first American writers to extol the value of natural places, so you should read their essays carefully to see how they begin the conversations. Leopold builds on this premise of the value of nature to consider the relationships and interconnections among all living things. Carson explores the impact of chemicals on natural systems and on our own bodies, and her book, *Silent Spring*, which is excerpted here, is often credited as the impetus for the American environmental movement. In many ways, the thoughts and writings of these four authors serve as a precursor to our contemporary understanding of sustainability.

The selection that concludes the chapter — Suzuki's "The Sacred Balance" — is more current, and reflects on human culture and its relationship with the environment. This is a vital aspect of the sustainability conversation, and this piece will provide further groundwork for understanding the connections between society and our planet's systems and resources. Suzuki introduces the notion of time (past, present, and future) as a significant aspect of sustainability, which is something you will see referenced in later selections in the book.

Collectively, the six essays in Chapter 1 provide a background to the sustainability conversation, preparing you for more specific and more detailed discussions that will follow. One of your goals as you read this chapter — perhaps a goal of your course — should be to look for the connections between the concepts of nature, environment, ecology, and sustainability. Although these concepts and terms are not identical, they are inextricably linked. Understanding these key words will help you develop your sustainability literacy and will enable you to form your own perspectives on sustainability.

From *Sustainability: A History*

Jeremy Caradonna

Jeremy Caradonna holds a PhD in History and teaches environmental studies courses at the University of Victoria in Canada. Caradonna is the former owner of Share Organics, a values-based business that connects organic farmers to local consumers. Caradonna also works as an environmental consultant, holds a position on the board of a biodiesel co-op, and assists on political campaigns for those who support green causes. He is the author of several articles and two books about sustainability.

This selection is an excerpt from Caradonna's 2014 book *Sustainability: A History*, which discusses the origins and conceptualization of the word *sustainability* and how it has grown into an idea that shapes the world around us. The selection discusses the origins of sustainability and defines what it means in simple terms, while also addressing critics who believe that sustainability is merely a "buzzword" with little meaning or focus. As you read, think about what "sustainability" means and how the concept has evolved over time.

> "We must aim for a continuous, resilient, and sustainable use [of forests]. . . ."
>
> —HANS CARL VON CARLOWITZ, 1713

> "Sustainability is a lifestyle designed for permanence."
>
> —CHRIS TURNER, 2010

As hard as it might be to believe, the world once made do without the words "sustainable" and "sustainability." Today they're nearly ubiquitous. At the grocery store we shop for "sustainable foods" that were produced, of course, from "sustainable agriculture"; ministries of natural resources in many parts of the world strive for "sustainable yields" in forestry; the United Nations (UN) has long touted "sustainable development" as a strategy for global stability; and woe be the city dweller who doesn't aim for a "sustainable lifestyle."

Sustainability first emerged as an explicit social, environmental, and economic ideal in the late 1970s and 1980s. By the 1990s, it had become a familiar term in the world of policy wonkery—President Bill Clinton's Council on Sustainable Development, for instance—but the embrace wasn't universal. Bill McKibben, perhaps the most prominent environmentalist of the past thirty years, wrote an opinion piece in the *New York Times* in 1996 in which he dismissed sustainability as a "buzzless buzzword" that was "born partly in an effort to obfuscate" and which would never catch on in mainstream society. In McKibben's view, sustainability "never made the leap to lingo"—and never would. "It's time to figure out why, and then figure out something else." (McKibben preferred the term "maturity.") Many others have since accused "sustainability" and "sustainable development" of being superficial terms that mask ongoing environmental degradation and facilitate business-as-usual economic growth. Those are debatable points that will be discussed in this book. But one thing is clear: McKibben was quite wrong about the quick decline of "sustainability."

One way to demonstrate this growing interest is to look at book titles that bear the word "sustainable" or "sustainability." It's difficult to find books published before 1976 that employ these words as titles or even as keywords. No book in the English language used either term in the title before 1970. But since 1980 there has been an explosion of books and articles that not only use those words as titles but also deal with the many facets of sustainability. Indeed, thousands of books make up this growing body of literature. What's more, a quick Google search for "sustainability" returns around 150 million hits.

Is sustainability a buzzword? Absolutely. But is it also "buzzless"? Assuredly not. Governments, communities, organizations, and individuals all over the world have sought to align themselves with the basic principles of what they call "sustainability"—a desire to create a society that is safe, stable, prosperous, and ecologically minded. The practices inspired by the concept of sustainability could give rise to the world's third major socioeconomic transformation, after the Agricultural Revolution that took place 10,000 years ago, and the Industrial Revolution(s) of the late eighteenth and nineteenth centuries. It is not only a buzzword but also a galvanizingly powerful term whose application subsumes a number of other movements, environmental perhaps most of all.

"Sustainability" is, first and foremost, used as a corrective, a counterbalance, and directly tied to climate change (a term that most governments would like to avoid). Those who use it argue that we are 250 years into an "unsustainable" ecological assault on the planet that was triggered by industrialization and that has left us with a lot of soul searching and cleaning up to do. "Sustainability" therefore is a way of acknowledging how humankind has created an imbalance. According to Jeffrey D. Sachs, we now live in the Age of the Anthropocene, in which "human activity" has become the "dominant driver of the natural environment. We *are* or have become a kind of natural disaster."

The Fifth Assessment Report (2014) from the Intergovernmental Panel on Climate Change, a team of scientists whose job it is to sort through and summarize the state of climate science, makes it clear that Earth's climate system is warming steadily due to "anthropogenic greenhouse gas concentrations," such as carbon dioxide, methane, and nitrous oxide, all of which trap heat (at infrared wavelengths) that would otherwise escape from the Earth's atmosphere. "It is extremely likely that human influence has been the dominant cause of the observed warming since the mid-20th century," the report concludes. Climate change has already begun to alter natural systems and the environment in troubling ways: increasingly unpredictable temperatures and weather patterns, changes in the hydrological cycle that generate droughts and larger and more frequent storms, rising sea levels from melting ice caps, the die-off of some species, and so on. Climate change also suffers from "positive feedback cycles" (the loss of reflective ice cover, the release of natural stores of methane, etc.) that act as a domino effect and accelerate the speed of global warming. If greenhouse gas emissions continue to grow, average global temperatures could rise by 8.1° F by 2100. Furthermore, the growing population of homo sapiens on the planet, which surpassed the 7 billion mark in 2012, combined with manmade pollutants and the appropriation of over 30 percent of the net primary production of organic material—that is, we use or alter much of what nature has to offer—has resulted in devastating consequences for the world's ecosystems.

This is what sustainability is meant to counteract: a moribund economic system that has drained the world of many of its finite resources, including fresh water and crude oil, generated a meltdown in global financial systems, exacerbated social inequality in many parts of the world, and driven human civilization to the brink of catastrophe by unwisely advocating for economic growth at the expense of resources and essential ecosystem services.

Those whom we'll call "sustainists"—from scientists and engineers to economists, educators, policymakers, and social activists—have taken on the many challenges listed above. What they seek—and how—is always a subject of intense debate, even among themselves, but the broad contours are easy to articulate: safe and livable cities with abundant green spaces; buildings that produce their own energy; public transportation networks to decrease reliance on cars; agricultural systems that can produce enough food to meet human needs without genetically modified organisms or monoculture and without degrading soils and waterways with petro-chemicals; and a healthy environment. To sustainists, sustainability means planning for the future and rejecting that which threatens the lives and well-being of future generations. It means creating a "green,"

"To sustainists, sustainability means planning for the future and rejecting that which threatens the lives and well-being of future generations."

"low-carbon," and "resilient" economy that runs on renewable energy and does not support growth that would impair the ability for humans and other organisms to live in perpetuity on the Earth. For many it has a utopic dimension: decentralized forms of democracy that support peace and social justice.

In short, for those who embrace sustainability in the fullest sense—as an environmental, social, economic, and political ideal—we're at a crossroads in our civilization. There are two paths to take: continue with business as usual, ignore the science of climate change, and pretend that our economic system isn't on life support or remake and redefine our society along the lines of sustainability.

Understanding the Text

1. In what ways is the term *sustainability* related to the Industrial Revolution of the eighteenth century and the imbalances it created?

2. What does prominent environmentalist Bill McKibben have to say about sustainability? Why does Caradonna disagree with him?

3. In what ways is sustainability a "buzzword"? Is that a good thing or a bad thing?

4. Who are the "sustainists" described near the end of this excerpt, and what are their goals?

Reflection and Response

5. Caradonna talks about climate change as one of the central issues related to sustainability. What is your understanding of or experience with that term?

6. Do you believe that humans are the dominant driver of the natural environment? Why or why not?

7. This excerpt ends by describing a crossroads with two paths. Which path do you believe we are headed down right now? Do you think that will change in the future?

Making Connections

8. In what ways is this excerpt similar to or different from the definition of sustainability offered in this book's "Introduction for Students"?

9. This reading mentions the United Nations, which has played an important role in sustainability initiatives. Why do you think the UN is so involved in sustainability?

10. Caradonna mentions that "a quick Google search for 'sustainability' returns around 150 million hits." Check that tally on Google now. Has it risen or fallen, and what might that indicate?

Where I Lived, and What I Lived For

Henry David Thoreau

Henry David Thoreau was one of the most important American authors of the nineteenth century. *Walden*, from which this essay is excerpted, is his most famous work. Published in 1854, *Walden* describes Thoreau's two-year experience living in a cabin he built himself in woodland close to Walden Pond, a few miles outside the town of Concord, Massachusetts. Thoreau writes: "I went to the woods because I wished to live deliberately, to front only the essential facts of life, and see if I could not learn what it had to teach." *Walden* remains a best-selling book today, and many readers are drawn to Thoreau's belief in finding truth and meaning in natural settings.

Thoreau's experiment in living simply and deliberately was inspired by the Transcendentalist philosophy, which identifies a spiritual connection between humans and nature. In many ways, the Transcendentalist movement was a precursor to more contemporary environmental and sustainability movements, as it highlights the individual's place in the world and in nature.

As you read this selection, think about what Thoreau is saying about a "deliberate" life in harmony with nature. Why did he choose to live away from other people? What does he say about simplicity and the necessities of life? What does he suggest about modern society?

At a certain season of our life we are accustomed to consider every spot as the possible site of a house. I have thus surveyed the country on every side within a dozen miles of where I live. In imagination I have bought all the farms in succession, for all were to be bought, and I knew their price. I walked over each farmer's premises, tasted his wild apples, discoursed on husbandry with him, took his farm at his price, at any price, mortgaging it to him in my mind; even put a higher price on it—took everything but a deed of it—took his word for his deed, for I dearly love to talk—cultivated it, and him too to some extent, I trust, and withdrew when I had enjoyed it long enough, leaving him to carry it on. This experience entitled me to be regarded as a sort of real-estate broker by my friends. Wherever I sat, there I might live, and the landscape radiated from me accordingly. What is a house but a *sedes*, a seat?—better if a country seat. I discovered many a site for a house not likely to be soon improved, which some might have thought too far from the village, but to my eyes the village was too far from it. Well, there I might live, I said; and there I did live, for an hour, a summer and a winter life; saw how I could let the years run off, buffet the winter through, and see the spring come in. The future inhabitants of this region, wherever they may place their houses, may be sure that they have

Walden Pond, near Concord, Massachusetts.
Library of Congress [LC-DIG-det-4a22665]

been anticipated. An afternoon sufficed to lay out the land into orchard, wood-lot, and pasture, and to decide what fine oaks or pines should be left to stand before the door, and whence each blasted tree could be seen to the best advantage; and then I let it lie, fallow, perchance, for a man is rich in proportion to the number of things which he can afford to let alone.

My imagination carried me so far that I even had the refusal of several farms—the refusal was all I wanted—but I never got my fingers burned by actual possession. The nearest that I came to actual possession was when I bought the Hollowell place, and had begun to sort my seeds, and collected materials with which to make a wheelbarrow to carry it on or off with; but before the owner gave me a deed of it, his wife—every man has such a wife—changed her mind and wished to keep it, and he offered me ten dollars to release him. Now, to speak the truth, I had but ten cents in the world, and it surpassed my arithmetic to tell, if I was that man who had ten cents, or who had a farm, or ten dollars, or all together. However, I let him keep the ten dollars and the farm too, for I had carried it far enough; or rather, to be generous, I sold him the farm for just what I gave for it, and, as he was not a rich man, made him a present of ten dollars, and still had my ten cents, and seeds, and materials for a wheelbarrow left. I found thus that I had been a rich man without any damage to my poverty. But I retained the landscape, and I have since annually carried off what it yielded without a wheelbarrow. With respect to landscapes,

"I am monarch of all I *survey*,

My right there is none to dispute."

I have frequently seen a poet withdraw, having enjoyed the most valu-   5
able part of a farm, while the crusty farmer supposed that he had got a few wild apples only. Why, the owner does not know it for many years when a poet has put his farm in rhyme, the most admirable kind of invisible fence, has fairly impounded it, milked it, skimmed it, and got all the cream, and left the farmer only the skimmed milk.

The real attractions of the Hollowell farm, to me, were: its complete retirement, being, about two miles from the village, half a mile from the nearest neighbor, and separated from the highway by a broad field; its bounding on the river, which the owner said protected it by its fogs from frosts in the spring, though that was nothing to me; the gray color and ruinous state of the house and barn, and the dilapidated

> "A man is rich in proportion to the number of things which he can afford to let alone."

fences, which put such an interval between me and the last occupant; the hollow and lichen-covered apple trees, nawed [*sic*] by rabbits, showing what kind of neighbors I should have; but above all, the recollection I had of it from my earliest voyages up the river, when the house was concealed behind a dense grove of red maples, through which I heard the house-dog bark. I was in haste to buy it, before the proprietor finished getting out some rocks, cutting down the hollow apple trees, and grubbing up some young birches which had sprung up in the pasture, or, in short, had made any more of his improvements. To enjoy these advantages I was ready to carry it on; like Atlas,° to take the world on my shoulders—I never heard what compensation he received for that—and do all those things which had no other motive or excuse but that I might pay for it and be unmolested in my possession of it; for I knew all the while that it would yield the most abundant crop of the kind I wanted, if I could only afford to let it alone. But it turned out as I have said.

All that I could say, then, with respect to farming on a large scale—I have always cultivated a garden—was, that I had had my seeds ready. Many think that seeds improve with age. I have no doubt that time discriminates between the good and the bad; and when at last I shall plant, I shall be less likely to be disappointed. But I would say to my fellows, once for all, As long as possible live free and uncommitted. It makes but little difference whether you are committed to a farm or the county jail.

Atlas: a Greek mythological figure who holds the earth on his shoulders.

Old Cato, whose "De Re Rustica" is my "Cultivator," says—and the only translation I have seen makes sheer nonsense of the passage—"When you think of getting a farm turn it thus in your mind, not to buy greedily; nor spare your pains to look at it, and do not think it enough to go round it once. The oftener you go there the more it will please you, if it is good." I think I shall not buy greedily, but go round and round it as long as I live, and be buried in it first, that it may please me the more at last.

The present was my next experiment of this kind, which I propose to describe more at length, for convenience putting the experience of two years into one. As I have said, I do not propose to write an ode to dejection, but to brag as lustily as chanticleer in the morning, standing on his roost, if only to wake my neighbors up.

When first I took up my abode in the woods, that is, began to spend my nights as well as days there, which, by accident, was on Independence Day, or the Fourth of July, 1845, my house was not finished for winter, but was merely a defense against the rain, without plastering or chimney, the walls being of rough, weather-stained boards, with wide chinks, which made it cool at night. The upright white hewn studs and freshly planed door and window casings gave it a clean and airy look, especially in the morning, when its timbers were saturated with dew, so that I fancied that by noon some sweet gum would exude from them. To my imagination it retained throughout the day more or less of this auroral character, reminding me of a certain house on a mountain which I had visited a year before. This was an airy and unplastered cabin, fit to entertain a travelling god, and where a goddess might trail her garments. The winds which passed over my dwelling were such as sweep over the ridges of mountains, bearing the broken strains, or celestial parts only, of terrestrial music. The morning wind forever blows, the poem of creation is uninterrupted; but few are the ears that hear it. Olympus° is but the outside of the earth everywhere.

The only house I had been the owner of before, if I except a boat, was a tent, which I used occasionally when making excursions in the summer, and this is still rolled up in my garret; but the boat, after passing from hand to hand, has gone down the stream of time. With this more substantial shelter about me, I had made some progress toward settling in the world. This frame, so slightly clad, was a sort of crystallization around me, and reacted on the builder. It was suggestive somewhat as a picture in outlines. I did not need to go outdoors to take the air, for the atmosphere within had lost none of its freshness. It was not so much within doors as behind a door where I sat, even in the rainiest weather. The Harivansa°

Olympus: mountain where Greek gods were thought to live.
Harivansa (Harivamsa): ancient religious Hindu text.

says, "An abode without birds is like a meat without seasoning." Such was not my abode, for I found myself suddenly neighbor to the birds; not by having imprisoned one, but having caged myself near them. I was not only nearer to some of those which commonly frequent the garden and the orchard, but to those smaller and more thrilling songsters of the forest which never, or rarely, serenade a villager—the wood thrush, the veery, the scarlet tanager, the field sparrow, the whip-poor-will, and many others.

I was seated by the shore of a small pond, about a mile and a half south of the village of Concord and somewhat higher than it, in the midst of an extensive wood between that town and Lincoln, and about two miles south of that our only field known to fame, Concord Battle Ground; but I was so low in the woods that the opposite shore, half a mile off, like the rest, covered with wood, was my most distant horizon. For the first week, whenever I looked out on the pond it impressed me like a tarn high up on the side of a mountain, its bottom far above the surface of other lakes, and, as the sun arose, I saw it throwing off its nightly clothing of mist, and here and there, by degrees, its soft ripples or its smooth reflecting surface was revealed, while the mists, like ghosts, were stealthily withdrawing in every direction into the woods, as at the breaking up of some nocturnal conventicle. The very dew seemed to hang upon the trees later into the day than usual, as on the sides of mountains.

This small lake was of most value as a neighbor in the intervals of a gentle rain-storm in August, when, both air and water being perfectly still, but the sky overcast, mid-afternoon had all the serenity of evening, and the wood thrush sang around, and was heard from shore to shore. A lake like this is never smoother than at such a time; and the clear portion of the air above it being, shallow and darkened by clouds, the water, full of light and reflections, becomes a lower heaven itself so much the more important. From a hill-top nearby, where the wood had been recently cut off, there was a pleasing vista southward across the pond, through a wide indentation in the hills which form the shore there, where their opposite sides sloping toward each other suggested a stream flowing out in that direction through a wooded valley, but stream there was none. That way I looked between and over the near green hills to some distant and higher ones in the horizon, tinged with blue. Indeed, by standing on tiptoe I could catch a glimpse of some of the peaks of the still bluer and more distant mountain ranges in the northwest, those true-blue coins from heaven's own mint, and also of some portion of the village. But in other directions, even from this point, I could not see over or beyond the woods which surrounded me. It is well to have some water in your neighborhood, to give buoyancy to and float the earth. One value even of the smallest well is, that when you look into it you see that earth is not continent but insular.

This is as important as that it keeps butter cool. When I looked across the pond from this peak toward the Sudbury meadows, which in time of flood I distinguished elevated perhaps by a mirage in their seething valley, like a coin in a basin, all the earth beyond the pond appeared like a thin crust insulated and floated even by this small sheet of interverting water, and I was reminded that this on which I dwelt was but *dry land.*

Though the view from my door was still more contracted, I did not feel crowded or confined in the least. There was pasture enough for my imagination. The low shrub oak plateau to which the opposite shore arose stretched away toward the prairies of the West and the steppes of Tartary, affording ample room for all the roving families of men. "There are none happy in the world but beings who enjoy freely a vast horizon" — said Damodara, when his herds required new and larger pastures.

Both place and time were changed, and I dwelt nearer to those parts 15 of the universe and to those eras in history which had most attracted me. Where I lived was as far off as many a region viewed nightly by astronomers. We are wont to imagine rare and delectable places in some remote and more celestial corner of the system, behind the constellation of Cassiopeia's Chair, far from noise and disturbance. I discovered that my house actually had its site in such a withdrawn, but forever new and unprofaned, part of the universe. If it were worth the while to settle in those parts near to the Pleiades or the Hyades, to Aldebaran or Altair, then I was really there, or at an equal remoteness from the life which I had left behind, dwindled and twinkling with as fine a ray to my nearest neighbor; and to be seen only in moonless nights by him. Such was part of creation where I had squatted, —

> "There was a shepherd that did live,
>   And held his thoughts as high
> As were the mounts whereon his flocks
>   Did hourly feed him by."

What should we think of the shepherd's life if his flocks always wandered to higher pastures than his thoughts?

Every morning was a cheerful invitation to make my life of equal simplicity, and I may say innocence, with Nature herself. I have been as sincere a worshipper of Aurora° as the Greeks. I got up early and bathed in the pond; that was a religious exercise, and one of the best things which I did. They say that characters were engraven on the bathing tub of King Tching Thang to this effect: "Renew thyself completely each day; do it again, and again, and forever again." I can understand that. Morning brings back the heroic ages. I was as much affected by the faint hum of a mosquito making its invisible

Aurora: the Roman goddess of dawn.

and unimaginable tour through my apartment at earliest dawn, when I was sitting with door and windows open, as I could be by any trumpet that ever sang of fame. It was Homer's requiem; itself an Iliad and Odyssey in the air, singing its own wrath and wanderings. There was something cosmical about it; a standing advertisement, till forbidden, of the everlasting vigor and fertility of the world. The morning, which is the most memorable season of the day, is the awakening hour. Then there is least somnolence in us; and for an hour, at least, some part of us awakes which slumbers all the rest of the day and night. Little is to be expected of that day, if it can be called a day, to which we are not awakened by our Genius, but by the mechanical nudgings of some servitor, are not awakened by our own newly acquired force and aspirations from within, accompanied by the undulations of celestial music, instead of factory bells, and a fragrance filling the air—to a higher life than we fell asleep from; and thus the darkness bear its fruit, and prove itself to be good, no less than the light. That man who does not believe that each day contains an earlier, more sacred, and auroral hour than he has yet profaned, has despaired of life, and is pursuing a descending and darkening way. After a partial cessation of his sensuous life, the soul of man, or its organs rather, are reinvigorated each day, and his Genius tries again what noble life it can make. All memorable events, I should say, transpire in morning time and in a morning atmosphere. The Vedas° say, "All intelligences awake with the morning." Poetry and art, and the fairest and most memorable of the actions of men, date from such an hour. All poets and heroes, like Memnon, are the children of Aurora, and emit their music at sunrise. To him whose elastic and vigorous thought keeps pace with the sun, the day is a perpetual morning. It matters not what the clocks say or the attitudes and labors of men. Morning is when I am awake and there is a dawn in me. Moral reform is the effort to throw off sleep. Why is it that men give so poor an account of their day if they have not been slumbering? They are not such poor calculators. If they had not been overcome with drowsiness, they would have performed something. The millions are awake enough for physical labor, but only one in a million is awake enough for effective intellectual exertion, only one in a hundred millions to a poetic or divine life. To be awake is to be alive. I have never yet met a man who was quite awake. How could I have looked him in the face?

We must learn to reawaken and keep ourselves awake, not by mechanical aids, but by an infinite expectation of the dawn, which does not forsake us in our soundest sleep. I know of no more encouraging fact than the unquestionable ability of man to elevate his life by a conscious endeavor. It is something to be able to paint a particular picture, or to

Vedas: Hindu book of knowledge.

carve a statue, and so to make a few objects beautiful; but it is far more glorious to carve and paint the very atmosphere and medium through which we look, which morally we can do. To affect the quality of the day, that is the highest of arts. Every man is tasked to make his life, even in its details, worthy of the contemplation of his most elevated and critical hour. If we refused, or rather used up, such paltry information as we get, the oracles would distinctly inform us how this might be done.

I went to the woods because I wished to live deliberately, to front only the essential facts of life, and see if I could not learn what it had to teach, and not, when I came to die, discover that I had not lived. I did not wish to live what was not life, living is so dear, nor did I wish to practice resignation, unless it was quite necessary. I wanted to live deep and suck out all the marrow of life, to live so sturdily and Spartan-like as to put to rout all that was not life, to cut a broad swath and shave close, to drive life into a corner, and reduce it to its lowest terms, and, if it proved to be mean, why then to get the whole and genuine meanness of it, and publish its meanness to the world; or if it were sublime, to know it by experience, and be able to give a true account of it in my next excursion. For most men, it appears to me, are in a strange uncertainty about it, whether it is of the devil or of God, and have *somewhat hastily* concluded that it is the chief end of man here to "glorify God and enjoy him forever."

Still we live meanly, like ants; though the fable tells us that we were 20 long ago changed into men; like pygmies we fight with cranes; it is error upon error, and clout upon clout, and our best virtue has for its occasion a superfluous and evitable wretchedness. Our life is frittered away by detail. An honest man has hardly need to count more than his ten fingers, or in extreme cases he may add his ten toes, and lump the rest. Simplicity, simplicity, simplicity! I say, let your affairs be as two or three, and not a hundred or a thousand; instead of a million count half a dozen, and keep your accounts on your thumb-nail. In the midst of this chopping sea of civilized life, such are the clouds and storms and quicksands and thousand-and-one items to be allowed for, that a man has to live, if he would not founder and go to the bottom and not make his port at all, by dead reckoning, and he must be a great calculator indeed who succeeds. Simplify, simplify. Instead of three meals a day, if it be necessary eat but one; instead of a hundred dishes, five; and reduce other things in proportion. Our life is like a German Confederacy, made up of petty states, with its boundary forever fluctuating, so that even a German cannot tell you how it is bounded at any moment. The nation itself, with all its so-called internal improvements, which, by the way are all external and superficial, is just such an unwieldy and overgrown establishment, cluttered with furniture and tripped up by its own traps, ruined by luxury and heedless expense, by want of calculation and a worthy aim, as the million households in the land; and the only cure for it, as for them, is in a rigid economy, a stern and more than Spartan simplicity of life and elevation of purpose. It lives too fast. Men think that it is essential that the *Nation* have commerce, and export ice, and talk through a telegraph, and ride thirty miles an hour, without a doubt, whether *they* do or not; but whether we should live like baboons or like men, is a little uncertain. If we do not get out sleepers, and forge rails, and devote days and nights to the work, but go to tinkering upon our *lives* to improve *them,* who will build railroads? And if railroads are not built, how shall we get to heaven in season? But if we stay at home and mind our business, who will want railroads? We do not ride on the railroad; it rides upon us. Did you ever think what those sleepers are that underlie the railroad? Each one is a man, an Irishman, or a Yankee man. The rails are laid on them, and they are covered with sand, and the cars run smoothly over them. They are sound sleepers, I assure you. And every few years a new lot is laid down and run over; so that, if some have the pleasure of riding on a rail, others have the misfortune to be ridden upon. And when they run over a man that is walking in his sleep, a supernumerary sleeper in the wrong position, and wake him up, they suddenly stop the cars, and make a hue and cry about it, as if this were an exception. I am glad to know that it takes a gang of men for every five miles to keep the sleepers down and level in their beds as it is, for this is a sign that they may sometime get up again.

Why should we live with such hurry and waste of life? We are determined to be starved before we are hungry. Men say that a stitch in time saves nine, and so they take a thousand stitches today to save nine tomorrow. As for *work,* we haven't any of any consequence. We have the Saint Vitus' dance,° and cannot possibly keep our heads still. If I should only give a few pulls at the parish bell-rope, as for a fire, that is, without setting the bell, there is hardly a man on his farm in the outskirts of Concord, notwithstanding that press of engagements which was his excuse so many times this morning, nor a boy, nor a woman, I might almost say, but would forsake all and follow that sound, not mainly to save property from the flames, but, if we will confess the truth, much more to see it burn, since burn it must, and we, be it known, did not set it on fire — or to see it put out, and have a hand in it, if that is done as handsomely; yes, even if it were the parish church itself. Hardly a man takes a half-hour's nap after dinner, but when he wakes he holds up his head and asks, "What's the news?" as if the rest of mankind had stood his sentinels. Some give directions to be waked every half-hour, doubtless

---

St. Vitus' dance: disease characterized by involuntary jerking movements.

for no other purpose; and then, to pay for it, they tell what they have dreamed. After a night's sleep the news is as indispensable as the breakfast. "Pray tell me anything new that has happened to a man anywhere on this globe"—and he reads it over his coffee and rolls, that a man has had his eyes gouged out this morning on the Wachito River, never dreaming the while that he lives in the dark unfathomed mammoth cave of this world, and has but the rudiment of an eye himself.

For my part, I could easily do without the post-office. I think that there are very few important communications made through it. To speak critically, I never received more than one or two letters in my life—I wrote this some years ago—that were worth the postage. The penny-post is, commonly, an institution through which you seriously offer a man that penny for his thoughts which is so often safely offered in jest. And I am sure that I never read any memorable news in a newspaper. If we read of one man robbed, or murdered, or killed by accident, or one house burned, or one vessel wrecked, or one steamboat blown up, or one cow run over on the Western Railroad, or one mad dog killed, or one lot of grasshoppers in the winter—we never need read of another. One is enough. If you are acquainted with the principle, what do you care for a myriad instances and applications? To a philosopher all *news*, as it is called, is gossip, and they who edit and read it are old women over their tea. Yet not a few are greedy after this gossip. There was such a rush, as I hear, the other day at one of the offices to learn the foreign news by the last arrival, that several large squares of plate glass belonging to the establishment were broken by the pressure—news which I seriously think a ready wit might write a twelve-month, or twelve years, beforehand with sufficient accuracy. As for Spain, for instance, if you know how to throw in Don Carlos and the Infanta, and Don Pedro and Seville and Granada, from time to time in the right proportions—they may have changed the names a little since I saw the papers—and serve up a bull-fight when other entertainments fail, it will be true to the letter, and give us as good an idea of the exact state or ruin of things in Spain as the most succinct and lucid reports under this head in the newspapers: and as for England, almost the last significant scrap of news from that quarter was the revolution of 1649; and if you have learned the history of her crops for an average year, you never need attend to that thing again, unless your speculations are of a merely pecuniary character. If one may judge who rarely looks into the newspapers, nothing new does ever happen in foreign parts, a French revolution not excepted.

What news! how much more important to know what that is which was never old! "Kieou-pe-yu (great dignitary of the state of Wei) sent a man to Khoung-tseu to know his news. Khoung-tseu caused the messenger to be seated near him, and questioned him in these terms: What is your master doing? The messenger answered with respect: My master desires to diminish the number of his faults, but he cannot accomplish it. The messenger being gone, the philosopher remarked: What a worthy messenger! What a worthy messenger!" The preacher, instead of vexing the ears of drowsy farmers on their day of rest at the end of the week—for Sunday is the fit conclusion of an ill-spent week, and not the fresh and brave beginning of a new one—with this one other draggle-tail of a sermon, should shout with thundering voice, "Pause! Avast! Why so seeming fast, but deadly slow?"

Shams and delusions are esteemed for soundest truths, while reality is fabulous. If men would steadily observe realities only, and not allow themselves to be deluded, life, to compare it with such things as we know, would be like a fairy tale and the Arabian Nights' Entertainments. If we respected only what is inevitable and has a right to be, music and poetry would resound along the streets. When we are unhurried and wise, we perceive that only great and worthy things have any permanent and absolute existence, that petty fears and petty pleasures are but the shadow of the reality. This is always exhilarating and sublime. By closing the eyes and slumbering, and consenting to be deceived by shows, men establish and confirm their daily life of routine and habit everywhere, which still is built on purely illusory foundations. Children, who play life, discern its true law and relations more clearly than men, who fail to live it worthily, but who think that they are wiser by experience, that is, by failure. I have read in a Hindoo book, that "there was a king's son, who, being expelled in infancy from his native city, was brought up by a forester, and, growing up to maturity in that state, imagined himself to belong to the barbarous race with which he lived. One of his father's ministers having discovered him, revealed to him what he was, and the misconception of his character was removed, and he knew himself to be a prince. So soul," continues the Hindoo philosopher, "from the circumstances in which it is placed, mistakes its own character, until the truth is revealed to it by some holy teacher, and then it knows itself to be *Brahme*." I perceive that we inhabitants of New England live this mean life that we do because our vision does not penetrate the surface of things. We think that that *is* which *appears* to be. If a man should walk through this town and see only the reality, where, think you, would the "Mill-dam" go to? If he should give us an account of the realities he beheld there, we should not recognize the place in his description. Look at a meeting-house, or a court-house, or a jail, or a shop, or a dwelling-house, and say what that thing really is before a true gaze, and they would all go to pieces in your account of them. Men esteem truth remote, in the outskirts of the system, behind the farthest star, before Adam and after the last man. In eternity there is indeed something true and sublime. But all these times and places and occasions are now and here. God himself culminates in the present moment, and will never be more divine in the lapse of all the ages. And we are enabled to apprehend at all what is sublime and noble only by the perpetual instilling and drenching of the reality that surrounds us. The universe constantly and obediently answers to our conceptions; whether we travel fast or slow, the track is laid for us. Let us spend our lives in conceiving then. The poet or the artist never yet had so fair and noble a design but some of his posterity at least could accomplish it.

Let us spend one day as deliberately as Nature, and not be thrown off 25 the track by every nutshell and mosquito's wing that falls on the rails. Let us rise early and fast, or break fast, gently and without perturbation; let company come and let company go, let the bells ring and the children cry—determined to make a day of it. Why should we knock under and go with the stream? Let us not be upset and overwhelmed in that terrible rapid and whirlpool called a dinner, situated in the meridian shallows. Weather this danger and you are safe, for the rest of the way is down hill. With unrelaxed nerves, with morning vigor, sail by it, looking another way, tied to the mast like Ulysses.° If the engine whistles, let it whistle till it is hoarse for its pains. If the bell rings, why should we run? We will consider what kind of music they are like. Let us settle ourselves, and work and wedge our feet downward through the mud and slush of opinion, and prejudice, and tradition, and delusion, and appearance, that alluvion which covers the globe, through Paris and London, through New York and Boston and Concord, through Church and State, through poetry and philosophy and religion, till we come to a hard bottom and rocks in place, which we can call *reality*, and say, This is, and no mistake; and then begin, having a *point d'appui*, below freshet and frost and fire, a place where you might found a wall or a state, or set a lamp-post safely, or perhaps a gauge, not a Nilometer, but a Realometer, that future ages might know how deep a freshet of shams and appearances had gathered from time to time. If you stand right fronting and face to face to a fact, you will see the sun glimmer on both its surfaces, as if it were a cimeter, and feel its sweet edge dividing you through the heart and marrow, and so you will happily conclude your mortal career. Be it life or death, we crave only reality. If we are really dying, let us hear the rattle in our throats and feel cold in the extremities; if we are alive, let us go about our business.

Time is but the stream I go a-fishing in. I drink at it; but while I drink I see the sandy bottom and detect how shallow it is. Its thin current slides away, but eternity remains. I would drink deeper; fish in the sky, whose bottom is pebbly with stars. I cannot count one. I know not the first

Ulysses: a character in Homer's *Iliad* and *Odyssey*.

letter of the alphabet. I have always been regretting that I was not as wise as the day I was born. The intellect is a cleaver; it discerns and rifts its way into the secret of things. I do not wish to be any more busy with my hands than is necessary. My head is hands and feet. I feel all my best faculties concentrated in it. My instinct tells me that my head is an organ for burrowing, as some creatures use their snout and fore paws, and with it I would mine and burrow my way through these hills. I think that the richest vein is somewhere hereabouts; so by the divining-rod and thin rising vapors I judge; and here I will begin to mine.

Understanding the Text

1. What does Thoreau mean when he says, "A man is rich in proportion to the number of things which he can afford to let alone" (par. 1)? How does this concept relate to what you know about environmentalism and sustainability?

2. How does Thoreau describe his location in paragraphs 10–13? Why is this important?

3. In paragraphs 14 and 15, Thoreau talks about waking up each morning. What does "waking up" mean to him literally, symbolically, and spiritually?

4. Near the end of this passage, Thoreau writes that "Time is but a stream I go a-fishing in" (par. 23). What is Thoreau saying about his place in the world?

Reflection and Response

5. Thoreau talks a lot about ownership. What are the benefits and liabilities of ownership? Do you agree or disagree with Thoreau's perspective?

6. What do you make of the many references to classical mythology in this excerpt? Why do you think Thoreau included them? What do they add to the text?

7. The word "simplicity" is used repeatedly in this text. Why does Thoreau repeat the term so often? What is his point?

8. How does Thoreau's location affect his way of thinking? Would he have had a different perspective if he had lived in a more urban environment? How do your landscape and location affect the way you think about things?

Making Connections

9. Thoreau is associated with the Transcendentalist philosophy. Do some research on Transcendentalism. What are its central beliefs? How does Transcendentalism relate to environmentalism and sustainability?

10. What is Walden Pond like today? How is it different from the place Thoreau lived? What would Thoreau think if he visited Walden Pond right now?

11. In paragraph 19, Thoreau discusses the communication technologies of his day. What is he saying about the ways in which we communicate? How does this relate to the communication technologies you use in your everyday life? How does technology connect or disconnect us from other people?

The American Forests

John Muir

John Muir is often described as the "father of the environmental movement" because he was one of the earliest and most persuasive advocates of environmental preservation in the United States. Born in Scotland in 1838, Muir moved to the United States as a boy and spent much of his early life exploring the American wilderness. After traveling to California, he spent many years exploring and writing about the Sierra Nevada mountain area. His writing and advocacy for the region helped establish the Yosemite and Sequoia National Parks.

Muir published a dozen books and hundreds of articles about his experiences in the wilderness, and his work has been read by millions. It is no understatement to say that Muir fundamentally shaped the way Americans envision their relationship with the natural world. Hiking trails, monuments, beaches, glaciers, bridges, and even a college have been named in his honor. Later in his life, Muir founded the Sierra Club, one of the oldest and most influential environmental organizations in the United States.

The essay excerpted here, "The American Forests," originally appeared in the *Atlantic* magazine in 1897. Muir wrote the essay to raise awareness about the decline of American forests, and the essay is often credited as one of the inspirations for the establishment of the U.S. Forest Service. Pay attention to Muir's central idea and the way he conveys it. What point is he making about natural resources? What does he hope to accomplish? How does he use language to persuade readers?

The forests of America, however slighted by man, must have been a great delight to God; for they were the best he ever planted. The whole continent was a garden, and from the beginning it seemed to be favored above all the other wild parks and gardens of the globe. To prepare the ground, it was rolled and sifted in seas with infinite loving deliberation and forethought, lifted into the light, submerged and warmed over and over again, pressed and crumpled into folds and ridges, mountains and hills, subsoiled with heaving volcanic fires, ploughed and ground and sculptured into scenery and soil with glaciers and rivers,—every feature growing and changing from beauty to beauty, higher and higher. And in the fullness of time it was planted in groves, and belts, and broad, exuberant, mantling forests, with the largest, most varied, most fruitful, and most beautiful trees in the world. Bright seas made its border with wave embroidery and icebergs; gray deserts were outspread in the middle of it, mossy tundras on the north, savannas on the south, and blooming prairies and plains; while lakes and rivers shone through all the vast forests and openings, and happy birds and beasts gave delightful animation. Everywhere, everywhere over all the blessed continent, there were beauty, and melody, and kindly, wholesome, foodful abundance.

These forests were composed of about five hundred species of trees, all of them in some way useful to man, ranging in size from twenty-five feet in height and less than one foot in diameter at the ground to four hundred feet in height and more than twenty feet in diameter,—lordly monarchs proclaiming the gospel of beauty like apostles. For many a century after the ice-ploughs were melted, nature fed them and dressed them every day; working like a man, a loving, devoted, painstaking gardener; fingering every leaf and flower and mossy furrowed bole; bending, trimming, modeling, balancing, painting them with the loveliest colors; bringing over them now clouds with cooling shadows and showers, now sunshine; fanning them with gentle winds and rustling their leaves; exercising them in every fibre with storms, and pruning them; loading them with flowers and fruit, loading them with snow, and ever making them more beautiful as the years rolled by. Wide-branching oak and elm in endless variety, walnut and maple, chestnut and beech, ilex and locust, touching limb to limb, spread a leafy translucent canopy along the coast of the Atlantic over the wrinkled folds and ridges of the Alleghanies,°—a green billowy sea in summer, golden and purple in autumn, pearly gray like a steadfast frozen mist of interlacing branches and sprays in leafless, restful winter.

To the southward stretched dark, level-topped cypresses in knobby, tangled swamps, grassy savannas in the midst of them like lakes of light, groves of gay sparkling spice-trees, magnolias and palms, glossy-leaved and blooming and shining continually. To the northward, over Maine and the Ottawa, rose hosts of spiry, rosiny evergreens,—white pine and spruce, hemlock and cedar, shoulder to shoulder, laden with purple cones, their myriad needles sparkling and shimmering, covering hills and swamps, rocky headlands and domes, ever bravely aspiring and seeking the sky; the ground in their shade now snow-clad and frozen, now mossy and flowery; beaver meadows here and there, full of lilies and grass; lakes gleaming like eyes, and a silvery embroidery of rivers and creeks watering and brightening all the vast glad wilderness.

Thence westward were oak and elm, hickory and tupelo, gum and liriodendron, sassafras and ash, linden and laurel, spreading on ever wider in glorious exuberance over the great fertile basin of the Mississippi,

---

Alleghanies: the Allegheny Mountains, which run through Pennsylvania, Maryland, West Virginia, and Virginia.

over damp level bottoms, low dimpling hollows, and round dotting hills, embosoming sunny prairies and cheery park openings, half sunshine, half shade; while a dark wilderness of pines covered the region around the Great Lakes. Thence still westward swept the forests to right and left around grassy plains and deserts a thousand miles wide: irrepressible hosts of spruce and pine, aspen and willow, nut-pine and juniper, cactus and yucca, caring nothing for drought, extending undaunted from mountain to mountain, over mesa and desert, to join the darkening multitudes of pines that covered the high Rocky ranges and the glorious forests along the coast of the moist and balmy Pacific, where new species of pine, giant cedars and spruces, silver firs and sequoias, kings of their race, growing close together like grass in a meadow, poised their brave domes and spires in the sky three hundred feet above the ferns and the lilies that enameled the ground; towering serene through the long centuries, preaching God's forestry fresh from heaven.

Here the forests reached their highest development. Hence they went 5 wavering northward over icy Alaska, brave spruce and fir, poplar and birch, by the coasts and the rivers, to within sight of the Arctic Ocean. American forests! the glory of the world! Surveyed thus from the east to the west, from the north to the south, they are rich beyond thought, immortal, immeasurable, enough and to spare for every feeding, sheltering beast and bird, insect and son of Adam; and nobody need have cared had there been no pines in Norway, no cedars and deodars on Lebanon and the Himalayas, no vine-clad selvas in the basin of the Amazon. With such variety, harmony, and triumphant exuberance, even nature, it would seem, might have rested content with the forests of North America, and planted no more.

So they appeared a few centuries ago when they were rejoicing in wildness. The Indians with stone axes could do them no more harm than could gnawing beavers and browsing moose. Even the fires of the Indians and the fierce shattering lightning seemed to work together only for good in clearing spots here and there for smooth garden prairies, and openings for sunflowers seeking the light. But when the steel axe of the white man rang out in the startled air their doom was sealed. Every tree heard the bodeful sound, and pillars of smoke gave the sign in the sky.

I suppose we need not go mourning the buffaloes. In the nature of things they had to give place to better cattle, though the change might have been made without barbarous wickedness. Likewise many of nature's five hundred kinds of wild trees had to make way for orchards and cornfields. In the settlement and civilization of the country, bread more than timber or beauty was wanted; and in the blindness of hunger, the early settlers, claiming Heaven as their guide, regarded God's

John Muir in 1902.
Library of Congress [LC-USZ62-52000]

trees as only a larger kind of pernicious weeds, extremely hard to get rid of. Accordingly, with no eye to the future, these pious destroyers waged interminable forest wars; chips flew thick and fast; trees in their beauty fell crashing by millions, smashed to confusion, and the smoke of their burning has been rising to heaven more than two hundred years. After the Atlantic coast from Maine to Georgia had been mostly cleared and scorched into melancholy ruins, the overflowing multitude of bread and money seekers poured over the Alleghanies into the fertile middle West, spreading ruthless devastation ever wider and farther over the rich valley of the Mississippi and the vast shadowy pine region about the Great Lakes. Thence still westward the invading horde of destroyers called settlers made its fiery way over the broad Rocky Mountains, felling and burning more fiercely than ever, until at last it has reached the wild side of the continent, and entered the last of the great aboriginal forests on the shores of the Pacific.

Surely, then, it should not be wondered at that lovers of their country, bewailing its baldness, are now crying aloud, "Save what is left of the forests!" Clearing has surely now gone far enough; soon timber will be scarce, and not a grove will be left to rest in or pray in. The remnant protected will yield plenty of timber, a perennial harvest for every right use, without further diminution of its area, and will continue to cover the springs of the rivers that rise in the mountains and give irrigating waters to the dry valleys at their feet, prevent wasting floods and be a blessing to everybody forever.

Every other civilized nation in the world has been compelled to care for its forests, and so must we if waste and destruction are not to go on to the bitter end, leaving America as barren as Palestine or Spain. In its calmer moments in the midst of bewildering hunger and war and restless over-industry, Prussia has learned that the forest plays an important part in human progress, and that the advance in civilization only makes it more indispensable. It has, therefore, as shown by Mr. Pinchot, refused to deliver its forests to more or less speedy destruction by permitting them to pass into private ownership. But the state woodlands are not allowed to lie idle. On the contrary, they are made to produce as much timber as is possible without spoiling them. In the administration of its forests, the state righteously considers itself bound to treat them as a trust for the nation as a whole, and to keep in view the common good of the people for all time.

In France no government forests have been sold since 1870. On the   10 other hand, about one half of the fifty million francs spent on forestry has been given to engineering works, to make the replanting of denuded° areas possible. The disappearance of the forests in the first place, it is claimed, may be traced in most cases directly to mountain pasturage. The provisions of the code concerning private woodlands are substantially these: No private owner may clear his woodlands without giving notice to the government at least four months in advance, and the forest service may forbid the clearing on the following grounds: to maintain the soil on mountains, to defend the soil against erosion and flooding by rivers or torrents, to insure the existence of springs and watercourses, to protect the dunes and seashore, etc. A proprietor who has cleared his forest without permission is subject to heavy fine, and in addition may be made to replant the cleared area.

In Switzerland, after many laws like our own had been found wanting, the Swiss forest school was established in 1865, and soon after the Federal Forest Law was enacted, which is binding over nearly two thirds of the country. Under its provisions, the cantons must appoint and pay the number of suitably educated foresters required for the fulfillment of the forest law; and in the organization of a normally stocked forest, the object of first importance must be the cutting each year of an amount of timber equal to the total annual increase, and no more.

denuded: made naked or bare; stripped.

The Russian government passed a law in 1888, declaring that clearing is forbidden in protection forests, and is allowed in others "only when its effects will not be to disturb the suitable relations which should exist between forest and agricultural lands."

Even Japan is ahead of us in the management of her forests. They cover an area of about 29,000,000 acres. The feudal lords valued the woodlands, and enacted vigorous protective laws; and when, in the latest civil war, the Mikado government destroyed the feudal system, it declared the forests that had belonged to the feudal lords to be the property of the state, promulgated a forest law binding on the whole kingdom, and founded a school of forestry in Tokio. The forest service does not rest satisfied with the present proportion of woodland, but looks to planting the best forest trees it can find in any country, if likely to be useful and to thrive in Japan.

"Now it is plain that the forests are not inexhaustible, and that quick measures must be taken if ruin is to be avoided."

In India systematic forest management was begun about forty years ago, under difficulties — presented by the character of the country, the prevalence of running fires, opposition from lumbermen, settlers, etc. — not unlike those which confront us now. Of the total area of government forests, perhaps 70,000,000 acres, 55,000,000 acres have been brought under the control of the forestry department, — a larger area than that of all our national parks and reservations. The chief aims of the administration are effective protection of the forests from fire, an efficient system of regeneration, and cheap transportation of the forest products; the results so far have been most beneficial and encouraging.

It seems, therefore, that almost every civilized nation can give us a lesson on the management and care of forests. So far our government has done nothing effective with its forests, though the best in the world, but is like a rich and foolish spendthrift who has inherited a magnificent estate in perfect order, and then has left his rich fields and meadows, forests and parks, to be sold and plundered and wasted at will, depending on their inexhaustible abundance. Now it is plain that the forests are not inexhaustible, and that quick measures must be taken if ruin is to be avoided. Year by year the remnant is growing smaller before the axe and fire, while the laws in existence provide neither for the protection of the timber from destruction nor for its use where it is most needed. . . .

It is not generally known that, notwithstanding the immense quantities of timber cut every year for foreign and home markets and mines, 15 from five to ten times as much is destroyed as is used, chiefly by running forest fires that only the federal government can stop. Travelers through the West in summer are not likely to forget the fire-work displayed along the various railway tracks. Thoreau,° when contemplating the destruction of the forests on the east side of the continent, said that soon the country would be so bald that every man would have to grow whiskers to hide its nakedness, but he thanked God that at least the sky was safe. Had he gone West he would have found out that the sky was not safe; for all through the summer months, over most of the mountain regions, the smoke of mill and forest fires is so thick and black that no sunbeam can pierce it. The whole sky, with clouds, sun, moon, and stars, is simply blotted out. There is no real sky and no scenery. Not a mountain is left in the landscape. At least none is in sight from the lowlands, and they all might as well be on the moon, as far as scenery is concerned.

The half dozen transcontinental railroad companies advertise the beauties of their lines in gorgeous many-colored folders, each claiming its as the "scenic route." "The route of superior desolation"—the smoke, dust, and ashes route—would be a more truthful description. Every train rolls on through dismal smoke and barbarous melancholy ruins; and the companies might well cry in their advertisements: "Come! travel our way. Ours is the blackest. It is the only genuine Erebus° route. The sky is black and the ground is black, and on either side there is a continuous border of black stumps and logs and blasted trees appealing to heaven for help as if still half alive, and their mute eloquence is most interestingly touching. The blackness is perfect. On account of the superior skill of our workmen, advantages of climate, and the kind of trees, the charring is generally deeper along our line, and the ashes are deeper, and the confusion and desolation displayed can never be rivaled. No other route on this continent so fully illustrates the abomination of desolation." Such a claim would be reasonable, as each seems the worst, whatever route you chance to take.

Of course a way had to be cleared through the woods. But the felled timber is not worked up into firewood for the engines and into lumber for the company's use; it is left lying in vulgar confusion, and is fired from time to time by sparks from locomotives or by the workmen camping along the line. The fires, whether accidental or set, are allowed to run into the woods as far as they may, thus assuring comprehensive destruction. The directors of a line that guarded against fires, and cleared a clean

---

Thoreau: Henry David Thoreau (1817–1862), U.S. naturalist and author.
Erebus: in classical mythology, it is the darkness under the earth, imagined either as the abode of sinners after death or of all the dead.

gap edged with living trees, and fringed and mantled with the grass and flowers and beautiful seedlings that are ever ready and willing to spring up, might justly boast of the beauty of their road; for nature is always ready to heal every scar. But there is no such road on the western side of the continent. Last summer, in the Rocky Mountains, I saw six fires started by sparks from a locomotive within a distance of three miles, and nobody was in sight to prevent them from spreading. They might run into the adjacent forests and burn the timber from hundreds of square miles; not a man in the State would care to spend an hour in fighting them, as long as his own fences and buildings were not threatened.

Notwithstanding all the waste and use which have been going on unchecked like a storm for more than two centuries, it is not yet too late, though it is high time, for the government to begin a rational adminis-tration of its forests. About seventy million acres it still owns,—enough for all the country, if wisely used. These residual forests are generally on mountain slopes, just where they are doing the most good, and where their removal would be followed by the greatest number of evils; the lands they cover are too rocky and high for agriculture, and can never be made as valuable for any other crop as for the present crop of trees. It has been shown over and over again that if these mountains were to be stripped of their trees and underbrush, and kept bare and sodless by hordes of sheep and the innumerable fires the shepherds set, besides those of the millmen, prospectors, shake-makers, and all sorts of adven-turers, both lowlands and mountains would speedily become little bet-ter than deserts, compared with their present beneficent fertility. During heavy rainfalls and while the winter accumulations of snow were melt-ing, the larger streams would swell into destructive torrents; cutting deep, rugged-edged gullies, carrying away the fertile humus and soil as well as sand and rocks, filling up and overflowing their lower channels, and covering the lowland fields with raw detritus.° Drought and barren-ness would follow.

In their natural condition, or under wise management, keeping out destructive sheep, preventing fires, selecting the trees that should be cut for lumber, and preserving the young ones and the shrubs and sod of herbaceous vegetation, these forests would be a never failing fountain of wealth and beauty. The cool shades of the forest give rise to moist beds and currents of air, and the sod of grasses and the various flowering plants and shrubs thus fostered, together with the network and sponge of tree roots, absorb and hold back the rain and the waters from melting snow, compelling them to ooze and percolate and flow gently through

detritus: any disintegrated material; debris or dirt.

the soil in streams that never dry. All the pine needles and rootlets and blades of grass, and the fallen decaying trunks of trees, are dams, storing the bounty of the clouds and dispensing it in perennial life-giving streams, instead of allowing it to gather suddenly and rush headlong in short-lived devastating floods. Everybody on the dry side of the continent is beginning to find this out, and, in view of the waste going on, is growing more and more anxious for government protection. The outcries we hear against forest reservations come mostly from thieves who are wealthy and steal timber by wholesale. They have so long been allowed to steal and destroy in peace that any impediment to forest robbery is denounced as a cruel and irreligious interference with "vested rights," likely to endanger the repose of all ungodly welfare.

Gold, gold, gold! How strong a voice that metal has!

"O wae for the siller, it is sae preva'lin'!"

Even in Congress, a sizable chunk of gold, carefully concealed, will outtalk and outfight all the nation on a subject like forestry, well smothered in ignorance, and in which the money interests of only a few are conspicuously involved. Under these circumstances, the bawling, blethering oratorical stuff drowns the voice of God himself. Yet the dawn of a new day in forestry is breaking. Honest citizens see that only the rights of the government are being trampled, not those of the settlers. Merely what belongs to all alike is reserved, and every acre that is left should be held together under the federal government as a basis for a general policy of administration for the public good. The people will not always be deceived by selfish opposition, whether from lumber and mining corporations or from sheepmen and prospectors, however cunningly brought forward underneath fables and gold.

Emerson° says that things refuse to be mismanaged long. An exception would seem to be found in the case of our forests, which have been mismanaged rather long, and now come desperately near being like smashed eggs and spilt milk. Still, in the long run the world does not move backward. The wonderful advance made in the last few years, in creating four national parks in the West, and thirty forest reservations, embracing nearly forty million acres; and in the planting of the borders of streets and highways and spacious parks in all the great cities, to satisfy the natural taste and hunger for landscape beauty and righteousness that God has put, in some measure, into every human being and animal, shows the trend of awakening public opinion. The making

Emerson: Ralph Waldo Emerson (1803–1882), U.S. essayist and poet.

of the far-famed New York Central Park was opposed by even good men, with misguided pluck, perseverance, and ingenuity; but straight right won its way, and now that park is appreciated. So we confidently believe it will be with our great national parks and forest reservations. There will be a period of indifference on the part of the rich, sleepy with wealth, and of the toiling millions, sleepy with poverty, most of whom never saw a forest; a period of screaming protest and objection from the plunderers, who are as unconscionable and enterprising as Satan. But light is surely coming, and the friends of destruction will preach and bewail in vain.

The United States government has always been proud of the welcome it has extended to good men of every nation, seeking freedom and homes and bread. Let them be welcomed still as nature welcomes them, to the woods as well as to the prairies and plains. No place is too good for good men, and still there is room. They are invited to heaven, and may well be allowed in America. Every place is made better by them. Let them be as free to pick gold and gems from the hills, to cut and hew, dig and plant, for homes and bread, as the birds are to pick berries from the wild bushes, and moss and leaves for nests. The ground will be glad to feed them, and the pines will come down from the mountains for their homes as willingly as the cedars came from Lebanon for Solomon's temple. Nor will the woods be the worse for this use, or their benign influences be diminished any more than the sun is diminished by shining. Mere destroyers, however, tree-killers, spreading death and confusion in the fairest groves and gardens ever planted, let the government hasten to cast them out and make an end of them. For it must be told again and again, and be burningly borne in mind, that just now, while protective measures are being deliberated languidly, destruction and use are speeding on faster and farther every day. The axe and saw are insanely busy, chips are flying thick as snowflakes, and every summer thousands of acres of priceless forests, with their underbrush, soil, springs, climate, scenery, and religion, are vanishing away in clouds of smoke, while, except in the national parks, not one forest guard is employed.

All sorts of local laws and regulations have been tried and found wanting, and the costly lessons of our own experience, as well as that of every civilized nation, show conclusively that the fate of the remnant of our forests is in the hands of the federal government, and that if the remnant is to be saved at all, it must be saved quickly.

Any fool can destroy trees. They cannot run away; and if they could, they would still be destroyed, — chased and hunted down as long as fun or a dollar could be got out of their bark hides, branching horns, or magnificent bole backbones. Few that fell trees plant them; nor would planting avail much towards getting back anything like the noble primeval forests. During a man's life only saplings can be grown, in the place of the old trees—tens of centuries old—that have been destroyed. It took more than three thousand years to make some of the trees in these Western woods,—trees that are still standing in perfect strength and beauty, waving and singing in the mighty forests of the Sierra. Through all the wonderful, eventful centuries since Christ's time—and long before that—God has cared for these trees, saved them from drought, disease, avalanches, and a thousand straining, leveling tempests and floods; but he cannot save them from fools,—only Uncle Sam can do that.

Understanding the Text

1. How does Muir describe the variation in American forests from region to region?
2. How does Muir use the passage of time — past, present, and future — to make a point about the American forests?
3. How do the policies regarding deforestation in other countries differ from those Muir describes? Why does he make this comparison?

Reflection and Response

4. Why does Muir use so much description of the forests and landscape? What is the purpose of this thick description?
5. At times, Muir uses biblical or spiritual terminology. Why do you think he would link the earth and forests to God? How did this appeal to his audience?
6. What impact does the last paragraph of this piece have on you? What was Muir's intended purpose?

Making Connections

7. Muir mentions Thoreau's fear for the forests and their future (par. 16). What are the other similarities between Thoreau's essay (earlier in this chapter) and Muir's?
8. Do some research on Yosemite or Sequoia National Park. What role did Muir play in their creation? Do you think he would be pleased with their current state?
9. Muir was one of the founders of the Sierra Club, a prominent environmental organization. Visit the Sierra Club's website and look for similarities between the essay you've just read and the content you find on the website. In what ways are Muir's ideas present in the organization today? How is it different from what he might have envisioned?
10. In what ways does this essay foreshadow current environmental and sustainability issues? In what ways are the issues it describes different from our current issues?

The Obligation to Endure

Rachel Carson

Writer, scientist, and conservationist Rachel Carson was born on a small family farm in Springdale, Pennsylvania, in 1907. Carson graduated from Pennsylvania College for Women (now Chatham College) in 1929; studied at the Marine Biological Laboratory in Woods Hole, Massachusetts; and received her master's degree in zoology from Johns Hopkins University in 1932. She began her career as an aquatic biologist for the U.S. Bureau of Fisheries and became a full-time writer in the 1950s.

Carson is known for two best-selling books: *The Sea around Us* (1951) and *Silent Spring* (1962). Her early writing, including *The Sea around Us*, focuses on the beauty of nature and combines scientific study and poetic description. Her later work focuses on the dangers of pesticides and other chemicals and their widespread use after World War II. Carson wrote *Silent Spring* to warn the public about the long-term effects of these chemicals, challenging the practices of agricultural scientists and the U.S. government. The basic premise of "The Obligation to Endure," the second chapter in *Silent Spring*, is that pesticides may do more harm than good and that public health and safety must be considered.

After the publication of *Silent Spring*, Carson was attacked as an alarmist by some in the chemical industry and in government, but she continued to speak out about the dangers of pesticides to humans, animals, and ecosystems. Testifying before Congress in 1963, Carson called for new policies to protect human health and the environment. Her work led to a nationwide ban on DDT and other pesticides, and it contributed to the creation of the U.S. Environmental Protection Agency (EPA). Carson was posthumously awarded the Presidential Medal of Freedom by President Jimmy Carter.

The history of life on earth has been a history of interaction between living things and their surroundings. To a large extent, the physical form and the habits of the earth's vegetation and its animal life have been molded by the environment. Considering the whole span of earthly time, the opposite effect, in which life actually modifies its surroundings, has been relatively slight. Only within the moment of time represented by the present century has one species—man—acquired significant power to alter the nature of his world.

During the past quarter century this power has not only increased to one of disturbing magnitude but it has changed in character. The most alarming of all man's assaults upon the environment is the contamination of air, earth, rivers, and sea with dangerous and even lethal materials. This pollution is for the most part irrecoverable; the chain of evil it initiates not only in the world that must support life but in living tissues is for the most part irreversible. In this now universal contamination of the environment, chemicals are the sinister and little recognized partners of radiation in

> "The history of life on earth has been a history of interaction between living things and their surroundings."

changing the very nature of the world—the very nature of its life. Strontium 90, released through nuclear explosions into the air, comes to earth in rain or drifts down as fallout, lodges in soil, enters into the grass or corn or wheat grown there, and in time takes up its abode in the bones of a human being, there to remain until his death. Similarly, chemicals sprayed on croplands or forests or gardens lie long in soil, entering into living organisms, passing from one to another in a chain of poisoning and death. Or they pass mysteriously by underground streams until they emerge and, through the alchemy of air and sunlight, combine into new forms, that kill vegetation, sicken cattle, and work unknown harm on those who drink from once pure wells. As Albert Schweitzer has said, "Man can hardly even recognize the devils of his own creation."

It took hundreds of millions of years to produce the life that now inhabits the earth, eons of time in which that developing and evolving and diversifying life reached a state of adjustment and balance with its surroundings. The environment, rigorously shaping and directing the life it supports, contained elements that were hostile as well as supporting. Certain rocks gave out dangerous radiation; even within the light of the sun, from which all life draws its energy, there were short-wave radiations with power to injure. Given time—time not in years but in millennia—life adjusts, and a balance has been reached. For time is the essential ingredient; but in the modern world there is no time.

The rapidity of change and the speed with which new situations are created follow the impetuous and heedless pace of man rather than the deliberate pace of nature. Radiation is no longer merely the background radiation of rocks, the bombardment of cosmic rays, the ultraviolet of the sun that have existed before there was any life on earth; radiation is now the unnatural creation of man's tampering with the atom. The chemicals to which life is asked to make its adjustment are no longer merely the calcium and silica and copper and all the rest of the minerals washed out of the rocks and carried in rivers to the sea; they are the synthetic creations of man's inventive mind, brewed in his laboratories, and having no counterparts in nature.

To adjust to these chemicals would require time on the scale that is nature's; it would require not merely the years of a man's life but the life of generations. And even this, were it by some miracle possible, would

5

be futile, for the new chemicals come from our laboratories in an endless stream; almost five hundred annually find their way into actual use in the United States alone. The figure is staggering and its implications are not easily grasped—500 new chemicals to which the bodies of men and animals are required somehow to adapt each year, chemicals totally outside the limits of biologic experience.

Among them are many that are used in man's war against nature. Since the mid-1940s over 200 basic chemicals have been created for use in killing insects, weeds, rodents, and other organisms described in the modern vernacular as "pests"; and they are sold under several thousand different brand names.

These sprays, dusts, and aerosols are now applied almost universally to farms, gardens, forests, and homes—nonselective chemicals that have the power to kill every insect, the "good" and the "bad," to still the song of birds and the leaping of fish in the streams, to coat the leaves with a deadly film, and to linger on in soil—all this though the intended target may be only a few weeds or insects. Can anyone believe it is possible to lay down such a barrage of poisons on the surface of the earth without making it unfit for all life? They should not be called "insecticides," but "biocides."

The whole process of spraying seems caught up in an endless spiral. Since DDT° was released for civilian use, a process of escalation has been going on in which ever more toxic materials must be found. This has happened because insects, in a triumphant vindication of Darwin's principle of the survival of the fittest, have evolved super races immune to the particular insecticide used, hence a deadlier one has always to be developed and then a deadlier one than that. It has happened also because, for reasons to be described later, destructive insects often undergo a "flareback," or resurgence, after spraying, in numbers greater than before. Thus the chemical war is never won, and all life is caught in its violent crossfire.

Along with the possibility of the extinction of mankind by nuclear war, the central problem of our age has therefore become the contamination of man's total environment with such substances of incredible potential for harm—substances that accumulate in the tissues of plants and animals and even penetrate the germ cells to shatter or alter the very material of heredity upon which the shape of the future depends.

Some would-be architects of our future look toward a time when   10
it will be possible to alter the human germ plasm by design. But we may easily be doing so now by inadvertence, for many chemicals, like

DDT: $C_{14}H_9Cl_5$; potent chemical used as an insecticide, prohibited for agricultural use in the United States since 1973.

radiation, bring about gene mutations. It is ironic to think that man might determine his own future by something so seemingly trivial as the choice of an insect spray.

All this has been risked — for what? Future historians may well be amazed by our distorted sense of proportion. How could intelligent beings seek to control a few unwanted species by a method that contaminated the entire environment and brought the threat of disease and death even to their own kind? Yet this is precisely what we have done. We have done it, moreover, for reasons that collapse the moment we examine them. We are told that the enormous and expanding use of pesticides is necessary to maintain farm production. Yet is our real problem not one of overproduction? Our farms, despite measures to remove acreages from production and to pay farmers not to produce, have yielded such a staggering excess of crops that the American taxpayer in 1962 is paying out more than one billion dollars a year as the total carrying cost of the surplus-food storage program. And is the situation helped when one branch of the Agriculture Department tries to reduce production while another states, as it did in 1958, "It is believed generally that reduction of crop acreages under provisions of the Soil Bank will stimulate interest in use of chemicals to obtain maximum production on the land retained in crops"?

All this is not to say there is no insect problem and no need of control. I am saying, rather, that control must be geared to realities, not to mythical situations, and that the methods employed must be such that they do not destroy us along with the insects.

The problem whose attempted solution has brought such a train of disaster in its wake is an accompaniment of our modern way of life. Long before the age of man, insects inhabited the earth—a group of extraordinarily varied and adaptable beings. Over the course of time since man's advent, a small percentage of the more than half a million species of insects have come into conflict with human welfare in two principal ways: as competitors for the food supply and as carriers of human disease.

Disease-carrying insects become important where human beings are crowded together, especially under conditions where sanitation is poor, as in time of natural disaster or war or in situations of extreme poverty and deprivation. Then control of some sort becomes necessary. It is a sobering fact, however, as we shall presently see, that the method of massive chemical control has had only limited success, and also threatens to worsen the very conditions it is intended to curb.

Under primitive agricultural conditions the farmer had few insect problems. These arose with the intensification of agriculture—the devotion of immense acreages to a single crop. Such a system set the stage for explosive increases in specific insect populations. Single-crop farming does not take advantage of the principles by which nature works; it is agriculture as an engineer might conceive it to be. Nature has introduced great variety into the landscape, but man has displayed a passion for simplifying it. Thus he undoes the built-in checks and balances by which nature holds the species within bounds. One important natural check is a limit on the amount of suitable habitat for each species. Obviously then, an insect that lives on wheat can build up its population to much higher levels on a farm devoted to wheat than on one in which wheat is intermingled with other crops to which the insect is not adapted.

The same thing happens in other situations. A generation or more ago, the towns of large areas of the United States lined their streets with the noble elm tree. Now the beauty they hopefully created is threatened with complete destruction as disease sweeps through the elms, carried by a beetle that would have only limited chance to build up large populations and to spread from tree to tree if the elms were only occasional trees in a richly diversified planting.

Another factor in the modern insect problem is one that must be viewed against a background of geologic and human history: the spreading of thousands of different kinds of organisms from their native homes to invade new territories. This worldwide migration has been studied and graphically described by the British ecologist Charles Elton in his recent book *The Ecology of Invasions*. During the Cretaceous

15

Period,° some hundred million years ago, flooding seas cut many land bridges between continents and living things found themselves confined in what Elton calls "colossal separate nature reserves." There, isolated from others of their kind, they developed many new species. When some of the land masses were joined again, about 15 million years ago, these species began to move out into new territories — a movement that is not only still in progress but is now receiving considerable assistance from man.

The importation of plants is the primary agent in the modern spread of species, for animals have almost invariably gone along with the plants, quarantine being a comparatively recent and not completely effective innovation. The United States Office of Plant Introduction alone has introduced almost 200,000 species and varieties of plants from all over the world. Nearly half of the 180 or so major insect enemies of plants in the United States are accidental imports from abroad, and most of them have come as hitchhikers on plants.

In new territory, out of reach of the restraining hand of the natural enemies that kept down its numbers in its native land, an invading plant or animal is able to become enormously abundant. Thus it is no accident that our most troublesome insects are introduced species.

These invasions, both the naturally occurring and those dependent on human assistance, are likely to continue indefinitely. Quarantine and massive chemical campaigns are only extremely expensive ways of buying time. We are faced, according to Dr. Elton, "with a life-and-death need not just to find new technological means of suppressing this plant or that animal"; instead we need the basic knowledge of animal populations and their relations to their surroundings that will "promote an even balance and damp down the explosive power of outbreaks and new invasions." Much of the necessary knowledge is now available but we do not use it. We train ecologists in our universities and even employ them in our governmental agencies, but we seldom take their advice. We allow the chemical death rain to fall as though there were no alternative, whereas in fact there are many, and our ingenuity could soon discover many more if given opportunity.

Have we fallen into a mesmerized state that makes us accept as inevitable that which is inferior or detrimental, as though having lost the will or the vision to demand that which is good? Such thinking, in the words of the ecologist Paul Shepard, "idealizes life with only its head out of water, inches above the limits of toleration of the corruption of its own

Cretaceous Period: from 135 million to 63 million years ago; end of the age of reptiles; appearance of modern insects and flowering plants.

environment. . . . Why should we tolerate a diet of weak poisons, a home in insipid surroundings, a circle of acquaintances who are not quite our enemies, the noise of motors with just enough relief to prevent insanity? Who would want to live in a world which is just not quite fatal?"

Yet such a world is pressed upon us. The crusade to create a chemically sterile, insect-free world seems to have engendered a fanatic zeal on the part of many specialists and most of the so-called control agencies. On every hand there is evidence that those engaged in spraying operations exercise a ruthless power. "The regulatory entomologists . . . function as prosecutor, judge and jury, tax assessor and collector and sheriff to enforce their own orders," said Connecticut entomologist Neely Turner. The most flagrant abuses go unchecked in both state and federal agencies.

It is not my contention that chemical insecticides must never be used. I do contend that we have put poisonous and biologically potent chemicals indiscriminately into the hands of persons largely or wholly ignorant of their potentials for harm. We have subjected enormous numbers of people to contact with these poisons, without their consent and often without their knowledge. If the Bill of Rights contains no guarantee that a citizen shall be secure against lethal poisons distributed either by private individuals or by public officials, it is surely only because our forefathers, despite their considerable wisdom and foresight, could conceive of no such problem.

I contend, furthermore, that we have allowed these chemicals to be used with little or no advance investigation of their effect on soil, water, wildlife, and man himself. Future generations are unlikely to condone our lack of prudent concern for the integrity of the natural world that supports all life.

There is still very limited awareness of the nature of the threat. This is   25
an era of specialists, each of whom sees his own problem and is unaware of or intolerant of the larger frame into which it fits. It is also an era dominated by industry, in which the right to make a dollar at whatever cost is seldom challenged. When the public protests, confronted with some obvious evidence of damaging results of pesticide applications, it is fed little tranquilizing pills of half truth. We urgently need an end to these false assurances, to the sugar coating of unpalatable facts. It is the public that is being asked to assume the risks that the insect controllers calculate. The public must decide whether it wishes to continue on the present road, and it can do so only when in full possession of the facts. In the words of Jean Rostand,° "The obligation to endure gives us the right to know."

Jean Rostand: (1894–1977), French biologist and philosopher.

Understanding the Text

1. What does Carson say about the power of humans to alter the natural world? In what ways is this power new, unique, or dangerous?

2. Why does Carson suggest that these chemicals should be called "biocides" rather than "insecticides"? What is the difference between these terms? Which term is more accurate?

3. In what two principal ways do insects conflict with humans? Does Carson believe that pesticides and other chemicals are the best methods for addressing these conflicts?

Reflection and Response

4. How does Carson appeal directly to the public? Is the public her primary audience in this piece? What other audiences do you think she imagined?

5. How does this excerpt discuss the notion of time? What are the differences in time that Carson discusses? How might these differences affect humans and natural environments?

6. The image on page 53 is taken from Carson's original text of *Silent Spring*. What does this image convey? How does it seek to persuade readers without using words? Do you think the image adds meaning to Carson's work?

Making Connections

7. Carson's work is credited for the ban of some pesticides, including DDT. Do some research to learn about DDT. How is it different from or similar to other pesticides that are still on the market?

8. Research some natural ways to control the pests that may destroy crops or gardens. Are these methods as effective as traditional pesticides? Which methods seem most appropriate to you?

9. Do some research on the EPA. What are the agency's goals? How are these goals similar to or different from Carson's ideas in this reading selection?

Thinking Like a Mountain

Aldo Leopold

Aldo Leopold (1887–1948) was an American writer, scientist, and conservationist. Leopold studied forestry at Yale University, worked for the U.S. Forest Service, and later became a professor of game management at the University of Wisconsin. Leopold is best known for his book *A Sand County Almanac* (1949), which has sold more than two million copies. The book is admired for its depiction of the land as a living organism, and "Thinking Like a Mountain" is one of the most famous passages in it.

Leopold was influential in the development of modern environmental ethics and in the movement for wilderness conservation. His ethics of nature and wildlife preservation had a profound impact on the environmental movement, and, like other environmentalists of his time, he warned of the dangers of short-term or limited thinking about natural resources. This essay describes Leopold's experience watching a wolf die and the realization this brought him about the interconnections among humans, animals, and nature. As you read the essay, think about what Leopold is saying about our connection to and dependence on the natural world.

A deep chesty bawl echoes from rimrock to rimrock, rolls down the mountain, and fades into the far blackness of the night. It is an outburst of wild defiant sorrow, and of contempt for all the adversities of the world.

Every living thing (and perhaps many a dead one as well) pays heed to that call. To the deer it is a reminder of the way of all flesh, to the pine a forecast of midnight scuffles and of blood upon the snow, to the coyote a promise of gleanings to come, to the cowman a threat of red ink at the bank, to the hunter a challenge of fang against bullet. Yet behind these obvious and immediate hopes and fears there lies a deeper meaning, known only to the mountain itself. Only the mountain has lived long enough to listen objectively to the howl of a wolf.

Those unable to decipher the hidden meaning know nevertheless that it is there, for it is felt in all wolf country, and distinguishes that country from all other land. It tingles in the spine of all who hear wolves by night, or who scan their tracks by day. Even without sight or sound of wolf, it is implicit in a hundred small events: the midnight whinny of a pack horse, the rattle of rolling rocks, the bound of a fleeing deer, the way shadows lie under the spruces. Only the ineducable tyro can fail to sense the presence or absence of wolves, or the fact that mountains have a secret opinion about them.

My own conviction on this score dates from the day I saw a wolf die. We were eating lunch on a high rimrock, at the foot of which a turbulent river elbowed its way. We saw what we thought was a doe fording the torrent, her breast awash in white water. When she climbed the bank toward us and shook out her tail, we realized our error: it was a wolf. A half-dozen others, evidently grown pups, sprang from the willows and all joined in a welcoming mêlée of wagging tails and playful maulings. What was literally a pile of wolves writhed and tumbled in the center of an open flat at the foot of our rimrock.

In those days we had never heard of passing up a chance to kill a wolf. In a second we were pumping lead into the pack, but with more excitement than accuracy: how to aim a steep downhill shot is always confusing. When our rifles were empty, the old wolf was down, and a pup was dragging a leg into impassable slide-rocks.

We reached the old wolf in time to watch a fierce green fire dying 5 in her eyes. I realized then, and have known ever since, that there was something new to me in those eyes—something known only to her and to the mountain. I was young then, and full of trigger-itch; I thought that because fewer wolves meant more deer, that no wolves would mean hunters' paradise. But after seeing the green fire die, I sensed that neither the wolf nor the mountain agreed with such a view.

● ● ●

Since then I have lived to see state after state extirpate° its wolves. I have watched the face of many a newly wolfless mountain, and seen the south-facing slopes wrinkle with a maze of new deer trails. I have seen every edible bush and seedling browsed, first to anaemic desuetude, and then to death. I have seen every edible tree defoliated to the height of a saddlehorn. Such a mountain looks as if someone had given God a new pruning shears, and forbidden Him all other exercise. In the end the starved bones of the hoped-for deer herd, dead of its own too-much, bleach with the bones of the dead sage, or molder under the high-lined junipers.

"In wildness is the salvation of the world."

I now suspect that just as a deer herd lives in mortal fear of its wolves, so does a mountain live in mortal fear of its deer. And perhaps with better cause, for while a buck pulled down by wolves can be replaced in two or three years, a range pulled down by too many deer may fail of replacement in as many decades.

So also with cows. The cowman who cleans his range of wolves does not realize that he is taking over the wolf's job of trimming the herd to fit

extirpate: to remove or destroy totally; exterminate.

the range. He has not learned to think like a mountain. Hence we have dustbowls, and rivers washing the future into the sea.

· · ·

We all strive for safety, prosperity, comfort, long life, and dullness. The deer strives with his supple legs, the cowman with trap and poison, the statesman with pen, the most of us with machines, votes, and dollars, but it all comes to the same thing: peace in our time. A measure of success in this is all well enough, and perhaps is a requisite to objective thinking, but too much safety seems to yield only danger in the long run. Perhaps this is behind Thoreau's dictum: In wildness is the salvation of the world. Perhaps this is the hidden meaning in the howl of the wolf, long known among mountains, but seldom perceived among men.

Understanding the Text

1. Why did Leopold kill the wolf? What did he learn from his experience?

2. Why does a mountain live "in mortal fear of its deer" (par. 8)?

3. What is the connection among wolves, deer, and the mountains in this essay? By extension, what is Leopold saying about the role of humans in this relationship?

Reflection and Response

4. What does it mean to "think like a mountain" (par. 9)?

5. In what ways does the wolf's howl have "meaning"? Do wolves, deer, people, and mountains communicate in different ways?

6. How does this excerpt address the notion of time? What does Leopold suggest about the perception of time?

7. Why does Leopold divide this essay into sections? Does each section have a different focus? How do these sections affect the way you read this essay?

Making Connections

8. Near the end of this passage, Leopold references Thoreau's dictum: "In wildness is the salvation of the world" (par. 10). What does this mean? Reread Thoreau's writing earlier in this chapter and look for similarities between the two writers' ideas as well as Thoreau's influences on Leopold's thinking.

9. How is "thinking like a mountain" related to what you know about sustainability? Do you think this short phrase captures the essence of sustainability? Why or why not?

10. Find an example of a natural place that has been damaged or destroyed by human activity. How does this relate to Leopold's essay?

The Sacred Balance: Rediscovering Our Place in Nature

David Suzuki

David Suzuki (b. 1936) is a Canadian academic and an environmental activist. Suzuki earned a PhD in zoology from the University of Chicago in 1961, and he was a professor in the genetics department at the University of British Columbia from 1963 until 2001. Suzuki was the host of several popular television and radio series about nature and the environment, including the long-running CBC Television science magazine, *The Nature of Things*, which was aired in more than forty countries.

The Sacred Balance was published in 2007 and was later adapted into a series of documentary films. The book highlights humankind's interconnection with the earth and with other living creatures. As you read the prologue to the book, think about the qualities that have made humans successful as a species and how some of those same qualities may threaten our future health and well-being.

S uppose that 200,000 years ago, biologists from another galaxy searching for life forms in other parts of the universe had discovered Earth and parked their space vehicle above the Rift Valley in Africa. At the moment of our species' birth, mammoths, saber-toothed cats, huge moa birds and giant sloths still roamed the planet. Those intergalactic visitors would have gazed upon vast grasslands filled with marvelous plants and animals, including a newly evolved species, *Homo sapiens*.°

It is highly unlikely that those alien scientists would have concentrated their attention on this infant upright ape species in anticipation of its meteoric rise to preeminence a mere two hundred millennia later. After all, those early humans lived in small family groups that didn't rival the immense herds of wildebeest and antelope. In comparison with many other species, they weren't especially large, fast or strong, or endowed with special sensory acuity. Those early humans possessed a survival trait that was invisible because it was locked within their skulls and only revealed through their behavior. Their immense and complex brains conferred tremendous intelligence, along with a vast capacity for memory, an insatiable curiosity and an astonishing creativity — abilities that more than compensated for their physical and sensory deficiencies.

That newly evolved human brain invented a novel concept called the "future." In reality, all that exists is the present and our memories

Homo sapiens: the species to which human beings belong.

of what is past, but by creating the notion of a future, we were unique in recognizing that we could influence events to come by what we do in the present. By looking ahead, we could anticipate potential danger and opportunities. Foresight was the great advantage that catapulted *Homo sapiens* into a position of dominance on the planet.

The eminent Nobel laureate François Jacob suggests that the human brain is "hardwired" to require order. Chaos is terrifying to us, because without some appreciation of cause and effect, we have no possibility of understanding and controlling the cosmic forces impinging on our lives. Early humans recognized that there are patterns in nature that are predictable—diurnal rhythm, or the movement of the sun; movement of the moon and stars; tides; seasons; animal migration; and plant succession. They were able to exploit these regularities for their own benefit and to avoid potential hazards.

Over time, every human society evolved a culture that inculcated an understanding of its place on Earth and in the cosmos. The collective knowledge, beliefs, languages and songs of each society make up what anthropologists call a worldview. In every worldview, there is an understanding that everything is connected to everything else, that nothing exists in isolation. People have always known that we are deeply embedded in and dependent upon the natural world.

In such a world of interconnectedness, every action has consequences, and since we were part of that world, we had a responsibility to act properly to keep the world in order. Many of our rituals, songs, prayers and ceremonies were reaffirmations of our dependence on nature and our commitment to behave properly. That is how it has been for most of human existence all over the world.

From Naked Ape to Superspecies

But suddenly in the last century, *Homo sapiens* has undergone a radical transformation into a new kind of force that I call a "superspecies." For the first time in the 3.8 billion years that life has existed on Earth, one species—humanity—is altering the biological, physical and chemical features of the planet on a geological scale. That shift to superspecies has occurred with explosive speed through a number of factors. One is population. It took all of human existence to reach a billion people in the early nineteenth century. A hundred years later, when I was born, in 1936, there were two billion people on Earth. In my lifetime, global population has tripled. Thus, by virtue of our numbers alone, our species' "ecological footprint" on the planet has grown explosively—we all have to eat, breathe and drink, and clothe and shelter ourselves.

We are now the most numerous mammalian species on the planet, but unlike all the others, our ecological impact has been greatly amplified by technology. Virtually all of modern technology has been developed within the past century, thereby escalating both the scale and scope of our ability to exploit our surroundings. Resource exploitation is fueled by an exploding consumer demand for products, and the fulfillment of that demand has become a critical component of economic growth. Hyper-consumption in the developed world serves as the model for people in developing countries now that globalization has rendered the entire world population a potential market. Taken together, human numbers, technology, consumption and a globalized economy have made us a new kind of force on the planet.

Throughout our evolutionary past, we were a local, tribal animal. We may have encountered a hundred humans over a range of a few hundred kilometers in a lifetime. We didn't have to worry about tribes on the other side of a mountain or across an ocean; nor did we have to consider the collective impact of our entire species, because our ecological footprint was so much lighter and nature seemed vast and endlessly self-renewing. Our new status of superspecies has been achieved so rapidly that we are only now becoming aware of a new level of collective responsibility, which reflects a dawning realization that taken all together, human activity is the main cause of the current decline in the biosphere's rich diversity and productivity that support all life on earth.

A Shattered World

As we have shifted our status to superspecies, our ancient understanding 10
of the exquisite interconnectivity of all life has been shattered. We find it increasingly difficult to recognize the linkages that once gave us a sense of place and belonging. After all, we are flooded with food and goods that come from all parts of the world, so we scarcely notice that it's the middle of winter when we are buying fresh strawberries and cherries. The constraints of locality and seasons are pushed aside by the global economy. Exacerbating the fragmentation of the world has been the stunning shift from predominant habitation in rural village communities to concentration in large cities. In big cities, it becomes easy to assume that we differ from all other species in that we create our own habitat and thereby escape the constraints of nature. It is nature that cleanses water, creates air, decomposes sewage, absorbs garbage, generates electricity and produces food, but in cities, these "ecosystem services" are assumed to be performed by the workings of the economy.

To make matters worse, as we look toward more and more esoteric sources for our information, the context, history and background needed to set new "facts" or events in place are lost, and our world is broken up into disconnected bits and pieces. While we look to science to reveal the secrets of the cosmos, its primary methodology of reductionism focuses on parts of nature. And as the world around us is examined in pieces, the rhythms, patterns and cycles within which those pieces are integrated are lost, and any insights we gain become illusions of understanding and mastery. Finally, as transnational corporations, politics and telecommunications move onto the global stage, the sense of the local is decimated.

This, then, is where we are at the beginning of the third millennium. With explosive speed, we have been transmogrified from a species like most others that live in balance with their surroundings into an unprecedented force. Like a species introduced into a new environment free of constraints, we have expanded beyond the capacity of our surroundings to support us. It is clear from the history of the past two centuries that the path we embarked on after the Industrial Revolution is leading us increasingly into conflict with life support systems of the natural world. Despite forty years of experience in the environmental movement we have not yet turned onto a different path.

The Growth of Environmentalism

Like millions of people around the world, I was galvanized° in 1962 by Rachel Carson's° eloquent call to action in her book *Silent Spring*. We were swept up in what was to become the "environmental movement." In British Columbia, that meant protesting such threats as the American testing of nuclear weapons at Amchitka in the Aleutian Islands (a protest that gave birth to Greenpeace° in Vancouver), clear-cut logging throughout the province, proposed offshore drilling for oil, the planned dam at Site C on the Peace River, and air and water pollution from pulp mills. In my mind, the problem was that we were taking too much from the environment and putting too much waste back into it. From that perspective, the solution was to set limits on how much and what could be removed from the biosphere for human use and how much and what could be put back into our surroundings, then make sure to enforce the regulations. So in addition to protesting, marching and blockading, many of us were

galvanized: startled into sudden activity; stimulated.
Rachel Carson: (1907–1964), U.S. marine biologist and author.
Greenpeace: an organization founded in 1971 that stresses the need to maintain a balance between human progress and environmental conservation.

lobbying politicians to set aside more parks, to enact Clean Water and Clean Air legislation, to pass Endangered Species Acts and to establish the agencies to enforce the regulations. When *Silent Spring* was published in 1962, no government on Earth had a Minister or Department of the Environment.

But Carson's book itself offered evidence of the need for a deeper analysis. As I read the book, I was shocked to realize that the experimental systems scientists study in flasks and growth chambers are artifacts, simplifications meant to mimic reality but lacking the context within which those simplified systems exist and devoid of the rhythms, patterns and cycles that impinge on the Earth. This realization came to me as a profound shock and impelled me to look beyond the lab into the real world.

The more involved I became in environmental issues, the clearer it became to me that my rather simple-minded approach wouldn't work, because we were too ignorant to anticipate the consequences of our activity and to set appropriate limits. Carson's book dealt with DDT.° In the 1930s when Paul Mueller, working for the chemical company Geigy in Switzerland, discovered that DDT killed insects, the economic benefits of a chemical pesticide were immediately obvious. Trumpeting the imminent scientific conquest of insect pests and their associated diseases and damage to crops, Geigy patented the discovery and went on to make millions, and Mueller was awarded the Nobel Prize in 1948. But years later, when bird watchers noted the decline of eagles and hawks, biologists investigated and discovered the hitherto unknown phenomenon of "biomagnification," whereby compounds become concentrated as they are ingested up the food chain. How could limits have been set on DDT in the early 1940s when we didn't even know about biomagnification as a biological process until birds began to disappear?

Similarly, CFCs° were hailed as a wonderful creation of chemistry. 15 These complex molecules were chemically inert, so they didn't react with other compounds and thus made excellent fillers in aerosol cans to go along with substances such as deodorants. No one anticipated that because of their stability, CFCs would persist in the environment and drift into the upper atmosphere, where ultraviolet radiation would break off ozone-scavenging chlorine free radicals. Most people had never heard of the ozone layer, and certainly no one could have anticipated the long-term effects of CFCs, so how could the compounds have been

---

DDT: $C_{14}H_9Cl_5$; potent chemical used as an insecticide, prohibited for agricultural use in the United States since 1973.
CFCs: chlorofluorocarbons, chemical compound used in various industrial, commercial, and household items that are hastening the depletion of the ozone layer.

regulated? I have absolutely no doubt that genetically modified organisms (GMOs) will also prove to have unexpected negative consequences despite the benefits claimed by biotech companies. But if we don't know enough to anticipate the long-term consequences of human technological innovation, how can its impact be managed? For me as a scientist, this posed a terrible conundrum.

A Way Out

I gained an important insight to free me from this quandary in the late 1970s. As host of the long-running television series *The Nature of Things*, I learned of the battle over clear-cut logging in the Queen Charlotte Islands, off the coast of British Columbia. For thousands of years, the islands have been home to the Haida, who refer to their lands as Haida Gwaii. The forestry giant MacMillan Bloedel had been clear-cutting huge areas of the islands for years, an activity that had generated increasingly vocal opposition. It was a good story, and I proposed to report it. In the early 1980s, I flew to Haida Gwaii to interview loggers, forestry officials, government bureaucrats, environmentalists and natives. One of the people I interviewed was a young Haida artist named Guujaaw who had led the opposition to logging for years.

Unemployment was very high in the Haida communities, and logging generated desperately needed jobs for the Haida. So I asked Guujaaw why he opposed the logging. He answered, "Our people have determined that Windy Bay and other areas must be left in their natural condition so that we can keep our identity and pass it on to following generations. The forests, those oceans, are what keep us as Haida people today." When I asked him what would happen if the logging continued and the trees were cleared, he answered simply, "If they're logged off, we'll probably end up the same as everyone else, I guess."

It was a simple statement whose implications escaped me at the time. But on reflection, I realized that he had given me a glimpse into a profoundly different way of seeing the world. Guujaaw's statement suggested that for his people, the trees, the birds, the fish, the water, and wind are all parts of Haida identity. Haida history and culture and the very meaning of why Haida are on earth reside in the land.

Ever since that interview, I have been a student learning from encounters with indigenous people in many parts of the world. From Japan to Australia, Papua New Guinea, Borneo, the Kalahari, the Amazon and the Arctic, aboriginal people have expressed to me that vital need to be connected to the land. They refer to Earth as their Mother, who they say gives birth to us. Moreover, skin enfolds our bodies but does not define our limits because water, gases and heat dissipating from our bodies radiate outward, joining us to the world around us. What I have learned is a perspective that we are an inseparable part of a community of organisms that are our kin.

In 2001, U.S. president Bill Clinton joined with scientists to announce [20] the completion of the Human Genome Project,° which elucidated the complete sequence of three billion letters in a single human nucleus. While politicians and scientists speculated about the potential benefits of understanding diseases, new drugs and cures for many ailments, the most amazing revelation was all but ignored. Not only is the human genome nearly identical to our closest relatives, the Great Apes, as well as our pet dogs and cats, we carry thousands of genes identical to those in fish, birds, insects and plants, a revelation that we share genes with all other life forms to whom we are related by our shared evolutionary history.

Changing Our Perspective

In 1990, my wife, Tara Cullis, and I established an organization that would examine the root causes of ecological destruction so that we could seek alternatives to our current practices. We decided to draft a document that would

> "We are intimately fused to our surroundings and the notion of separateness or isolation is an illusion."

express the foundation's worldview and perspective and could be offered to the Earth Summit in Rio de Janeiro in 1992. We called it a Declaration of Interdependence. Tara and I formulated a rough draft and asked for input from Guujaaw, ethnobiologist Wade Davis and the children's singer Raffi. When I was working on the first draft, I tried writing "We are made up of molecules from the air, water and soil," but this sounded like a scientific treatise and failed to convey the simple truth of our relationship with Earth in a powerful, emotional way. After spending days pondering the lines, I suddenly thought, "We *are* the air, we *are* the water, we *are* the earth, we *are* the Sun."

With this realization, I also saw that environmentalists like me had been framing the issue improperly. There is no environment "out there" that is separate from us. We can't manage our impact on the environment if we *are* our surroundings. Indigenous people are absolutely correct: we are born of the earth and constructed from the four sacred elements of earth, air, fire and water. (Hindus list these four and add a fifth element, space.)

Human Genome Project: a federally funded U.S. scientific project to identify both the genes and the entire sequence of DNA base pairs that make up the human genome.

Once I had finally understood the truth of these ancient wisdoms, I also realized that we are intimately fused to our surroundings and the notion of separateness or isolation is an illusion. Through reading I came to understand that science reaffirms the profundity of these ancient truths over and over again. Looked at as biological beings, despite our veneer of civilization, we are no more removed from nature than any other creature, even in the midst of a large city. Our animal nature dictates our essential needs: clean air, clean water, clean soil, clean energy. This led me to another insight, that these four "sacred elements" are created, cleansed and renewed by the web of life itself. If there is to be a fifth sacred element, it is biodiversity itself. And whatever we do to these elements, we do directly to ourselves.

As I read further, I discovered the famed psychologist Abraham Maslow, who pointed out that we have a nested series of fundamental needs. At the most basic level, we require the five sacred elements in order to live rich, full lives. But when those basic necessities are met, a new set of needs arises. We are social animals, and the most profound force shaping our humanity is love. And when that vital social requirement is fulfilled, then a new level of spiritual needs arises as an urgent priority. This is how I made the fundamental reexamination of our relationship with Earth that led to *The Sacred Balance*.

In the years since, I have yet to meet anyone who would dispute the reality and primacy of these fundamental needs. And everything in my reading and experiences since then has merely reaffirmed and amplified my understanding of these basic needs. The challenge of this millennium is to recognize what we need to live rich, rewarding lives without undermining the very elements that ensure them.

Understanding the Text

1. What characteristics enabled humans to survive and become the dominant species on the planet?

2. How does Suzuki define a "superspecies," and what factors have contributed to the impact of humans on the global environment?

3. According to Suzuki, what are the solutions to our global environmental problems? What are the major features and movements within environmentalism that have influenced Suzuki's thinking?

Reflection and Response

4. The introduction to this piece asks you to imagine that you're a biologist from another planet, visiting earth 200,000 years ago. Why does Suzuki create this fictional situation? What does he hope readers will gain from it?

5. What is the "sacred balance" that Suzuki refers to in the title of the essay?

6. Suzuki writes that "we have expanded beyond the capacity of our surroundings to support us" (par. 12). Do you agree with this statement? Why or why not?

7. What does Suzuki mean when he writes, "We *are* the air, we *are* the water, we *are* the earth, we *are* the Sun" (par. 22)? Does he mean this literally or metaphorically?

Making Connections

8. Suzuki mentions the impact that *Silent Spring* had on the world. What other books, speeches, or movies may have had similar impacts on our collective thinking about environmentalism and sustainability?

9. In the section titled "A Shattered World," Suzuki talks about the "reductionist" methodology that predominates science. How is this similar to what Fritjof Capra suggests in his essay in Chapter 4? What alternatives do the two authors offer?

10. Suzuki suggests that humans are unique because of our ability to envision a future but that we have neglected this ability with regard to global sustainability. Think of something that you do on a daily or weekly basis that might work for you now but may be unsustainable (or unhealthy) in the long run.

2 | How Is Sustainability a Political Issue?

S ustainability is a complex issue, and the conversations surrounding it involve a wide range of people, organizations, companies, institutions, governments, and nations. All of the participants in these conversations operate from their own perspectives, and they all have different goals and motivations in engaging with sustainability. Each writer seeks to persuade others to think about the subject in certain ways and to act on those thoughts.

As you will discover through reading this chapter, these participants envision sustainability as a political issue — that is, they seek to sway public opinion and influence government policies to achieve their goals. Many of the authors in this chapter are politicians themselves or are active in politics, and for those individuals, shaping the opinions of the public is very important. In fact, most articles in this chapter are written for a general public audience. You are a part of that audience; as you read these selections, consider the ways in which each author attempts to change your thinking about sustainability.

The readings in this chapter are intentionally diverse. They cover a wide range of genres, from government reports to magazine articles to blog postings. All of these genres and many more are part of our collective public discourse about sustainability, and each genre and subject has a different goal. More important, the readings in Chapter 2 span the political spectrum from liberal to conservative. One primary goal of the chapter is to help you compare and contrast the ways in which different groups and individuals use language to shape public understanding about sustainability.

The chapter begins with what is arguably the most important document written about sustainability: the United Nations World Commission report entitled "Our Common Future." This report, often referred to as the "Brundtland Report," was written by an international group of politicians, and it put sustainability on the worldwide political agenda for the first time. The next few articles are from authors who are identified (or who self-identify) as politically liberal — most notably Gore and Thorpe. Political

photo: Thomas Goeppert/EyeEm/Getty Images

liberals are generally seen as the strongest advocates for environmental preservation and sustainability programs. The authors who appear later in this chapter are generally more skeptical of the goals, aims, and possibilities of sustainability and environmental efforts — including Manzi and Wehner as well as Scruton — and they represent more politically conservative views. The final reading selection, by Buchanan, seeks to bridge the political gap between liberals and conservatives on the issue of sustainability. Your own perspective may fall somewhere along this political spectrum, and it may change as you read these articles — that's a good thing.

As you read, pay close attention to the ways in which key words like *environment* and *sustainability* are defined. Each author expresses a different outlook on these key terms and, consequently, suggests different methods of addressing the issues surrounding them. Although it may seem confusing to read contrasting or opposing definitions of a term like *sustainability*, keep in mind that these definitions can reveal the author's viewpoints, objectives, and goals concerning the subject.

Our Common Future: From One Earth to One World (Brundtland Report)

World Commission on Environment and Development

In 1983 the United Nations convened the World Commission on Environment and Development (WCED) to address the accelerating deterioration of natural resources and the global impact of human development. Four years later, the WCED published a report titled "Our Common Future," which is also known as the Brundtland Report in recognition of the chair of the WCED, Norway's Prime Minister Gro Harlem Brundtland.

The Brundtland Report has been viewed as a landmark text in the debates concerning global sustainability. The report examines the role of governments, businesses, and individuals in sustainability, and it provides a comprehensive overview of the major global environmental crises as well as suggestions on how to address these problems. "Our Common Future" is also responsible for a key (and frequently quoted) definition of sustainable development: development that "meets the needs of the present without compromising the ability of future generations to meet their own needs" (par. 11).

As you read this excerpt from "Our Common Future," think about the ways in which sustainability is a global issue and the role that worldwide organizations like the UN and the WCED might play in creating a more sustainable world.

I n the middle of the 20th century, we saw our planet from space for the first time. Historians may eventually find that this vision had a greater impact on thought than did the Copernican revolution° of the 16th century, which upset the human self-image by revealing that the Earth is not the center of the universe. From space, we see a small and fragile ball dominated not by human activity and edifice but by a pattern of clouds, oceans, greenery, and soils. Humanity's inability to fit its activities into that pattern is changing planetary systems, fundamentally. Many such changes are accompanied by life-threatening hazards. This new reality, from which there is no escape, must be recognized — and managed.

Fortunately, this new reality coincides with more positive developments new to this century. We can move information and goods faster around

---

Copernican revolution: the now-accepted theory that all planets revolve around the sun as opposed to the earth, proposed by Nicolaus Copernicus (Polish astronomer, 1473–1543).

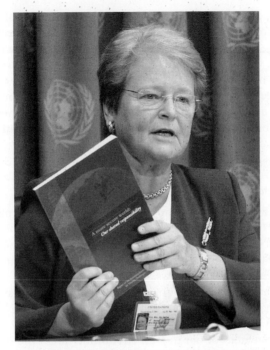

Dr. Gro Harlem Brundtland at UN Headquarters in 2004.
STAN HONDA/Getty Images

the globe than ever before; we can produce more food and more goods with less investment of resources; our technology and science gives us, at least, the potential to look deeper into and better understand natural systems. From space, we can see and study the Earth as an organism whose health depends on the health of all its parts. We have the power to reconcile human affairs with natural laws and to thrive in the process. In this our cultural and spiritual heritages can reinforce our economic interests and survival imperatives.

This Commission believes that people can build a future that is more prosperous, more just, and more secure. Our report, *Our Common Future*, is not a prediction of ever increasing environmental decay, poverty, and hardship in an ever more polluted world among ever decreasing resources. We see instead the possibility for a new era of economic growth, one that must be based on policies that sustain and expand the environmental resource base. And we believe such growth to be absolutely essential to relieve the great poverty that is deepening in much of the developing world.

But the Commission's hope for the future is conditional on decisive political action now to begin managing environmental resources to ensure both sustainable human progress and human survival. We are not forecasting a future; we are serving a notice — an urgent notice based on the latest and best scientific evidence — that the time has come to make the decisions needed to secure the resources to sustain this and coming generations. We do not offer a detailed blueprint for action, but instead a pathway by which the peoples of the world may enlarge their spheres of cooperation.

The Global Challenge

Successes and Failures

Those looking for success and signs of hope can find many: infant 5
mortality is falling; human life expectancy is increasing; the proportion of the world's adults who can read and write is climbing; the proportion of children starting school is rising; and global food production increases faster than the population grows.

But the same processes that have produced these gains have given rise to trends that the planet and its people cannot long bear. These have traditionally been divided into failures of "development" and failures in the management of our human environment. On the development side, in terms of absolute numbers there are more hungry people in the world than ever before, and their numbers are increasing. So are the numbers who cannot read or write, the numbers without safe water or safe and sound homes, and the numbers short of woodfuel with which to cook and warm themselves. The gap between rich and poor nations is widening — not shrinking — and there is little prospect, given present trends and institutional arrangements, that this process will be reversed.

There are also environmental trends that threaten to radically alter the planet, that threaten the lives of many species upon it, including the human species. Each year another 6 million hectares° of productive dry-land turns into worthless desert. Over three decades, this would amount to an area roughly as large as Saudi Arabia. More than 11 million hectares of forests are destroyed yearly, and this, over three decades, would equal an area about the size of India. Much of this forest is converted to low-grade farmland unable to support the farmers who settle it. In Europe, acid precipitation kills forests and lakes and damages the artistic and architectural heritage of nations; it may have acidified vast tracts of soil beyond reasonable hope of repair. The burning of fossil fuels puts into

hectares: a unit of surface, or land, measure equal to 100 acres, or 10,000 square meters.

the atmosphere carbon dioxide, which is causing gradual global warming.° This "greenhouse effect"° may by early next century[1] have increased average global temperatures enough to shift agricultural production areas, raise sea levels to flood coastal cities, and disrupt national economies. Other industrial gases threaten to deplete the planet's protective ozone shield to such an extent that the number of human and animal cancers would rise sharply and the oceans' food chain would be disrupted, industry and agriculture put toxic substances into the human food chain and into underground water tables beyond reach of cleansing.

There has been a growing realization in national governments and multilateral institutions that it is impossible to separate economic development issues from environment issues; many forms of development erode the environmental resources upon which they must be based, and environmental degradation can undermine economic development. Poverty is a major cause and effect of global environmental problems. It is therefore futile to attempt to deal with environmental problems without a broader perspective that encompasses the factors underlying world poverty and international inequality.

These concerns were behind the establishment in 1983 of the World Commission on Environment and Development by the UN General Assembly. The Commission is an independent body, linked to but outside the control of governments and the UN system. The Commission's mandate gave it three objectives: to re-examine the critical environment and development issues and to formulate realistic proposals for dealing with them; to propose new forms of international cooperation on these issues that will influence policies and events in the direction of needed changes; and to raise the levels of understanding and commitment to action of individuals, voluntary organizations, businesses, institutes, and governments.

Through our deliberations and the testimony of people at the public 10 hearings we held on five continents, all the commissioners came to focus on one central theme: many present development trends leave increasing numbers of people poor and vulnerable, while at the same time degrading the environment. How can such development serve next century's world of twice as many people relying on the same environment? This realization broadened our view of development. We came to see it not

global warming: an increase in the earth's average atmospheric temperature that causes corresponding changes in climate and that may result from the greenhouse effect.
greenhouse effect: an atmospheric heating phenomenon caused by gases, such as carbon dioxide, water vapor, methane, and others, that trap heat within the earth's atmosphere.
[1]This report was written in 1987.—Ed.

in its restricted context of economic growth in developing countries. We came to see that a new development path was required, one that sustained human progress not just in a few pieces for a few years, but for the entire planet into the distant future. Thus "sustainable development" becomes a goal not just for the "developing" nations, but for industrial ones as well. . . .

Sustainable Development

Humanity has the ability to make development sustainable to ensure that it meets the needs of the present without compromising the ability of future generations to meet their own needs. The concept of sustainable development does imply limits—not absolute limits but limitations imposed by the present state of technology and social organization on environmental resources and by the ability of the biosphere° to absorb the effects of human activities. But technology and social organization can be both managed and improved to make way for a new era of economic growth. The Commission believes that widespread poverty is no longer inevitable. Poverty is not only an evil in itself, but sustainable development requires meeting the basic needs of all and extending to all the opportunity to fulfill their aspirations for a better life. A world in which poverty is endemic will always be prone to ecological and other catastrophes.

"Sustainable development . . . meets the needs of the present without compromising the ability of future generations to meet their own needs."

Meeting essential needs requires not only a new era of economic growth for nations in which the majority are poor, but an assurance that those poor get their fair share of the resources required to sustain that growth. Such equity would be aided by political systems that secure effective citizen participation in decision making and by greater democracy in international decision making.

Sustainable global development requires that those who are more affluent adopt life-styles within the planet's ecological means—in their use of energy, for example. Further, rapidly growing populations can increase the pressure on resources and slow any rise in living standards; thus sustainable development can only be pursued if population size and growth are in harmony with the changing productive potential of the ecosystem.

Yet in the end, sustainable development is not a fixed state of harmony, but rather a process of change in which the exploitation of

---

biosphere: the part of the earth's crust, waters, and atmosphere that supports life.

resources, the direction of investments, the orientation of technological development, and institutional change are made consistent with future as well as present needs. We do not pretend that the process is easy or straightforward. Painful choices have to be made. Thus, in the final analysis, sustainable development must rest on political will.

The Institutional Gaps

The objective of sustainable development and the integrated nature of the global environment/development challenges pose problems for institutions, national and international, that were established on the basis of narrow preoccupations and compartmentalized concerns. Governments' general response to the speed and scale of global changes has been a reluctance to recognize sufficiently the need to change themselves. The challenges are both interdependent and integrated, requiring comprehensive approaches and popular participation.

Yet most of the institutions facing those challenges tend to be independent, fragmented, working to relatively narrow mandates with closed decision processes. Those responsible for managing natural resources and protecting the environment are institutionally separated from those responsible for managing the economy. The real world of interlocked economic and ecological systems will not change; the policies and institutions concerned must.

There is a growing need for effective international cooperation to manage ecological and economic interdependence. Yet at the same time, confidence in international organizations is diminishing and support for them dwindling.

The other great institutional flaw in coping with environment/ development challenges is governments' failure to make the bodies whose policy actions degrade the environment responsible for ensuring that their policies prevent that degradation. Environmental concern arose from damage caused by the rapid economic growth following the Second World War. Governments, pressured by their citizens, saw a need to clean up the mess, and they established environmental ministries and agencies to do this. Many had great success within the limits of their mandates—in improving air and water quality and enhancing other resources. But much of their work has of necessity been after-the-fact repair of damage: reforestation, reclaiming desert lands, rebuilding urban environments, restoring natural habitats, and rehabilitating wild lands.

The existence of such agencies gave many governments and their citizens the false impression that these bodies were by themselves able to protect and enhance the environmental resource base. Yet many industrialized and most developing countries carry huge economic burdens from inherited problems such as air and water pollution, depletion of groundwater, and the proliferation of toxic chemicals and hazardous wastes. These have been joined by more recent problems—erosion, desertification, acidification, new chemicals, and new forms of waste—that are directly related to agricultural, industrial, energy, forestry, and transportation policies and practices.

The mandates of the central economic and sectoral ministries are also often too narrow, too concerned with quantities of production or growth. The mandates of ministries of industry include production targets, while the accompanying pollution is left to ministries of environment. Electricity boards produce power, while the acid pollution they also produce is left to other bodies to clean up. The present challenge is to give the central economic and sectoral ministries the responsibility for the quality of those parts of the human environment affected by their decisions, and to give the environmental agencies more power to cope with the effects of unsustainable development.

The same need for change holds for international agencies concerned with development lending, trade regulation, agricultural development, and so on. These have been slow to take the environmental effects of their work into account, although some are trying to do so.

The ability to anticipate and prevent environmental damage requires that the ecological dimensions of policy be considered at the same time as the economic, trade, energy, agricultural, and other dimensions. They should be considered on the same agendas and in the same national and international institutions.

This reorientation is one of the chief institutional challenges of the 1990s and beyond. Meeting it will require major institutional development and reform. Many countries that are too poor or small or that have limited managerial capacity will find it difficult to do this unaided. They will need financial and technical assistance and training. But the changes required involve all countries, large and small, rich and poor. . . .

A Call for Action

Over the course of this [the twentieth] century, the relationship between the human world and the planet that sustains it has undergone a profound change.

When the century began, neither human numbers nor technology had the power radically to alter planetary systems. As the century closes, not only do vastly increased human numbers and their activities have that power, but major, unintended changes are occurring in the atmosphere, in soils, in waters, among plants and animals, and in the relationships among all of these. The rate of change is outstripping the ability of scientific disciplines and our current capabilities to assess and advise. It is frustrating the attempts of political and economic institutions, which evolved in a different, more fragmented world, to adapt and cope. It deeply worries many people who are seeking ways to place those concerns on the political agendas.

The onus lies with no one group of nations. Developing countries face the obvious life-threatening challenges of desertification, deforestation, and pollution, and endure most of the poverty associated with environmental degradation. The entire human family of nations would suffer from the disappearance of rain forests in the tropics, the loss of plant and animal species, and changes in rainfall patterns. Industrial nations face the life-threatening challenges of toxic chemicals, toxic wastes, and acidification. All nations may suffer from the releases by industrialized countries of carbon dioxide and of gases that react with the ozone layer, and from any future war fought with the nuclear arsenals controlled by those nations. All nations will have a role to play in changing trends, and in righting an international economic system that increases rather than decreases inequality, that increases rather than decreases numbers of poor and hungry.

The next few decades are crucial. The time has come to break out of past patterns. Attempts to maintain social and ecological stability through old approaches to development and environmental protection will increase instability. Security must be sought through change. The Commission has noted a number of actions that must be taken to reduce risks to survival and to put future development on paths that are sustainable. Yet we are aware that such a reorientation on a continuing basis is simply beyond the reach of present decision-making structures and institutional arrangements, both national and international.

This Commission has been careful to base our recommendations on the realities of present institutions, on what can and must be accomplished today. But to keep options open for future generations, the present generation must begin now, and begin together.

To achieve the needed changes, we believe that an active follow-up of this report is imperative. It is with this in mind that we call for the UN General Assembly, upon due consideration, to transform this report into a UN Programme on Sustainable Development. Special follow-up conferences could be initiated at the regional level. Within an appropriate period after the presentation of this report to the General Assembly, an international conference could be convened to review progress made, and to promote follow-up arrangements that will be needed to set benchmarks and to maintain human progress.

First and foremost, this Commission has been concerned with people—of all countries and all walks of life. And it is to people that we address our report. The changes in human attitudes that we call for depend on a vast campaign of education, debate, and public participation. This campaign must start now if sustainable human progress is to be achieved.

The members of the World Commission on Environment and Development came from 21 very different nations. In our discussions, we disagreed often on details and priorities. But despite our widely differing backgrounds and varying national and international responsibilities, we were able to agree to the lines along which change must be drawn.

We are unanimous in our conviction that the security, well-being, and very survival of the planet depend on such changes, now.

Understanding the Text

1. Who do you see as the primary audience for this report? How does the report engage that audience? Who are the secondary audiences?

2. This report attempts to balance hope for the future with the current realities of the global environment. What are some of the primary successes and challenges described here?

3. How does this text describe and define sustainable development? Do you think the definition is accurate and comprehensive? Why or why not?

Reflection and Response

4. The first sentence of this piece reminds us of our accomplishment in seeing our planet from outer space for the first time. Why do you think the authors chose this as an opening sentence?

5. In what ways are poverty and environmental issues connected? Why do the authors address poverty? What problems can poverty cause for natural environments?

6. What is the "Call for Action" identified in the last section of this excerpt? How does it affect you personally?

Making Connections

7. Population growth remains one of the biggest threats to humanity and our ability to maintain a sustainable world. Do you think that governments and international organizations should try to control population growth? What methods should they pursue? What methods should they not pursue?

8. This text is referenced in many other sources throughout this book. Why do you think this is an important piece in the history of sustainability?

9. This document suggests that time is a crucial factor and that efforts toward sustainability must begin immediately. Do some research to determine what steps have been taken toward global sustainability since the report was published in 1987.

Climate of Denial

Al Gore

Al Gore Jr. was the forty-fifth vice president of the United States (1993–2001) under President Bill Clinton. Gore is well-known for his environmental advocacy work as well as for his popular writing about environmental issues. He has founded a number of nonprofit organizations, including the Alliance for Climate Protection, and he has received a Nobel Peace Prize for his work in climate change activism. Gore was the subject of the Academy Award–winning documentary film *An Inconvenient Truth* (2007), which followed Gore's nationwide speaking tour to educate Americans about global climate change.

"Climate of Denial" was published in 2011 in *Rolling Stone* magazine. In the essay, Gore addresses the role of television news media in the debate about global climate change. He argues that business "special interest" groups play an undue role in the debate, at the expense of scientific data. As you read the essay, think about the ways in which debates about climate change and sustainability are portrayed in news broadcasts. ✻ liberals

The first time I remember hearing the question "Is it real?" was when I went as a young boy to see a traveling show put on by "professional wrestlers" one summer evening in the gym of the Forks River Elementary School in Elmwood, Tennessee.

The evidence that it was real was palpable: "They're really hurting each other! That's real blood! Look a'there! They can't fake that!" On the other hand, there was clearly a script (or in today's language, a "narrative"), with good guys to cheer and bad guys to boo.

But the most unusual and in some ways most interesting character in these dramas was the referee: Whenever the bad guy committed a gross and obvious violation of the "rules"—such as they were—like using a metal folding chair to smack the good guy in the head, the referee always seemed to be preoccupied with one of the cornermen, or looking the other way. Yet whenever the good guy—after absorbing more abuse and unfairness than any reasonable person could tolerate—committed the slightest infraction, the referee was all over him. The answer to the question "Is it real?" seemed connected to the question of whether the referee was somehow confused about his role: Was he too an entertainer?

That is pretty much the role now being played by most of the news media in refereeing the current wrestling match over whether global warming is "real," and whether it has any connection to the constant dumping of 90 million tons of heat-trapping emissions into the Earth's thin shell of atmosphere every 24 hours.

Admittedly, the contest over global warming is a challenge for the ref-   5
eree because it's a tag-team match, a real free-for-all. In one corner of the
ring are Science and Reason. In the other corner: Poisonous Polluters and
Right-wing Ideologues.°

The referee—in this analogy, the news media—seems confused about
whether he is in the news business or the entertainment business. Is he
responsible for ensuring a fair match? Or is he part of the show, selling
tickets and building the audience? The referee certainly seems distracted:
by Donald Trump, Charlie Sheen, the latest reality show—the list of
serial obsessions is too long to enumerate here.

But whatever the cause, the referee appears not to notice that the
Polluters and Ideologues are trampling all over the "rules" of democratic
discourse. They are financing pseudoscientists whose job is to manufacture doubt about what is true and what is false; buying elected officials
wholesale with bribes that the politicians themselves have made "legal"
and can now be made in secret; spending hundreds of millions of dollars
each year on misleading advertisements in the mass media; hiring four
anti-climate lobbyists for every member of the U.S. Senate and House of
Representatives. (Question: Would Michael Jordan have been a star if he
was covered by four defensive players every step he took on the basket-
ball court?)

This script, of course, is not entirely new: A half-century ago, when
Science and Reason established the linkage between cigarettes and lung
diseases, the tobacco industry hired actors, dressed them up as doctors,
and paid them to look into television cameras and tell people that the
linkage revealed in the Surgeon General's Report was not real at all. The
show went on for decades, with more Americans killed each year by
cigarettes than all of the U.S. soldiers killed in all of World War II.

This time, the scientific consensus is even stronger. It has been
endorsed by every National Academy of science of every major country
on the planet, every major professional scientific society related to the
study of global warming and 98 percent of climate scientists throughout the world. In the latest and most authoritative study by 3,000 of
the very best scientific experts in the world, the evidence was judged
"unequivocal."

But wait! The good guys transgressed the rules of decorum, as   10
evidenced in their private e-mails that were stolen and put on the
Internet. The referee is all over it: Penalty! Go to your corner! And in their
3,000-page report, the scientists made some mistakes! Another penalty!

Right-wing Ideologue: a person who zealously advocates an extreme conservative
political position.

And if more of the audience is left confused about whether the climate crisis is real? Well, the show must go on. After all, it's entertainment. There are tickets to be sold, eyeballs to glue to the screen.

Part of the script for this show was leaked to the *New York Times* as early as 1991. In an internal document, a consortium of the largest global-warming polluters spelled out their principal strategy: "Reposition global warming as theory, rather than fact." Ever since, they have been sowing doubt even more effectively than the tobacco companies before them.

To sell their false narrative, the Polluters and Ideologues have found it essential to undermine the public's respect for Science and Reason by attacking the integrity of the climate scientists. That is why the scientists are regularly accused of falsifying evidence and exaggerating its implications in a greedy effort to win more research grants, or secretly pursuing a hidden political agenda to expand the power of government. Such slanderous insults are deeply ironic: extremist ideologues—many financed or employed by carbon polluters—accusing scientists of being greedy extremist ideologues.

After World War II, a philosopher studying the impact of organized propaganda on the quality of democratic debate wrote, "The conversion of all questions of truth into questions of power has attacked the very heart of the distinction between true and false."

Is the climate crisis real? Yes, of course it is. Pause for a moment to 15 consider these events of just the past 12 months:

- **Heat.** According to NASA, 2010 was tied with 2005 as the hottest year measured since instruments were first used systematically in the 1880s. Nineteen countries set all-time high temperature records. One city in Pakistan, Mohenjo-Daro, reached 128.3 degrees Fahrenheit, the hottest temperature ever measured in an Asian city. Nine of the 10 hottest years in history have occurred in the last 13 years. The past decade was the hottest ever measured, even though half of that decade represented a "solar minimum"—the low ebb in the natural cycle of solar energy emanating from the sun.

- **Floods.** Megafloods displaced 20 million people in Pakistan, further destabilizing a nuclear-armed country; inundated an area of Australia larger than Germany and France combined; flooded 28 of the 32 districts that make up Colombia, where it has rained almost continuously for the past year; caused a "thousand-year" flood in my home city of Nashville; and led to all-time record flood levels in the Mississippi River Valley. Many places around the world are now experiencing larger and more frequent extreme downpours

and snowstorms; last year's "Snowmageddon" in the northeastern United States is part of the same pattern, notwithstanding the
guffaws of deniers.

- **Drought.** Historic drought and fires in Russia killed an estimated
  56,000 people and caused wheat and other food crops in Russia,
  Ukraine and Kazakhstan to be removed from the global market,
  contributing to a record spike in food prices. "Practically everything is burning," Russian president Dmitry Medvedev declared.
  "What's happening with the planet's climate right now needs to be
  a wake-up call to all of us." The drought level in much of Texas has
  been raised from "extreme" to "exceptional," the highest category.
  This spring the majority of the counties in Texas were on fire, and
  Governor Rick Perry requested a major disaster declaration for all
  but two of the state's 254 counties. Arizona is now fighting the
  largest fire in its history. Since 1970, the fire season throughout
  the American West has increased by 78 days. Extreme droughts
  in central China and northern France are currently drying up
  reservoirs and killing crops.

- **Melting Ice.** An enormous mass of ice, four times larger than
  the island of Manhattan, broke off from northern Greenland last
  year and slipped into the sea. The acceleration of ice loss in both
  Greenland and Antarctica has caused another upward revision of
  global sea-level rise and the numbers of refugees expected from
  low-lying coastal areas. The Arctic ice cap, which reached a record
  low volume last year, has lost as much as 40 percent of its area
  during summer in just 30 years.

These extreme events are happening in real time. It is not uncommon   20
for the nightly newscast to resemble a nature hike through the Book of
Revelation. Yet most of the news media completely ignore how such
events are connected to the climate crisis, or dismiss the connection as
controversial; after all, there are scientists on one side of the debate and
deniers on the other. A Fox News executive, in an internal e-mail to the
network's reporters and editors that later became public, questioned the
"veracity of climate change data" and ordered the journalists to "refrain
from asserting that the planet has warmed (or cooled) in any given
period without IMMEDIATELY pointing out that such theories are based
upon data that critics have called into question."

But in the "real" world, the record droughts, fires, floods and mud-
slides continue to increase in severity and frequency. Leading climate
scientists like Jim Hansen and Kevin Trenberth now say that events like
these would almost certainly not be occurring without the influence of

man-made global warming. And that's a shift in the way they frame these impacts. Scientists used to caution that we were increasing the probability of such extreme events by "loading the dice"—pumping more carbon into the atmosphere. Now the scientists go much further, warning that we are "painting more dots on the dice." We are not only more likely to roll 12s; we are now rolling 13s and 14s. In other words, the biggest storms are not only becoming more frequent, they are getting bigger, stronger and more destructive.

"The only plausible explanation for the rise in weather-related catastrophes is climate change," Munich Re, one of the two largest reinsurance companies in the world, recently stated. "The view that weather extremes are more frequent and intense due to global warming coincides with the current state of scientific knowledge."

Many of the extreme and destructive events are the result of the rapid increase in the amount of heat energy from the sun that is trapped in the atmosphere, which is radically disrupting the planet's water cycle. More heat energy evaporates more water into the air, and the warmer air holds a lot more moisture. This has huge consequences that we now see all around the world.

When a storm unleashes a downpour of rain or snow, the precipitation does not originate just in the part of the sky directly above where it falls. Storms reach out—sometimes as far as 2,000 miles—to suck in water vapor from large areas of the sky, including the skies above oceans, where water vapor has increased by four percent in just the last 30 years. (Scientists often compare this phenomenon to what happens in a bathtub when you open the drain; the water rushing out comes from the whole tub, not just from the part of the tub directly above the drain. And when the tub is filled with more water, more goes down the drain. In the same way, when the warmer sky is filled with a lot more water vapor, there are bigger downpours when a storm cell opens the "drain.")

In many areas, these bigger downpours also mean longer periods 25 between storms—at the same time that the extra heat in the air is also drying out the soil. That is part of the reason so many areas have been experiencing both record floods and deeper, longer-lasting droughts.

Moreover, the scientists have been warning us for quite some time—in increasingly urgent tones—that things will get much, much worse if we continue the reckless dumping of more and more heat-trapping pollution into the atmosphere. *Drought is projected to spread across significant, highly populated areas of the globe throughout this century.* Look at what the scientists say is in store for the Mediterranean nations. Should we care about the loss of Spain, France, Italy, the Balkans, Turkey, Tunisia? Look at what they say is in store for Mexico. Should we notice? Should we care?

Former U.S. Vice President Al Gore speaking about climate change in
December 2008.
JANEK SKARZYNSKI/AFP/Getty Images

Maybe it's just easier, psychologically, to swallow the lie that these
scientists who devote their lives to their work are actually greedy deceiv-
ers and left-wing extremists—and that we should instead put our faith
in the pseudoscientists financed by large carbon polluters whose business plans depend on their continued use of the atmospheric commons
as a place to dump their gaseous, heat-trapping waste without limit or
constraint, free of charge. very effective

The truth is this: What we are doing is functionally insane. If we do
not change this pattern, we will condemn our children and all future
generations to struggle with ecological curses for several millennia to
come. Twenty percent of the global-warming pollution we spew into the
sky each day will still be there 20,000 years from now!

We do have another choice. Renewable energy sources are coming into
their own. Both solar and wind will soon produce power at costs that
are competitive with fossil fuels; indications are that twice as many solar
installations were erected worldwide last year as compared to 2009. The
reductions in cost and the improvements in efficiency of photovoltaic
cells over the past decade appear to be following an exponential curve
that resembles a less dramatic but still startling version of what happened
with computer chips over the past 50 years.

Enhanced geothermal energy is potentially a nearly limitless source   30
of competitive electricity. Increased energy efficiency is already saving
businesses money and reducing emissions significantly. New generations

of biomass energy—ones that do not rely on food crops, unlike the mistaken strategy of making ethanol from corn—are extremely promising. Sustainable forestry and agriculture both make economic as well as environmental sense. And all of these options would spread even more rapidly if we stopped subsidizing Big Oil and Coal and put a price on carbon that reflected the true cost of fossil energy—either through the much-maligned cap-and-trade approach, or through a revenue-neutral tax swap.

All over the world, the grassroots movement in favor of changing public policies to confront the climate crisis and build a more prosperous, sustainable future is growing rapidly. But most governments remain paralyzed, unable to take action—even after years of volatile gasoline prices, repeated wars in the Persian Gulf, one energy-related disaster after another, and a seemingly endless stream of unprecedented and lethal weather disasters.

Continuing on our current course would be suicidal for global civilization. But the key question is: How do we drive home that fact in a democratic society when questions of truth have been converted into questions of power? When the distinction between what is true and what is false is being attacked relentlessly, and when the referee in the contest between truth and falsehood has become an entertainer selling tickets to a phony wrestling match?

The "wrestling ring" in this metaphor is the conversation of democracy. It used to be called the "public square." In ancient Athens, it was the Agora. In the Roman Republic, it was the Forum. In the Egypt of the recent Arab Spring, "Tahrir Square" was both real and metaphorical—encompassing Facebook, Twitter, Al-Jazeera and texting.

In the America of the late 18th century, the conversation that led to our own "Spring" took place in printed words: pamphlets, newsprint, books, the "Republic of Letters." It represented the fullest flower of the Enlightenment, during which the oligarchic power of the monarchies, the feudal lords and the Medieval Church was overthrown and replaced with a new sovereign: the Rule of Reason.

The public square that gave birth to the new consciousness of the Enlightenment emerged in the dozen generations following the invention of the printing press—"the Gutenberg Galaxy," the scholar Marshall McLuhan called it—a space in which the conversation of democracy was almost equally accessible to every literate person. Individuals could both find the knowledge that had previously been restricted to elites and contribute their own ideas.

Ideas that found resonance with others rose in prominence much the way Google searches do today, finding an ever larger audience and becoming a source of political power for individuals with neither wealth nor force of arms. Thomas Paine, to take one example, emigrated from England to Philadelphia with no wealth, no family connections and no power other than that which came from his ability to think and write clearly—yet his *Common Sense* became the *Harry Potter* of Revolutionary America. The "public interest" mattered, was actively discussed and pursued.

But the "public square" that gave birth to America has been transformed beyond all recognition. The conversation that matters most to the shaping of the "public mind" now takes place on television. Newspapers and magazines are in decline. The Internet, still in its early days, will one day support business models that make true journalism profitable—but up until now, the only successful news websites aggregate content from struggling print publications. Web versions of the newspapers themselves are, with few exceptions, not yet making money. They bring to mind the classic image of Wile E. Coyote running furiously in midair just beyond the edge of the cliff, before plummeting to the desert floor far beneath him.

The average American, meanwhile, is watching television an astonishing five hours a day. In the average household, at least one television set is turned on more than eight hours a day. Moreover, approximately 75 percent of those using the Internet frequently watch television at the same time that they are online.

Unlike access to the "public square" of early America, access to television requires large amounts of money. Thomas Paine could walk out of his front door in Philadelphia and find a dozen competing, low-cost print shops within blocks of his home. Today, if he traveled to the nearest TV station, or to the headquarters of nearby Comcast—the dominant television provider in America—and tried to deliver his new ideas to the American people, he would be laughed off the premises. The public square that used to be a commons has been refeudalized, and the gatekeepers charge large rents for the privilege of communicating to the American people over the only medium that really affects their thinking. "Citizens" are now referred to more commonly as "consumers" or "the audience."

That is why up to 80 percent of the campaign budgets for candidates   40 in both major political parties is devoted to the purchase of 30-second TV ads. Since the rates charged for these commercials increase each year, the candidates are forced to raise more and more money in each two-year campaign cycle.

Of course, the only reliable sources from which such large sums can be raised continuously are business lobbies. Organized labor, a shadow of its former self, struggles to compete, and individuals are limited by law to making small contributions. During the 2008 campaign, there was a bubble of hope that Internet-based fundraising might even the scales, but in the end, Democrats as well as Republicans relied far more on traditional sources of large contributions. Moreover, the recent deregulation of unlimited—and secret—donations by wealthy corporations has made the imbalance even worse.

In the new ecology of political discourse, special-interest contributors of the large sums of money now required for the privilege of addressing voters on a wholesale basis are not squeamish about asking for the quo they expect in return for their quid. Politicians who don't acquiesce don't get the money they need to be elected and re-elected. And the impact is doubled when special interests make clear—usually bluntly—that the money they are withholding will go instead to opponents who are more than happy to pledge the desired quo. Politicians have been racing to the bottom for some time, and are presently tunneling to new depths. It is now commonplace for congressmen and senators first elected decades ago—as I was—to comment in private that the whole process has become unbelievably crass, degrading and horribly destructive to the core values of American democracy.

Largely as a result, the concerns of the wealthiest individuals and corporations routinely trump the concerns of average Americans and small businesses. There are a ridiculously large number of examples: eliminating the inheritance tax paid by the wealthiest one percent of families is considered a much higher priority than addressing the suffering of the millions of long-term unemployed; Wall Street's interest in legalizing gambling in trillions of dollars of "derivatives" was considered way more important than protecting the integrity of the financial system and the interests of middle-income home buyers. It's a long list. . . .

We haven't gone nuts—but the "conversation of democracy" has become so deeply dysfunctional that our ability to make intelligent collective decisions has been seriously impaired. Throughout American history, we relied on the vibrancy of our public square—and the quality of our democratic discourse—to make better decisions than most nations in the history of the world. But we are now routinely making really bad decisions that completely ignore the best available evidence of what is true and what is false. When the distinction between truth and falsehood is systematically attacked without shame or consequence—when a great nation makes crucially important decisions on the basis of completely false information that is no longer adequately filtered through the fact-checking function of a healthy and honest public discussion—the public interest is severely damaged.

That is exactly what is happening with U.S. decisions regarding the climate crisis. The best available evidence demonstrates beyond any reasonable doubt that the reckless spewing of global-warming pollution in obscene quantities into the atmospheric commons is having exactly the consequences long predicted by scientists who have analyzed the known facts according to the laws of physics.

The emergence of the climate crisis seems sudden only because of a relatively recent discontinuity in the relationship between human civilization and the planet's ecological system. In the past century, we have quadrupled global population while relying on the burning of carbon-based fuels — coal, oil and gas — for 85 percent of the world's energy. We are also cutting and burning forests that would otherwise help remove some of the added CO_2 from the atmosphere, and have converted agriculture to an industrial model that also runs on carbon-based fuels and strip-mines carbon-rich soils.

The cumulative result is a radically new reality — and since human nature makes us vulnerable to confusing the unprecedented with the improbable, it naturally seems difficult to accept. Moreover, since this new reality is painful to contemplate, and requires big changes in policy and behavior that are at the outer limit of our ability, it is all too easy to fall into the psychological state of denial. As with financial issues like subprime mortgages and credit default swaps, the climate crisis can seem too complex to worry about, especially when the shills for the polluters constantly claim it's all a hoax anyway. And since the early impacts of climatic disruption are distributed globally, they masquerade as an abstraction that is safe to ignore.

These vulnerabilities, rooted in our human nature, are being manipulated by the tag-team of Polluters and Ideologues who are trying to deceive us. And the referee — the news media — is once again distracted. As with the invasion of Iraq, some are hyperactive cheerleaders for the deception, while others are intimidated into complicity, timidity and silence by the astonishing vitriol heaped upon those who dare to present the best evidence in a professional manner. Just as TV networks who beat the drums of war prior to the Iraq invasion were rewarded with higher ratings, networks now seem reluctant to present the truth about the link between carbon pollution and global warming out of fear that conservative viewers will change the channel — and fear that they will receive a torrent of flame e-mails from deniers. . . .

All things are not equally true. It is time to face reality. We ignored reality in the marketplace and nearly destroyed the world economic system. We are likewise ignoring reality in the environment, and the consequences could be several orders of magnitude worse. Determining what is real can be a challenge in our culture, but in order to make wise choices in the presence of such grave risks, we must use common sense and the rule of reason in coming to an agreement on what is true.

So how can we make it happen? How can we as individuals make a 50 difference? In five basic ways:

First, become a committed advocate for solving the crisis. You can start with something simple: Speak up whenever the subject of climate arises. When a friend or acquaintance expresses doubt that the crisis is real, or that it's some sort of hoax, don't let the opportunity pass to put down your personal marker. The civil rights revolution may have been driven by activists who put their lives on the line, but it was partly won by average Americans who began to challenge racist comments in everyday conversations.

Second, deepen your commitment by making consumer choices that reduce energy use and reduce your impact on the environment. The demand by individuals for change in the marketplace has already led many businesses to take truly significant steps to reduce their global-warming pollution. Some of the corporate changes are more symbolic than real—"green-washing," as it's called—but a surprising amount of real progress is taking place. Walmart, to pick one example, is moving aggressively to cut its carbon footprint by 20 million metric tons, in part by pressuring its suppliers to cut down on wasteful packaging and use lower-carbon transportation alternatives. Reward those companies that are providing leadership.

Third, join an organization committed to action on this issue. The Alliance for Climate Protection (climateprotect.org), which I chair, has grassroots action plans for the summer and fall that spell out lots of ways to fight effectively for the policy changes we need. We can also enable you to host a slide show in your community on solutions to the climate crisis—presented by one of the 4,000 volunteers we have trained. Invite your friends and neighbors to come and then enlist them to join the cause.

Fourth, contact your local newspapers and television stations when they put out claptrap on climate—and let them know you're fed up with their stubborn and cowardly resistance to reporting the facts of this issue. One of the main reasons they are so wimpy and irresponsible about global warming is that they're frightened of the reaction they get from the deniers when they report the science objectively. So let them know that deniers are not the only ones in town with game. Stay on them! Don't let up! It's true that some media outlets are getting instructions from their owners on this issue, and that others are influenced by big advertisers, but many of them are surprisingly responsive to a genuine outpouring of opinion from their viewers and readers. It is way past time for the ref to do his job.

Finally, and above all, don't give up on the political system. Even 55 though it is rigged by special interests, it is not so far gone that candidates and elected officials don't have to pay attention to persistent, engaged and committed individuals. President Franklin Roosevelt once told civil rights leaders who were pressing him for change that he agreed with them about the need for greater equality for black Americans. Then, as the story goes, he added with a wry smile, "Now go out and make me do it."

"The climate crisis, in reality, is a struggle for the soul of America."

To make our elected leaders take action to solve the climate crisis, we must forcefully communicate the following message: "I care a lot about global warming; I am paying very careful attention to the way you vote and what you say about it; if you are on the wrong side, I am not only going to vote against you, I will work hard to defeat you—regardless of party. If you are on the right side, I will work hard to elect you."

Why do you think President Obama and Congress changed their game on "don't ask, don't tell"? It happened because enough Americans delivered exactly that tough message to candidates who wanted their votes. When enough people care passionately enough to drive that message home on the climate crisis, politicians will look at their hole cards, and enough of them will change their game to make all the difference we need.

This is not naïve; trust me on this. It may take more individual voters to beat the Polluters and Ideologues now than it once did—when special-interest money was less dominant. But when enough people speak this way to candidates, and convince them that they are dead serious about it, change will happen—both in Congress and in the White House. As the great abolitionist leader Frederick Douglass once observed, "Power concedes nothing without a demand. It never did, and it never will."

What is now at risk in the climate debate is nothing less than our ability to communicate with one another according to a protocol that binds all participants to seek reason and evaluate facts honestly. The ability to perceive reality is a prerequisite for self-governance. Wishful thinking and denial lead to dead ends. When it works, the democratic process helps clear the way toward reality, by exposing false argumentation to the best available evidence. That is why the Constitution affords such unique protection to freedom of the press and of speech.

The climate crisis, in reality, is a struggle for the soul of America. It 60 is about whether or not we are still capable—given the ill health of our democracy and the current dominance of wealth over reason—of perceiving important and complex realities clearly enough to promote and protect the sustainable well-being of the many. What hangs in the balance is the future of civilization as we know it.

Understanding the Text

1. In the debates about global climate change, Gore compares the news media to referees in professional wrestling. Explain this analogy. Do you believe it is accurate? Why or why not?

2. What are the four main climate events that support the idea that there is a climate crisis?

3. According to Gore, what are the five basic ways that individuals can make a difference in the climate crisis?

Reflection and Response

4. What is the "scientific consensus" about climate change? Why, according to Gore, is this consensus ignored, doubted, and distorted in the news?

5. Gore suggests that climate change deniers are similar to tobacco lobbyists from half a century earlier. Do you agree or disagree? Explain the connection.

6. In what ways has the "public square" for political debates changed throughout history? How do recent changes impact our understanding of climate change?

Making Connections

7. More recently, Gore has compared climate change debates to civil rights debates in America (such as those on race, gender, and sexual equality). Do some research on these issues. Do you see a correlation? Explain.

8. Gore is one of the most visible figures in current environmental and sustainability debates. As a result, he is revered by some and despised by others. Find an example of a "strong opinion" concerning Gore and climate change, and analyze the strengths and weaknesses of that opinion.

9. There are many video interviews of Gore discussing environmental issues and sustainability. Watch one of these on YouTube, and analyze Gore's message, approach, persuasive tactics, and body language, as well as other aspects of the presentation. In your opinion, is Gore a persuasive speaker? Why or why not?

What Exactly Is Ecofeminism?

JR Thorpe

JR Thorpe is an award-winning British author who holds a Master's degree in creative writing from Oxford University and a PhD in Literature from the University of Manchester. Thorpe is a regular contributor to *Bustle*, an online women's magazine, where she writes on science, feminism, and history. This article appeared in *Bustle* in 2016.

The article provides an overview of *ecofeminism*, a movement that examines the connections between women, ecology, and nature. The article describes many of these connections, including the ways in which environmental damage to the earth and the repression of women are linked in modern cultures. At the same time, the article describes the ecofeminist view that women have a unique connection to the environment and its natural processes. As you read the article, think about these various definitions of ecofeminism and consider the ways in which ecofeminism is tied to other political and social movements.

When it comes to environmental damage and the health of our natural resources, gender definitely plays a role: in who's affected, who can do what, and how we can move forward. The United Nations Environment Program puts it pretty succinctly, saying: "Around the world, environmental conditions impact the lives of women and men in different ways as a result of existing inequalities. Gender roles often create differences in the ways men and women act in relation to the environment, and in the ways men and women are enabled or prevented from acting as agents of environmental change." When it comes to putting a gendered lens on climate change and environmental issues, there's one particular school of thought that prioritizes women: the concept of ecofeminism. The name implies the basic idea, but what exactly is ecofeminism?

Emerging in the 1970s, alongside the anti-nuclear proliferation movement and the beginnings of green political activism, the concept of ecofeminism relates environmental damage to women's exploitation and lack of empowerment. To quote Professor Mary Mellor, a UK academic, "ecofeminism is a movement that sees a connection between the exploitation and degradation of the natural world and the subordination and oppression of women. . . . Ecofeminism brings together elements of the feminist and green movements, while at the same time offering a challenge to both." But it's not as simple as just women going out to fight for ecological issues. (Although we're very good at that.)

When it comes to actually defining ecofeminism, there's an issue: it's not actually one movement. Instead, it's more like a group of concepts and thoughts that emerged as part of a cultural movement in the 1970s, or what Dr. Richard Twine calls "differing accounts that wove together a perceived interconnection between the domination of women and nature." As we'll discover, there are some aspects of ecofeminism where people radically disagree. Some attitudes are widespread, but this is going to get complicated.

This will only be the most basic of primers; I can't summarize decades of complicated academic argument into one article (I wish). If you're interested in ecofeminism, and want to get into the theory and see the real complexity of it, do also read longer resources that give you more detail.

Ecofeminism Sees a Parallel between the Earth and Women

Basically, ecofeminism sees a relationship between the serious environmental damage done to the earth and the repression of women. But that one relationship can take many forms, depending on what kind of ecofeminist you are.

> "Ecofeminism sees a relationship between the serious environmental damage done to the earth and the repression of women."

One form of ecofeminism takes it very literally, saying that women are viewed in the same way as natural resources: as something to be taken, plundered, or used. Activist Ynestra King has stated, "We see the devastation of the earth and her beings by the corporate warriors, and the threat of nuclear annihilation by the military warriors, as feminist concerns. It is the masculinist mentality which would deny us our right to our own bodies and our own sexuality, and which depends on multiple systems of dominance and state power to have its way." This is the perspective of radical ecofeminism: that women and the environment are exploited in the same way by the same patriarchal dominating forces, who are seen as creating order and deriving value from "chaotic" things (like women and forests). Some radical ecofeminists also take the same position about animal welfare, saying animals are being unfairly exploited by current power structures in a way that harms the environment, too.

But there's another perspective: Cultural ecofeminism makes out the link between nature and women to be empowering, picturing our gender as uniquely connected to the environment and natural processes through things like menstruation and childbirth. This perspective posits that when it comes to feeling the real damage of environmental harm and doing something about it, we're better-placed to take action. Basically, the academic Leigh Brammer summed it up this way: "some ecofeminists view the link between woman and nature as empowering, others believe it's imposed by patriarchy and is degrading." The first belief is cultural ecofeminism, the second is radical ecofeminism.

Ecofeminism Challenges Power Hierarchies

One of the big aims of ecofeminism is to change the world's way of relating to things like women and the environment: instead of domination and power hierarchies, they want to install equality and communities that interact on a level playing field. Two of the most famous ecofeminists, Maria Mies and Vandana Shiva, declared in their introduction to the book *Ecofeminism* in 1993, "Our aim is to go beyond this narrow perspective [patriarchy and hierarchies] and to express our diversity and, in different ways, address the inherent inequalities in world structures which permit the North to dominate the South, men to dominate women, and the frenetic plunder of ever more resources for ever more unequally distributed economic gain to dominate nature."

Radical ecofeminism talks about this in particular; depicting women as natural and irrational, they say, created a hierarchy where men needed to come in and control and develop them, just as they do to nature.

Ecofeminism Points Out Women's Unique Involvement in Environmental Damage

Beyond the theoretical stuff, much ecofeminism points to the very real 10 interactions that women, particularly in developing countries, have with environment degradation, and how their disempowerment is related to serious ecological problems. For instance, women are often the gatherers of food and water (what's called "natural resource managers") for their households, which means that their lives are pretty heavily intertwined with a healthy, flourishing landscape. Sara Alcid at Everyday Feminism points out, for instance, that young girls who have to work with their mothers to find scarce water are less likely to be able to go to school, and that low-income women of color are disproportionately exposed to toxic chemicals in the workplace. Women are both invested in preventing environmental damage and very vulnerable to it.

Writer Leigh Grammar points out that this vulnerability is a patriarchal thing: "Women are hurt most by the exploitation of the earth because they are the most vulnerable in patriarchal society. The main focus is on women who are more at risk because they suffer double oppression of poverty, race, education, or nation." And it goes further than just disempowerment and cycles of poverty—women in their capacity as natural resource managers might have unique perspectives on how to help stop environmental damage, but if their voices are silenced, they can't help.

What Might Be Problematic about Ecofeminism

Aside from the problem of not being a coherent ideology, cultural ecofeminism in particular is often criticized for its tie between women and nature, as Yale University's "Ecofeminism: An Overview" explains. Isn't this just more gender stereotyping? As Dr. Catherine Roach, author of *Mother/Nature*, points out, it's hardly as if men aren't natural beings: "they do share all other human biological processes (eating, sleeping, eliminating wastes, getting sick, dying), and in addition, in their ejaculation of semen they have experience of a tangible stuff of the reproduction of life." For some commentators, like Anne Archambault, the idea that women are somehow more "natural" is nonsense and actually hamstrings the whole idea. "The claim that women are biologically closer to nature," she says, "reinforces the patriarchal ideology of domination and limits ecofeminism's effectiveness." Ecofeminists of the radical strain don't believe this either, causing conflict within the movement.

(There's also a bit of a cultural issue, too. For instance, Dr. Twine points out that Chinese society doesn't have the same "women equal nature" idea, even though it has similar issues about female inferiority; he cites the Chinese academic Huey-li Li, who says, "The association of women and nature is not a cross-cultural phenomenon, since nature as a whole is not identified with women in Chinese culture.")

People are worried about radical ecofeminism, too. One of the more popular critiques of ecofeminism, over at Green Fuse, makes the argument that it seems to clash with conventional feminism these days, which wants to put women into positions of power (Hilary 2016!) and give them a chance to be part of the hierarchy. Radical ecofeminism wants to eliminate those structures and replace them with communal decision-making and equal valuing of all people, and it's worried that it's not a realistic point of view.

The Bottom Line

Whatever your interpretation, ecofeminism is a unique feminist lens on the very real relationship between gender and environmental issues. Damage to the environment is definitely a feminist issue; it desperately needs the involvement of empowered, educated women to succeed in protecting communities and stopping further serious degradation.

Understanding the Text

1. Why are there so many definitions of ecofeminism, and how might that relate to the issues the movement faces?
2. How does ecofeminism challenge the typical models of hierarchy?
3. What are the three forms of ecofeminism and how do they differ?
4. What challenges does ecofeminism face as a movement?

Reflection and Response

5. How is ecofeminism connected to sustainability?
6. Do you believe that ecofeminism is mostly or exclusively for and about women?
7. Do you think that some aspects of ecofeminism might discourage men from joining the cause?
8. Do you think of nature as masculine or feminine? How does this influence your beliefs and actions regarding nature and the environment?

Making Connections

9. Conduct some research on ecofeminism. What other definitions or perspectives do you find, and how do they relate to Thorpe's perspective?
10. If you've read Rachel Carson's essay in Chapter 1 of this textbook, you may recognize that Carson faced much scrutiny and criticism. Do you see any parallels between Carson's difficulties in spreading her message and the challenges facing ecofeminism?
11. How have depictions of women in mythology or folklore been linked to the environment? How does this relate to the concept of ecofeminism?

Conservatives and Climate Change

Jim Manzi and Peter Wehner

Jim Manzi is the founder and chairman of Applied Predictive Technologies, an applied artificial intelligence software company, and an avid commentator on American politics and policies. He is a frequent contributor to publications such as the *Weekly Standard*, the *Atlantic*, and *Slate*, and the author of *Uncontrolled: The Surprising Power of Trial and Error for Business, Politics, and Society.*

Peter Wehner is the former Deputy Assistant to the President, Director of the White House Office of Strategic Initiatives, and Deputy Director of Speech Writing to Ronald Reagan, George H.W. Bush, and George W. Bush. Wehner has written on conservative issues in publications including the *Washington Post*, the *National Review*, and the *Wall Street Journal*. He is currently a Senior Fellow at the Ethics and Public Policy Center in Washington, DC.

"Conservatives and Climate Change" was published in 2015 in *National Affairs*, a quarterly journal of articles on national policy, politics, and society. The article discusses "unsustainable" conservative views on climate change. While focusing on the Republican viewpoint, the authors discuss the logic and stance of conservative climate change deniers and urge them to consider scientific evidence so that the government can push innovators to keep searching for ways to lessen the impact of our changing environment. The article maintains that technology is the key to combatting climate change, rather than taxation or emissions regulation. As you read, consider how technological advancements can reduce or mitigate the effects of climate change.

The political debate over climate change has long resembled a contest to see which party can discredit itself more. Liberals have seized upon outlandishly improbable climate scenarios to urge drastic and immediate action. Former vice president Al Gore, a leading liberal voice on the subject, has compared global warming to "an asteroid colliding with the Earth and wreaking havoc." "Our food systems, our cities, our people and our very way of life developed within a stable range of climatic conditions on Earth," Gore has written. "Without immediate and decisive action, these favorable conditions on Earth could become a memory if we continue to make the climate crisis worse day after day after day."

The truth is that the most authoritative, mainstream scientific predictions envision some serious, undesirable changes, but hardly the dystopia of Gore's imagination. Yet, as liberals have yelled that the sky is falling, conservatives have plugged their own ears not only to ludicrous exaggerations, but also to the available facts. Liberal alarmism could be countered with arguments and with constructive policy alternatives to the administrative power grabs that the left prefers. Instead, for years those conservatives with access to the biggest megaphones have announced that the science underlying global warming is somewhere between highly speculative and "the greatest hoax," to quote from the title of a book on the subject by Senator James Inhofe, a Republican with significant influence on climate matters.

Many more Republicans are uncomfortable making accusations of corruption and conspiracy against so much of the scientific community, but they too have struggled to sustain an untenable position. Senate majority leader Mitch McConnell, House speaker John Boehner, presidential candidates Bobby Jindal and Marco Rubio, and rising star Senator Joni Ernst have all adopted the new talking point on the issue: "I'm not a scientist." This is an attempt to invoke ignorance in order to avoid embarrassment.

Scientific ignorance is not an excuse for refusing to stake out a position. Politicians rely on engineers to help them figure out which bridges are worth building, on physicists to suggest which defense projects are most feasible, and on biologists to better understand the threat of Ebola or Swine Flu. There is no reason why climate change should be different.

Of course, there are always a few scientists who challenge this mainstream   5
view. But too often politicians have chosen the side of the outlier scientist whose conclusion they like instead of the widely accepted view that might challenge their own preferences. Now and then scientific paradigms will be radically rethought by some inventive thinker, but politicians are not to be relied upon to figure out who is a Galileo and who is a quack. Where there is an almost universally held scientific conclusion, politicians—absent some extraordinary circumstance—should take it seriously.

The Republican position—either avowed ignorance or conspiracy theorizing—is ultimately unsustainable, but some still cling to it because they believe that accepting the premise that some climate change is occurring as a result of human action means accepting the conclusions of the most rabid left-wing climate activists. They fear, at least implicitly, that the politics of climate change is just a twisted road with a known destination: supporting new carbon taxes, a cap-and-trade system, or other statist means of energy rationing, and in the process ceding yet another key economic sector to government control. Conservatives seem to be on the horns of a dilemma: They will have to either continue to ignore real scientific findings or accept higher taxes, energy rationing, and increased regulation.

This kind of conundrum is not a new problem for conservatives. In his famous essay "Why I Am Not a Conservative," written more than half a century ago, the great Austrian economist Friedrich Hayek pointed to exactly this "propensity to reject well-substantiated new knowledge because [the conservative] dislikes some of the consequences which seem to follow from it" as the most objectionable feature of conservatism. Yet in the same essay Hayek pointed to the resolution to this problem: "By refusing to face the facts, the conservative only weakens his own position. Frequently the conclusions which rationalist presumption draws from new scientific insights do not at all follow from them." Hayek's "rationalist"—akin to today's progressive—sees the expansion of centralized state power as the eternal solution. Every new problem revealed by science, in the progressive view, can be solved by empowering expert administrators. The conservative's response should be to embrace new scientific insights when they seem validated by available knowledge, while offering superior, market-based alternatives to the progressive's favored solutions.

The truth is that the best approach to the problem of climate change is one rooted in deeply held conservative ideas. The right kind of approach will build on the tried policy of economic growth rather than the untried policy of carbon rationing and pricing schemes. It will recognize that society as a whole, working through its free institutions, is more adaptable and more inventive than regulators with limited imaginations tend to expect. It will seek to safeguard the future through the example of the past and the energies of the present. And it will be rooted in the most modern and reliable science.

What to Expect from Climate Change

First, we should acknowledge the science as we know it today. Greenhouse gases absorb and redirect longer-wavelength radiation, but not shorter-wavelength radiation. When radiation from the sun hits the earth, some of it is absorbed by the land and the sea, which are consequently warmed by the energy. As a result, when the earth re-emits the sun's radiation in the form of heat, it is disproportionately of the lower-energy, longer-wavelength sort that the greenhouse gases, carbon dioxide (CO_2) foremost among them, trap or send back to earth. Thus, more carbon-dioxide emissions lead to a hotter planet. How much hotter is a complicated question that has been the subject of intense scientific inquiry over the past several decades.

The United Nations Intergovernmental Panel on Climate Change 10 has the task of integrating the best available knowledge on technical questions relating to climate change. The IPCC produces an Assessment Report every five to seven years that seeks to forecast climate change given fairly reasonable assumptions for world population and economic growth. These projections are therefore premised on various potential global-development scenarios for the 21st century. The fifth and most recent Assessment Report (known as AR5), published last year, projects that, without significant interventions to reduce emissions, global temperatures will rise on the order of two degrees Celsius by the end of the century in moderate emissions scenarios, and closer to four degrees in the most aggressive emissions scenarios.

Advocates for emissions controls, such as the Copenhagen Accord that the United States signed, often argue that scientific findings imply that we must keep the total global-temperature increase below two degrees Celsius in order to avoid disaster. So, it is argued, disaster looms unless we take decisive action.

Unfortunately for such advocates, the IPCC also estimates the economic impacts of various levels of warming. AR5 estimates that "global annual economic losses for additional temperature increases of ~2°C are between 0.2% and 2.0% of income"—no one's idea of economic disaster. The median estimate of the six studies cited by the report was that three to five degrees of warming would cause a reduction of approximately 3.6% in global gross economic product (the total gross domestic product of all the world's nations) at the end of the century. This is broadly consistent with the panel's previous Assessment Report 4 of 2007, which itself "confirm[ed]" the results of Assessment Report 3 of 2001. AR3 estimated that a four-degree increase in global temperatures should cause a reduction in global economic output of 1% to 5%. These estimates have been stable for more than a decade.

The key takeaway is this: According to the IPCC, the expected economic costs of global warming over a hundred years from now are likely to be about 3% of GDP. Now, of course, there is more to the world than GDP, and climate change would put more than just the economy at risk, like the well-being of different species and plant life. Moreover, the damage won't be uniformly distributed—some countries could have their economies damaged by much more than 3% and some countries by much less. The point is that 3% as a world figure signals that the challenge posed by climate change is not one of averting a global disaster in which Manhattan becomes an underwater theme park. Rather, climate change is likely to involve a modest risk that will have to be managed and a series of tradeoffs to be hotly debated.

If we are to seek to reduce the damage of greenhouse gases a hundred years from now, we will have to constrain emissions somehow in the near term. Since carbon dioxide is produced by nearly every aspect of the industrial economy, that means we would need to reduce current-day economic growth by some amount. We have to weigh the near-term and long-term costs to economic growth from emissions-abatement policies against the long-term benefits of those policies—namely, the extent to which global warming is avoided.

This kind of tradeoff presents a classic economic problem. Some individuals are consuming an item (like carbon) that damages the well-being of others who are not involved in the transaction (such as those who will suffer from whatever effects a slightly warmer world could cause decades from now). One common way of solving the problem is to tax the item so that the amount the consumer pays is closer to the actual cost society bears. If the tax is set at the right amount, everyone is, in aggregate, better off.

Yet, even in this imagined, perfectly efficient scheme, a policy of carbon mitigation shows few net benefits. According to the modeling group led by William Nordhaus, a Yale professor widely considered to be the world's leading expert on this kind of assessment, an optimally designed and implemented global carbon tax would provide an expected net benefit of about 0.2% of the present value of global GDP over the next several centuries. Even in Nordhaus's theoretical world, the tax would be set at a level that would still allow about 75% of the unconstrained damages from emissions to take place, since it would be economically more damaging to set the tax high enough to prevent them.

A gain of 0.2% of future global GDP is in fact a lot of money, about $3 trillion in present value. Usually a policy predicted to net $3 trillion would be attractive. Yet, in this case, it would be unwise to work toward a global carbon tax or carbon-auctioning system. To understand why, we must move from the world of academic model-building to the real world of geostrategic competition and domestic politics. To realize this gain of $3 trillion, every nation would have to agree to and then enforce a global, harmonized tax on all significant uses of carbon and other greenhouse gases in any material form. This would require the agreement of—just to take a few examples—the Parliament of India, the Brazilian National Congress, the Chinese Politburo, the authoritarian leader of Russia, and the U.S. Congress. Each of these entities and individuals has been known throughout history to elevate narrow, sectarian interests above the comprehensive good of all mankind, to put it kindly.

For the sake of argument, let's suppose we actually could negotiate such a binding agreement. All the side deals that would be required to get this done—ranging from grandfathering provisions for pre-existing factories and power plants, to special exemptions for "strategically important" industries, to carve-outs for poorer countries, to offsets for often dubious promises not to clear rainforests, and the like—may well create enough economic drag to more than offset the benefit of 0.2% of the present value of global output. Our track record of closing and implementing deals like the Kyoto Protocol, or even the recent rounds of WTO and regional trade deal negotiations (which, remember, are supposed to make the signatories richer), shouldn't inspire much confidence that the theoretical net benefits will outweigh the costs created by a global greenhouse-gas agreement.

In recent years, the U.S. government has not seriously considered a carbon tax, which is the carbon-mitigation policy preferred by almost all academic economists. Instead, Congress considered a cap-and-trade system, a form of emissions rationing, and the Obama administration is currently proposing sector-specific regulation of coal plants, because it is more politically palatable to hide the costs to consumers through such profoundly inefficient tools. Yet even all the side deals, offsets, special auctions, and so forth that were added to the Waxman-Markey cap-and-trade bill in 2009 were not enough to build a winning congressional coalition.

Further, even if we got to an agreement, we would then have to　20 enforce, for hundreds of years, a set of global rules that would run directly contrary to the narrow self-interest of most people currently alive on the planet. How likely is it, for example, that a rural Chinese or Indian official would enforce the rules on a local coal-fired power plant? These bottom-up pressures would likely render such an agreement a dead letter, or at least effectively make it a tax applicable only to the law-abiding developed countries that represent an ever-shrinking share of global carbon emissions.

Despite the dire warnings from progressives, the best models show us that global warming is a problem that is expected to have only a limited impact on the world economy. Any attempt to do anything about those damages would be rife with unintended consequences and, in any case, is geopolitical fantasy. Sober minds should select laissez faire as the best of imperfect options.

Confronting Worst Cases

But what if our best estimate is wrong and devastatingly optimistic? After all, it's only an estimate. Predicting the cost impact of various potential warming scenarios requires us to concatenate these climate predictions with economic models that predict the cost impact of these predicted temperature changes on the economy in the 21st, 22nd, and 23rd centuries. It is hubris to imagine that these can guarantee accuracy, and it is impossible to validate such a claim in any event.

Though three degrees Celsius is the most likely case, competent modelers don't assume that the most likely case is the only case. Rather, they build probability distributions for levels of warming and their associated economic impacts. For instance, there is an X% chance of warming that is four and a half degrees or greater, a Y% chance of four degrees or greater, and so on. The concern is thus with the inherently unquantifiable possibility that our probability distribution itself is wrong.

A sense of caution might lead us to suggest emissions caps as a form of insurance against the sort of devastating global warming that lies outside of the IPCC distribution. But standard cost-benefit analysis would suggest that such a precautionary policy is extraordinarily expensive. Suspend disbelief about the real-world politics for a moment, and assume that we could have a perfectly implemented global carbon tax. If the whole world introduced a tax high enough to keep atmospheric carbon concentration to no more than 420 parts per million — that's one-and-a-half times the pre-industrial average and well above what many environmentalists worried about worst-case scenarios would deem "safe" — we would expect, using the Nordhaus analysis as a reference point, to spend about $14 trillion more than the benefits that we would achieve. To put that in context, it is an amount on the order of the annual GDP of the United States. That's a heck of an insurance premium for an event so unlikely that it is literally outside of the probability distribution.

So what should we do? On some intuitive level, it is clear that rational 25 doubt about our probability distribution of forecasts for climate change over the next century should be greater than our doubt surrounding the likelihood that a flipped quarter will land on heads around 500 times of 1,000. Yet we cannot incorporate this doubt into an alternative probability distribution without doing our own armchair climate science in place of the IPCC, nor is it responsible to set a goal and announce "whatever it takes!" Furthermore, taking drastic action would also ignore the possibility that our models might be overestimating the risks involved. It makes sense to try to prepare for the possibility of greater harm than we now project, but that goal has to be pursued in a way that takes account of the actual risks and costs involved.

As it happens, the problem of climate catastrophe is not without likenesses. There are other potential, unquantifiable dangers that are of comparable likelihood and severity to that of outside-of-distribution climate change. Our policy toward these dangers is never one of unreserved caution.

Start with the example of an asteroid striking the Earth. The consensus scientific estimate is that there is a 1-in-10,000 chance that an asteroid large enough to kill a large fraction of the world's population will hit the earth in the next 100 years. That is, we face a 0.01% chance of sudden death for most people in the world, likely followed by massive climate change on the scale of that which killed off the non-avian dinosaurs. This scenario seems reasonably comparable to outside-of-distribution climate change. The U.S. government currently spends about $4 million per year on asteroid detection, in spite of an estimate that $1 billion per year spent on detection plus interdiction would be sufficient to reduce the probability of impact by 90%. Clearly for some potentially lethal threats we are unwilling to insure ourselves at spending levels that are orders of magnitude less than what is proposed for mitigating climate change.

Unfortunately for humanity, we face many dimly understood dangers: bioengineering technology gone haywire; a regional nuclear war in central Asia kicking off massive global climate change (in addition to its horrific direct effects); a global pandemic triggered by a modified version of the HIV or Avian Flu virus; or a rogue state weaponizing genetic-engineering technology. This list could go on almost indefinitely. To do everything conceivably possible to prevent catastrophic climate change is to become lost in the hot house of single-issue monomaniacs and to ignore the array of dangers and opportunities that we confront.

A healthy society is constantly scanning the horizon for threats and developing contingency plans to meet them. Yet the loss of economic and technological development that would be required to eliminate all theorized climate-change risk—or all risk from genetic and computational technologies or, for that matter, all risk from killer asteroids—would cripple our ability to deal with virtually every other foreseeable and unforeseeable risk, not to mention our ability to lead productive and satisfying lives in the meantime.

We can be confident that humanity will face many difficulties in the 30 upcoming century, as it has in every century. We just don't know which ones they will be. In the face of massive uncertainty, hedging one's bets and keeping one's options open is almost always the right strategy. Money, technology, and a flexible and creative political and economic culture are the raw materials that will give us the most options to deal with physical dangers. Markets, democratic political institutions, and economic growth are therefore the means toward greater adaptability in the future.

The Energy Innovation Example

America faces a tradeoff in which neither option is appealing. On the one hand, we could continue to create wealth and, because of carbon emissions, see meaningful reductions in the rate of economic growth in less than a century. On the other hand, we could significantly clip the wings of the American economy, making ourselves poorer now and, because of compounding, possibly poorer later.

When presented with option A or option B, neither being ideal, the entrepreneur chooses to invent C. This is, in a way, what has happened in the energy sector over the past decade and can continue to happen. America has experienced a technology-driven energy revolution with little inducement or guidance from Washington. Within the last decade, the United States has developed a new green-energy technology, leading to the fastest rate of reduction in CO_2 emissions of any major country in the world and to permanent reductions in absolute emissions. The Department of Energy expects that energy-related carbon emissions will remain below 2005 levels for decades, despite population growth.

This enduring, structural change in the American energy sector is the result of a series of innovations allowing us to extract so-called unconventional fossil fuels. The most important of these innovations has been hydraulic fracturing, often called "fracking," but other important developments include tight-oil extraction, horizontal drilling, and new applications of information technology. These combined efforts have allowed us to produce much more energy—an increase nearly equivalent to the total output of Iraq or Kuwait—and far cleaner energy. The fracking revolution has shifted American energy sources toward gas and away from coal. Since natural gas emits about half the carbon dioxide that coal does, our impact on the climate has been reduced. America's reduction in emissions—to say nothing of the jobs we've created and the energy independence we're obtaining—is cause for celebration.

The elaborate climate models don't account for this kind of innovation. Although they are, in a sense, models of change, they actually tend to be very static compared to the real world, as they can't predict large structural shifts due to technological innovation. In the future, radically cleaner fuel sources or technologies that could remove carbon from the atmosphere would be game-changers in the debate about climate policy, just as the fracking revolution has already changed the conversation. The question is how to bring about such game-changers.

The American energy revolution provides an example. It is important 35 to remember that less than a decade ago, virtually no one saw the rapid development of an alternative energy source on the horizon. In 2008 the International Energy Agency projected that U.S. oil and natural-gas production would remain flat or decline somewhat through about 2030. The discussion of technological solutions focused on far-off, highly speculative, panacea-like technologies such as wind and solar energy. Yet there was something latent in the American economy that allowed it to dramatically and unexpectedly disprove policymakers' lack of imagination.

The United States was able to launch its recent energy revolution for the same reason it has had revolutions in information technology, biotechnology, and certain other sectors. Three core elements undergird all these revolutions: a foundation of free markets and strong property rights; the new-economy innovation paradigm of entrepreneurial start-ups with independent financing and competitive-cooperative relationships with industry leaders; and support by government technology investments.

The primary driver has been the regulatory framework of strong property rights and free pricing. Among the world's key petroleum-producing countries, only the United States allows private entities to control large-scale oil and gas reserves. And outside of North America, hydrocarbon pricing is typically governed by detailed regulatory frameworks that are built around the realities of conventional petroleum production. Freer pricing, in combination with ownership of mineral rights, allows innovators in America to reap the economic rewards of their imagination and risk-taking.

Most of the recent technological advances have been made through trial-and-error and incremental improvements—a kind of Darwinian competition among a network of independent companies—as opposed to huge one-time projects by industry giants or quasi-governmental organizations. That is a credit to America's more flexible regulatory structure.

Finally, government has served the role of catalyst rather than manager. The Breakthrough Institute has produced reliable evidence that government subsidies for speculative technologies and research over at least 35 years have played a role in the development of the energy boom's key technology enablers, such as 3-D seismology, diamond drill bits, and horizontal drilling. Government-led efforts that are less obviously related—such as detailed geological surveys and earlier defense-related expenditures that enabled the U.S.-centered information-technology revolution, which has in turn created the capacity to more rapidly develop "smart drilling" technology—have also been important.

While various government ministers in well-tailored suits spent 40 lots of time over the last several decades meeting in Copenhagen and Rio de Janeiro to talk ad nauseam about how the key to ameliorating climate change is to make human beings do as they are told, the American system rode to the rescue by inventing and deploying new technology at scale. It is a system that conservatives routinely defend against progressives who want government to manage more and more. And it is a system that has done more than any other to substantially reduce carbon emissions. It would be foolish to think that system couldn't do it again.

Technology, Not Taxes

In *How to Think Seriously about the Planet*, the conservative philosopher Roger Scruton argues that conservatism and conservation share a root that is not just etymological. They are both policies of "husbanding resources and ensuring their renewal." Just as conservatives have championed the enduring value of our constitutional order, the institutions that have supported the free market, and our cultural capital, so too should they preserve and maximize our material capital on this planet. And the way to preserve our ecological riches is through those very same systems conservatives have long worked to conserve: a free market and a limited, flexible state.

The science is in. It is dubious at best to argue that large-scale attempts to manage the economy and mitigate carbon emissions will make us wealthier in the long run. The best models show that any realistic carbon tax — or worse, any set of command-and-control regulations or any crony-capitalist, carbon-credit auction scheme — will make us poorer, not richer. The first rule of conservative policymaking is to do no harm. Conservatives should oppose every large-scale, government-run carbon-mitigation plan, including the carbon tax that some on the right, like former congressman Bob Inglis, have hailed. Rigorous examination shows it would be better to do nothing than to accept the progressives' favored options.

Conservatives, however, should not limit themselves to merely opposing Waxman-Markey. They can champion an agenda that understands human beings to be much more imaginative than the economic models expect. By fostering the legal and economic ecosystems most conducive to breakthrough energy technologies, conservatives can help lessen the harms of climate change. As stated above, this includes the property rights and modest regulatory state that allow would-be innovators to learn through trial and error.

The second priority should be the kinds of public policies that actually help foster innovation. Investment in general infrastructure — both classic projects, like roads and bridges, and newer ones, in the area of digital infrastructure — grease the economic wheels. We also need to invest in visionary technologies that are too long-term, too speculative, or have benefits too diffuse to be funded by private companies.

During the 1980s and '90s, the Department of Energy drastically 45 increased its micromanagement of its labs in response to Congressional pressure to reduce waste and increase safety. This removed responsibility for core operating decisions—including personnel, travel, and project management—from the contractors that operate the labs to the DOE itself. This has greatly constrained the ability of the labs to flexibly pursue new innovations. The labs should be returned to a more independent contractor-led model with clearer goals but greater operational flexibility. We might, for example, set for one lab the goal of driving the true unit-cost of energy produced by a solar cell below that of coal, and a second lab the same task for nuclear power.

> "There is no reason why we should seek only technologies that lower our carbon use when the real goal is to avoid the damaging effects of a much warmer world."

At least one lab should be devoted to the geo-engineering technologies that can remove carbon dioxide from the atmosphere or mollify its heating effects. There is no reason why we should seek only technologies that lower our carbon use when the real goal is to avoid the damaging effects of a much warmer world. Because it tries to "engineer" a system we know very little about, geo-engineering should be pursued with utmost prudence and held in reserve as a "break glass in case of emergency" option.

We should also reckon with the fact that discovering breakthrough technologies is not guaranteed, so our best option might be to adapt to a slightly warmer world. Trees and reflective paint are proven to cool urban areas substantially. There are likely other adaptations to be made. As the world becomes warmer, local municipalities are going to demand adaptive technologies, and innovators will work to produce better and better solutions.

Third, innovation will require human capital. Greater high-skill immigration will bring innovators here, and a better education system will make innovators out of today's young people. Rather than ask government to "know" how to procure certain innovations by funding this or regulating that, public policy should help procure problem-solvers for the private sector. The focus of government action under this approach is to help create greater capabilities, not to direct resources.

There are many unknowns surrounding the question of climate change. We don't know how much the world will warm. We don't quite know how that will affect our day-to-day well-being. We can only estimate economic and ecological effects, and we can only speculate about future technologies—we don't know what kind of energy revolutions or geo-engineering feats are scientifically and practically possible. The proper response to a future we do not know is to build upon what we do know: the systems, institutions, and dispositions that have helped us solve problems and improve our lives.

All of these proposed policies build upon successes. When it comes 50
to climate change, the Republican Party need not theorize about
conspiracies or hide behind ignorance. It should confront the facts
as scientists generally understand them, as well as the limits of that
understanding, and it should seek to empower innovators looking for
solutions. The answer to the complex question of climate change will
be neither a regulatory Rube Goldberg machine nor a massive new tax.
Rather, conservatives should champion what they so frequently suggest
as the best way to solve complex problems: policies that open the space
for the private sector to innovate and adapt.

Understanding the Text

1. What are the authors' suggestions to combat climate change? Do you
   believe these suggestions would be supported by conservative Republicans?

2. How do the authors perceive Al Gore's vision of climate change?

3. In what ways can we begin to address climate change without resorting to
   economic solutions?

4. How does the quote from the Austrian economist Friedrich Hayek relate to
   the current conversation surrounding climate change?

Reflection and Response

5. The authors suggest that some conservatives deny climate change because
   of their economic ideologies. Are there other reasons why some conservatives reject climate change?

6. Do you believe that technology can play a major role in combating climate
   change? Or do you think that policies will have to be created to limit the
   amount of waste?

7. Do the authors portray different political beliefs about climate change in a
   fair and balanced way? Why or why not?

Making Connections

8. Do the political views on climate change in this article differ from those in
   other media forums? Find specific examples and compare them.

9. The authors mention Al Gore, whose essay, "Climate of Denial," is also featured in this chapter. What are the similarities and differences between these
   two pieces?

How to Think Seriously about the Planet: A Case for Environmental Conservatism

Roger Scruton

Sir Roger Scruton is an English writer and philosopher who has published over fifty books on conservative politics and contemporary culture. He currently holds a position as a Senior Fellow with the Ethics and Public Policy Center in Washington, D.C., and teaches both abroad and in the United States.

The following passage is from Chapter 1 of Scruton's book *How to Think Seriously about the Planet: A Case for Environmental Conservatism*. The passage argues that conservatism tied to sustainability is the only way to make environmentalism appealing to audiences on both the left and right of the political spectrum. The excerpt discusses the disparities in logic between different political views on sustainability. As you read, consider the relationship between the terms "conservatism" and "conservation."

The environmental movement has recently been identified, both by its supporters and by many of its opponents, as in some way "on the left": a protest on behalf of the poor and the powerless against big business, consumerism and the structures of social power. But that image is highly misleading. In Britain the environmental movement has its roots in the Enlightenment cult of natural beauty and in the nineteenth-century reaction to the Industrial Revolution, in which Tories and radicals played an equal part; and the early opposition to industrial farming joined guild socialists like H. J. Massingham, Tories like Lady Eve Balfour, secular gurus like Rudolf Steiner, and eccentric radicals like Rolf Gardiner, who borrowed ideas from left and right and who has even been identified (by Patrick Wright) as a kind of fascist. American environmentalism incorporates the nature worship of John Muir, the radical individualism of Thoreau, the transcendentalism of Emerson, the "ecocentrism" of Aldo Leopold and the social conservatism of the Southern Agrarians—a group of writers typified by the nostalgic poet Allen Tate, and represented in our day by Wendell Berry. French environmentalism is the child of *pays réel* conservatives like Gustave Thibon and Jean Giono, while the German Greens have inherited some of the romanticism of the early twentieth-century *Wandervogel* movement, as well as the vision of home and settlement so beautifully expressed by the German Romantic poets and taken up in our time both by the ex-Nazi Martin Heidegger and, in more lucid and liberal vein, by his Jewish student Hans Jonas.

Moreover, environmentalists today are aware of the ecological damage done by revolutionary socialism—as in the forced collectivization, frenzied industrialization and gargantuan plans to shift populations, rivers and whole landscapes that we have witnessed in the Soviet Union and China. Left-leaning thinkers will not regard those abuses as the inevitable result of their ideas. Nevertheless, they will recognize that more work is needed, if the normal conscience is to be persuaded that socialism is the answer, rather than one part of the problem. At the same time, they seldom recognize any affinity with "the right," and often seem to regard "conservatism" as a dirty word, with no semantic connection to the "conservation" that they favor.

The explanation, I believe, is that environmentalists have been habituated to see conservatism as the ideology of free enterprise, and free enterprise as an assault on the earth's resources, with no motive beyond short-term gain. Furthermore, there is a settled tendency on the left to confuse rational self-interest, which powers the market, with greed, which is a form of irrational excess. Thus the Green Party manifesto of 1989 identifies the "'false gods' of markets, greed, consumption and growth," and says "a Green Government would replace the false gods with cooperation, self-sufficiency, sharing and thrift." This manifesto echoes a widespread feeling that to rely exclusively on markets to solve our problems is to drift inevitably in an anti-social direction. And accusation goes hand in hand with the view that there are other, more altruistic motives that can be called upon, and which *would* be called upon by a left-wing government. I agree that there are those other motives. But I doubt that they would be called upon by a left-wing government.

Those who have called themselves conservatives in the political context are in part responsible for this misperception. For they have tended to see modern politics in terms of a simple dichotomy between individual freedom on the one hand, and state control on the other. Individual freedom means economic freedom, and this, in turn, means the freedom to exploit natural resources for financial gain. The timber merchant who cuts down a rainforest, the mining corporation that decapitates a mountain, the motor manufacturer that churns out an unending stream of cars, the cola producer that sends out a million plastic bottles each day—all are (or at any rate seem to be) obeying the laws of the market, and all, unless checked, are destroying some part of our shared inheritance. Because, in a market economy, the biggest actors do the most damage, environmentalists turn their hostility on big businesses, and on the free economies that produce them. Abolish the market economy, however, and the normal result is enterprises that are just as large and just as destructive but which, because they are in the hands of the state, are usually answerable to no sovereign power that can limit their predations.

It is a plausible conservative response, therefore, not to advocate economic freedom at all costs, but to recognize the costs or economic freedom, and to take all steps to reduce them.

We need free enterprise, but we also need the rule of law that contains 5 it, and law must keep pace with the threats. When enterprise is the prerogative of the state, the entity that controls the law is identical with the entity that has the most powerful motive to evade it—a sufficient explanation, it seems to me, of the ecological catastrophe of socialist economies. Studies have shown that free economies, with private property rights and an enforceable rule of law, not only consume far less energy per comparable product than economies where private property is insecure or absent, but also are able to adapt far more rapidly to the demand for clean energy, and for the reduction of emissions. And while markets cannot solve all our environmental problems, and are indeed the cause of some of them, the alternatives are almost always worse.

There is another and better reason for thinking that conservatism and environmentalism are natural bedfellows. Conservatism, as I understand it, means the maintenance of the social ecology. It is true that individual freedom is a part of that ecology, since without it social organisms cannot adapt. But freedom is not the only goal of politics.

"Conservatism and conservation are two aspects of a single long-term policy."

Conservatism and conservation are two aspects of a single long-term policy, which is that of husbanding resources and ensuring their renewal. These resources include the social capital embodied in laws, customs and institutions; they also include the material capital contained in the environment, and the economic capital contained in a free but law-governed economy. According to this view, the purpose of politics is not to rearrange society in the interests of some overarching vision or ideal, such as equality, liberty or fraternity. It is to maintain a vigilant resistance to the entropic forces that threaten our social and ecological equilibrium. The goal is to pass on to future generations, and meanwhile to maintain and enhance, the order of which we are the temporary trustees.

Understanding the Text

1. The author repeatedly uses the term "shared inheritance." What does he mean by this term and how is it related to sustainability?
2. Scruton notes that American environmentalism was inspired by a wide range of ideas and visionaries. How does he use this fact to support his argument?
3. How does Scruton argue that conservative, free markets could help improve environmental problems?

Reflection and Response

4. Do you believe that consumer habits have a direct impact on the state of the environment?
5. In what ways do you believe companies could or should improve their environmental impacts?
6. In the first sentence of the excerpt, Scruton observes that environmentalism is seen by some conservatives as a "leftist" movement that opposes big business, consumerism, and "the structures of social power." Do you agree or disagree with this position? What does Scruton believe?

Making Connections

7. How does Scruton's argument compare to Jim Manzi and Peter Wehner's in "Conservatives and Climate Change"?
8. Visit the website of a company whose products you appreciate or purchase. Does the website discuss sustainability, conservation, or environmental protection? Does this information (or lack of information) impact the way you view the company?
9. Conduct separate searches for the terms *conservation* and *conservatism*. Do the two definitions have anything in common?

How to Sell Conservatives on Climate Change

Mark Buchanan

Physicist and author Mark Buchanan has written three books about the way humans interact with science through social and societal institutions. His writing has also appeared in publications such as the *New York Times*, *New Scientist*, and the *MIT Technology Review*. As the co-creator of the workshop "Write about Science," Buchanan holds regular seminars dedicated to teaching students the fundamentals of scientific writing. He is currently working on his upcoming fourth novel and blog, which share the title *The Physics of Finance*.

Originally published on Bloomberg.com, "How to Sell Conservatives on Climate Change" argues that the Trump administration's view toward climate change makes bipartisan cooperation on sustainability more important than ever. The author discusses how lawmakers and environmental groups can recast the terms and language they use to describe sustainability efforts to appeal to a conservative audience. As you read, consider how word choice can shape one's emotions surrounding a certain topic or issue.

With Republican backing, Trump has set about nixing regulations on a host of environmental issues. He has annulled regulations preventing industries from leaking chemicals into wetlands, rivers and streams, and looks set to roll back automobile fuel efficiency standards. He wants to slash the budget of the Environmental Protection Agency, and has appointed an EPA head who doesn't believe that humans are responsible for climate change. From this and the media, one could get the impression that conservatives and Republicans are pretty much unanimous on such issues.

Yet the kind of deregulation that Trump is pursuing doesn't necessarily reflect conservative values. As Ronald Reagan put it, preserving the environment is "not a partisan challenge; it's common sense." More than a dozen significant conservative groups agree. ConservAmerica—known before 2012 as Republicans for Environmental Protection—recently unveiled a proposal to give tax breaks to companies that produce energy with zero carbon dioxide emissions. The Michigan Conservative Energy Forum fights utilities' attempts to block the growth of solar energy, while Conservatives for Energy Freedom works to support renewable and decentralized energy sources.

Learning how the views of these conservatives differ from typical liberal orthodoxy may be key to building a larger coalition. In a recent study,

"As Ronald Reagan put it, preserving the environment is 'not a partisan challenge; it's common sense.'" for example, sociologists David Hess and Kate Pride Brown found that conservatives on both sides of the environmental debate tend to appeal to the same set of values: national security, small government, free markets, personal liberty and job creation. Framing issues in such terms can thus be useful. Psychological studies indicate that when protecting the environment is cast as being about defending the purity of nature, expressing patriotism or obeying authority—or when the message comes from other conservatives—they respond much more favorably.

For this reason, pro-environment conservative groups could be decisive. As Republicans have moved strongly to the right, sociologist Aaron McCright argues, such groups have occupied the abandoned center. This actually leaves them well-positioned to recruit other conservatives, cooperate on specific policies with more liberal groups and help dispel the notion that being on the right means you must agree with Trump's policies. At the state and local level, where officials must deal with the practical consequences of climate change, many do very much care about the environment.

To that end, liberal groups must be willing to cooperate with, rather than criticize, their counterparts at the other end of the political spectrum—a sort of goodwill that ConservAmerica President Rob Sisson says isn't always forthcoming. Especially now, the environment needs all the allies it can get, and conservatives are probably the most valuable.

Understanding the Text

1. Why does the author believe that appealing to a more conservative audience on behalf of sustainability is increasingly important?

2. What were the results of the sociological study and how do they support the author's argument?

3. How do the current efforts made by conservative environmental groups align with the results of the study?

Reflection and Response

4. The author mentions the conservative group ConservAmerica, who were previously known as Republicans for Environmental Protection. How might their name change impact the ways in which they are perceived by conservatives and Republicans? Do you believe the name change was a smart move? Why or why not?

5. Do you believe that by simply using more appealing terms, environmental groups can increase their audience to include conservatives and Republicans?

Making Connections

6. Consider how the author uses language to support his argument. How do his word choice, use of quotations, and tone impact your perception of the article? How does that compare to his argument as a whole?

7. The article mentions that framing sustainability as "maintaining the purity of nature" is appealing to conservatives. How does that appeal compare to JR Thorpe's article "What Exactly Is Ecofeminism?"

3

How Do Crises and Disasters Create Challenges for Sustainability?

P eople are often drawn to sustainability when they identify a problem, encounter a difficulty, or experience something that makes them change their views about the world. We recognize an unsustainable situation now or in the future, and we look for ways to counteract that predicament. Sometimes this recognition is gradual and subtle — we begin to notice that our communities are not as clean as they used to be, or we are asked to choose "paper or plastic" at the grocery store checkout — and our thinking changes over time. Other times, though, we recognize the need for sustainability when we encounter or perceive a disaster or an emergent critical situation. Drastic changes or disruptions in the world can force us to reconsider our current ways of doing things, and sustainable solutions can help minimize the impact of catastrophes and crises and lessen their impact in the future.

This chapter examines several recent or ongoing crises and disasters and their relationship to sustainability. The reading selections begin with two specific disasters that have affected the United States in the recent past: Hurricane Katrina and the BP oil spill in the Gulf of Mexico. Abrams's article addresses the ongoing challenges of sustainability ten years after Hurricane Katrina made landfall near New Orleans in August 2005. Biello's essay focuses on the impact to wildlife following the BP oil spill in April 2010. Other transnational disasters are addressed in Chapter 5, most notably the tsunami that struck Japan in March 2011. These essays could be read in sequence to focus on sudden, catastrophic disasters in recent history, though they are separated into chapters based on their relative geographic locations.

The other crises and disasters addressed in this chapter may be less immediate, but they are no less serious or damaging. Essays by Singer and Brady address the challenges of extracting and transporting oil and other fossil fuels, speculating on the environmental and human costs of such practices. Kolbert and Diamond examine even broader, more slowly evolving crises that emerge from unsustainable human practices, including species extinction, climate change, and degradation of the environment.

photo: Thomas Goeppert/EyeEm/Getty Images

As you read the articles in this chapter, consider the relationship between human activity and crises and disasters involving sustainability. Although some of the issues addressed in the chapter are considered "natural" disasters, those disasters are often exacerbated by the choices we make in regard to our world. Think about the ways in which new, different, and more sustainable activities might mitigate or counteract such problems, offering hope for the future.

Hurricane Katrina's Unheeded Lesson: The Climate Refugee Crisis We Still Won't Address

Lindsay Abrams

Lindsay Abrams is the Program Coordinator of the Journalism and Design Program at The New School in New York City. Her writing has appeared in *Salon* magazine where she worked as a staff writer, as well as in the *Atlantic* during her time as an assistant editor.

The article printed below appeared in *Salon* in August 2015, exactly ten years after Hurricane Katrina destroyed coastlines from Florida to Texas, killing at least 1,245 people in the most costly natural disaster in U.S. history. As the article points out, New Orleans took the worst of the storm, with a majority of the city and bordering neighborhoods flooded for weeks after the storm ended. Over one million New Orleans residents evacuated the city, and many of them returned to find their homes destroyed. Abrams documents the long-term consequences and lessons to be learned from the storm in this article. As you read, think about the causes and effects of Hurricane Katrina, and consider whether or not the "lessons" of Katrina have gone unheeded in our society.

In the immediate lead-up to Hurricane Katrina and the devastating flooding that followed, some 1.5 million people were driven from their homes in Louisiana, Mississippi and Alabama. It was America's largest forced exodus since the Dust Bowl, and it all went down in just two weeks' time.

Two and a half years after the storm hit, 40 percent of those people still hadn't returned home. And a decade after the fact, we're still struggling to learn one the storm's most important lessons. Since Katrina, hundreds of thousands of people have been displaced, at least temporarily, by extreme weather events. Recovery, more often than not, is painfully slow: Hurricane Sandy displaced tens of thousands of people, some 39,000 of which still await housing assistance; it took years to rebuild the public housing wiped out by Hurricane Ike.

"We talk about climate resilience, and making our structures more able to withstand extreme weather events, and in their aftermath, we focus on a safe evacuation process—which is exactly what we should be doing," said Danielle Baussan, the managing director of energy policy at the Center for American Progress and the author of a new report on climate displacement in the wake of Katrina. "But we aren't necessarily looking at how we're bringing people home."

As New Orleans Mayor Mitch Landrieu recently put it, his city "is a canary in the coal mine for this country." And so far as displacement from extreme weather events goes, this couldn't be more true—though he may as well have said that Katrina was a warning to the entire world. According to the Internal Displacement Monitoring Center, the average number of people forced from their homes by natural disasters has doubled since 1970. And as the 21st century progresses, found the Intergovernmental Panel on Climate Change's Fifth Assessment report, the number of people displaced from their homes is expected to increase, a function of rising sea levels and the extreme weather events that scientists say are already being made worse by climate change. This is captured most dramatically in the public imagination by the image of entire low-lying island nations disappearing under the waves, but the growing class of so-called "climate refugees" can be taken to include anyone forced to abandon their homes due to the impacts of a changing climate. This can include migrations undertaken as the result of "slow-onset disasters" like drought and even people displaced by conflicts—of which climate change is being increasingly understood as a contributing factor.

Hurricane Katrina refugees evacuating New Orleans.
Mario Tama/Getty Images

And as is practically the rule with the impacts of climate change, it is 5
the already disadvantaged who will be disproportionately affected by displacement. In her report, Baussan highlights several reasons why this is
the case in the United States: low-income housing tends to be less resilient
to climate change in the first place; historically, low-income neighborhoods have been built in regions that are more vulnerable to extreme
weather. And then there's the question of having the resources, financial,
social and otherwise, to rebuild one's life after disaster strikes. "Weather is
going to impact everybody," Baussan told Salon. "But the aftermath will
be different for people who don't have the same resources to draw on."

In [the August 25, 2015] issue of the *New Yorker*, Malcolm Gladwell
offered a counterintuitive (of course) look at how being forced to leave
home—and in some cases, having no home to return to—may have
accidentally ended up benefitting some of Katrina's victims. The argument is that this allowed them, albeit through incredibly tragic means,
to escape their previous circumstance and start over in a place that
could offer them better opportunities. He cites the work of sociologist
David Kirk, who found that after the hurricane, parolees that weren't
able to return to their old neighborhoods and thus, their own ways, were
far less likely to end up back in prison. Katrina, Gladwell writes, "reminds
us that sometimes a clean break with the past has its advantages."

"Five years after the storm,
researchers found that more
than a third of the 163,000
children it displaced were
at least a year behind in
school."

But the full body of sociological
research suggests that while some of
the displaced may have come out of
the experience for the better—the
Vietnamese population is another
example of a "success story"—such an
outcome is hardly the rule. A major reason for that, Baussan posits, is because
of how utterly unprepared the United
States was to follow up with and provide services for the displaced. Gladwell describes the way Katrina's destruction prodded New Orleans to
overhaul its entire public school system, but five years after the storm,
researchers found that more than a third of the 163,000 children it displaced were at least a year behind in school; they were 4.5 more likely
than other children to have symptoms consistent with serious emotional
disturbance.

Surveys undertaken by researchers at Harvard Medical School in 2007
offered a similarly bleak perspective on Katrina's long-term impact on
mental health. Typically, the prevalence of mental illness following a
natural disaster decreases over time. But when the researchers followed
up with survivors nearly two years after the storm, they found that the

number of people with mood or anxiety disorders hadn't changed from when they were first surveyed, in the storm's more immediate aftermath. What's more, the prevalence of severe mental illness and suicidality had, in many instances, actually increased. The authors posited that part of the reason why mental health problems remained so pervasive may have had to do with the survivors' need for practical assistance, which for many, two years later, remained largely unmet. That many of these people were now living in different parts of the country, they noted, made it particularly difficult to get them the required services; still, they concluded, "it is especially important to reach these geographically displaced people because of their comparatively high risk of serious mental illness."

This is all to say nothing, meanwhile, of the people who were left behind—victims themselves, in a way, of displacement. The large-scale abandonment or, more recently, rapid gentrification of New Orleans' most heavily impacted neighborhoods has, ten years later, left the low-income and African American population that wasn't displaced are also, by many measures, worse off now than they were before the storm. Having a system in place to rapidly return the displaced to their homes, when possible, could help prevent such community-wide decay in the future.

"We're only going to see an increase in the number of storms," Baussan   10
said. "We're only going to see an increase in the number of people who are at least temporarily displaced from their homes. So if we don't try to think of a safety net for them beforehand, chances are they're not going to have a very successful return."

Understanding the Text

1. What does the article state about the number of people who have been impacted by natural disasters since the 1970s? What are the reasons for this?

2. Which group of people are more affected by natural disasters and why?

3. How is mental illness connected to the aftermath of Hurricane Katrina?

Reflection and Response

4. How is sustainability connected to the consequences of Hurricane Katrina?

5. The article cites journalist Malcolm Gladwell, who argues that the displacement caused by Hurricane Katrina has had unexpected positive outcomes. Do you agree or disagree with Gladwell's observation?

6. How do many of the long-term, undisplaced residents of New Orleans feel about their city today? What is that the case?

Making Connections

7. Consider other natural disasters that may threaten the United States. Do you feel that mass displacement is more likely for certain types of natural disasters? Why?

8. Research the current number of displaced New Orleans residents. Have the numbers changed since this article was published in 2015? Why or why not?

9. Hurricane Sandy had a devastating impact on parts of the East Coast. Do some research on the effects of Hurricane Sandy. How were the impacts of these two hurricanes similar or different?

How Did the BP Oil Spill Affect Gulf Coast Wildlife?

David Biello

David Biello is a writer who focuses on environmental and energy-related topics. He is also an associate editor at *Scientific American* and a host of *Scientific American's* news podcast *60-Second Earth.* He is currently working on a documentary with Detroit Public Television about the future of electricity.

This article from 2011 deals with the BP oil spill, which occurred in the Gulf of Mexico in April 2010. Biello describes some of the short-term and long-term effects of the spill, particularly focusing on the wildlife of the Gulf Coast. Although scientists are certain that marine and bird life has been affected, the consequences may also be more profound than they know.

Cocodrie, La.—The tendrils of coastline here were some of the first shores to see oil after BP's Macondo well blowout last year. On May 7, 2010—two days before the start of the annual fishing season—oil bounced off Grand Isle and flowed into Terrebonne Bay, remembers Michel Claudet, Terrebonne Parish president. In fact, oil fouled 35 percent of the U.S. Gulf Coast's 2,625 kilometers of shoreline before the spill was done.

"The people of Terrebonne are still trying to recover from the spill," Claudet says. "No one knew and we still do not know what might be the long-term effects."

The murky waters of the Mississippi River Delta obscure a profusion of life, hence the abundant local commercial and sport fishing. They also do an excellent job of hiding the long-term impacts of last year's oil spill. The oil that reached shore has been absorbed into the sponge-like wetlands or drifted to the sediment bottom, impacting shoreline that serves as a nursery for sealife, coastal habitat and a stopover for migrating birds.

"This spill is significant and, in all likelihood, will affect fish and wildlife across the Gulf, if not all of North America, for years, if not decades," warned Rowan Gould, then acting director of the U.S. Fish and Wildlife Service last May. "We will recover a small number of oil-covered birds. The concern is what we can't see. . . . We may never know the spill's impacts on many species of birds and marine life, given how far offshore they are found."

Six years after Hurricane Katrina, the storm's impact is still visible 5 throughout New Orleans, as evidenced by the emptied neighborhoods or the new houses in the Ninth Ward that resemble fresh scar tissue, easily distinguished from the former housing stock. One year after BP's oil spill, however, its impacts are largely invisible, hidden by the deep, cold waters of the Gulf and dispersed in that vast volume of water or tucked away into the endless marshes of the Louisiana coast.

"We may never know the spill's impacts on many species of birds and marine life, given how far offshore they are found."

A massive scientific effort is ongoing to precisely quantify the environmental damage caused by the oil spill — whether measured in oily sediments or missing generations of sealife. This is part of the National Oceanic and Atmospheric Administration (NOAA) Natural Resource Damage Assessment Process to determine what and how much BP will have to pay as well as an undertaking to understand a unique oil spill: one that happened more than 1,500 meters beneath the sea surface, spewing roughly five million barrels of oil before it was plugged.

As a result of this looming legal fight, much of what could be known about ecological impacts remains hidden. "Free and open access to scientific information concerning oil spills is not a given," noted the authors of a Congressional Research Service report on the oil spill's ecosystem impacts last October. For example, dead dolphins that washed ashore earlier this spring have been seized by the U.S. government. "NOAA and other federal agencies came into every lab with a dolphin in the fridge and confiscated it," says Casi Callaway, baykeeper for Mobile Bay in Alabama. "All data, all studies, all work on dolphins was sequestered."

Known Unknowns

Long-term impacts of the oil spill will not be known for years: After the *Exxon Valdez* spill in Alaska, it took three years before the local herring fishery collapsed. "A lot of species were spawning during the Deepwater Horizon [spill]," notes biological oceanographer Edward Chesney of the Louisiana Universities Marine Consortium (LUMCON). "We undoubtedly lost a lot of those fish and egg larvae — they can't move and are highly vulnerable to oil toxicity." The loss of entire generations of young marine life may also propagate up the food chain — over time. Already, scientists have found evidence of oil passing into plankton, which serve as the broad base of the food web.

Impacts to marine life range from outright death to reduced reproduction, altered development, impaired feeding as well as compromised immune systems. Even exposure to low concentrations of oil that fish embryos survive can alter the shape of their hearts as adults and

A large plume of smoke rises from fires on BP's Deepwater Horizon offshore oil rig on April 21, 2010.

Gerald Herbert/AP Images

reduce their ability to swim, according to research published April 11 in *Proceedings of the National Academy of Sciences*.

And simply because scientists had little information on certain spe- 10 cies before the spill—such as the denizens of the deep that bore the brunt of the dispersed oil—its impacts may prove impossible to measure, although research continues into the array of nematodes, fungi, mollusks and other organisms that thrive on the seafloor. "We don't have a lot of information on deep water species in general," Chesney notes.

Known Knowns

What is clear, however, is that the approximately five million barrels of Louisiana sweet (low-sulfur) crude that spewed into the Gulf of Mexico was toxic—a toxicity exacerbated by the use of 1.8 million gallons of dispersant both in the deep sea and at the surface. The oil itself sports an array of so-called polycyclic aromatic hydrocarbons (PAHs)—benzene, toluene and the like that are known to cause cancer. NOAA testing found more than 800 oil-related compounds in the water during the spill. "Those components are very toxic," says toxicologist Scott Miles of Louisiana State University. "Those are the ones you're sniffing when filling up the gas tank."

At the same time, they are compounds that fish and other organisms are efficient at not taking up into their tissues. "Accumulation of PAH is very difficult," notes toxicologist Joe Griffitt of the University of Southern Mississippi, who is studying how oil exposures that do not kill an animal can affect its reproductive success.

And these different compounds have different effects, some of which cancel each other out. "You have a very complex situation, very quickly," says Griffitt. PAH can have impacts that don't kill the marine organism directly but reduce its reproductive success or promote tumors—even interfere with the process of copying the genetic code. "There is some evidence that PAH can affect methylation patterns," Griffitt says. "You stick a methyl group on DNA somewhere and then effect gene transcription. It's theoretically heritable."

Further, it is difficult to tell whether a decline in reproduction or an increase in cancer is a direct result of the BP oil spill, a natural oil seep, some combination of causes or another cause entirely—in addition to being difficult to detect in the first place. "We are starting to see some tumors and lesions in fish exposed to Deepwater Horizon [spilled oil]," Chesney notes. In fact, fish caught in the Gulf, such as red snapper, are showing signs of weakened immune systems that have allowed opportunistic infections. The cause may or may not be BP's oil spill.

Evidence from prior spills, such as the *Exxon Valdez*, suggests further 15 long-term effects. "Salmon embryos exposed to oil, when they grow up, their babies are compromised, through mechanisms such as messing with the [hormonal] system," says biologist Andrew Whitehead of Louisiana State University, who studied Louisiana marshes both before and after the oil spill. Alaskan shorebirds also did not breed as much, had smaller eggs when they did breed, and those chicks that did hatch died more frequently.

In addition, BP's Macondo well oil itself smothered birds; more than 8,000 such birds representing 102 different species were collected—2,263 of them already dead—by government workers. Of course, this is likely just a fraction of the birds impacted because an oil-coated bird at sea sinks. "It is this phenomenon that makes an accurate estimate of bird deaths extremely difficult," wrote the Congressional Research Service in an October report on oil spill ecosystem impacts. The Center for Biological Diversity estimates that the oil spill killed or harmed approximately 82,000 birds as well as more than 6,000 sea turtles and 25,000 marine mammals, such as various species of dolphins.

And, unfortunately, the oil that did reach the coast—nearly 700 kilometers of marshland and 235 kilometers of beach was oiled, according to the government's Shoreline Cleanup Assessment Teams—"is very persistent once it gets up in the marsh grass," Miles says. "We still have a lot of oil in the Louisiana marshlands." That oil killed the spartina marsh grass at times, reducing coastal wetlands and, ultimately, exacerbating coastal erosion. "If it does kill the grass in high enough concentrations and a big storm comes up, it's going to start eroding," Miles adds.

Deep Clean?

At the same time, the closure of Gulf fisheries during the oil spill last year removed the enormous pressure from commercial fishing on populations ranging from shrimp to the tiny fish known as menhaden, the latter of which is caught to be ground up into meal. As a result, fishing this year is some of the best ever. "There are some fish species that are not as prolific as they have been. Others, there are millions, because we didn't fish them last year," Mobile Bay's Callaway says. "The food web has been touched and changed. We just don't know what that means."

And the fact that the spill occurred at sea—and beneath 1,500 meters of water—spared some of the most productive fisheries and spawning grounds in the world. "What is arriving at shore is much less toxic, much less difficult to deal with than what is coming out of the wellhead," says biologist Christopher D'Elia, dean of the School of the Coast and Environment at Louisiana State University. "If [the spill] had been closer, we would have been in much more trouble."

In the meantime, the Gulf shores enjoy a profusion of tarballs and tar 20 mats in excess of the ones that are always present as a result of natural seeps. "I have spent every summer of my life in Gulf Shores [Alabama], and I have never seen anything that is remotely close to what we have here now," Callaway says. "You just run your fingers through the sand and you've got hundreds, depending on when the last time they did a deep clean."

Such "deep cleans" have their own impacts. "There weren't sand crab holes anywhere—those are a major chunk of the food web," Callaway adds. "I didn't see periwinkles or clams along the shoreline. I'm hoping that is temporary and not long-lasting."

But evidence from prior oil spills suggests that Macondo well oil will be a part of the Gulf Coast for a very long time. "Oil persisted for much longer in the environment than anyone expected," Whitehead notes of the *Exxon Valdez* spill. "The oil was gone from the surface pretty quickly but sediment-associated organisms were persistently exposed to oil over long periods of time—we're talking five to 10 years after the spill."

Only that kind of time will tell what the abundance of life in the Mississippi Delta and the Gulf of Mexico reveals about the long-term impacts of the oil that spewed from BP's Macondo well in 2010. "We are trying to link exposure to effect," Whitehead says. "We are asking the organisms themselves to tell us: 'Has there been a relevant exposure?'"

Understanding the Text

1. How was Terrebonne Bay affected by the BP oil spill?
2. This article was written one year after the disaster. What effects remained from the spill at that time?
3. What are some of the plants and animals that have been affected by the spill?

Reflection and Response

4. How did the National Oceanic and Atmospheric Administration work to quantify the environmental damage caused by the oil spill?
5. What are the "known knowns" and the "known unknowns" concerning the oil spill?

Making Connections

6. This article was written a year after the BP disaster occurred. Do some research to find out how Terrebonne Bay and other affected areas along the Gulf of Mexico have recovered since this article was published.
7. Tourism is a major economic factor in the Gulf Coast region affected by the oil spill. Do some research on how the tourism industry has addressed these problems.

Fracking: The Solution? Or the Problem?

Alison Singer

Alison Singer is a PhD candidate in Community Sustainability at Appalachian State University in Boone, North Carolina. Singer also holds two Master's degrees from Appalachian State in Geography and Political Science. "Fracking: The Solution?" was published on Worldwatch Institute's blog, where Singer worked as an intern in 2013.

This blog article describes fracking: a process involving a high-pressure water mixture pumped deep into the earth to extract fossil fuels. It explains the process of fracking as well as the potential economic benefits and environmental consequences that fracking may produce. As you read, contemplate the pros and cons of fracking and how it could impact you, your family, and the environment you live in.

As the world hurtles towards catastrophic climate change, it is imperative to evaluate current policies, implement new policies, and transition towards a planet less dependent on fossil fuels. Easily accessible fossil fuels have been depleted due to our dependence on them, and hydraulic fracturing (fracking) has been touted as a way to increase extraction efficiency and help sustain our current energy consumption rates. However, fracking has also been roundly criticized as environmentally damaging, and as a simple band-aid strategy to delay the inevitable end of fossil fuels.

Fracking is a way to increase the efficiency of oil and gas wells, as well as access previously untapped reserves, and is performed by pumping fracturing fluid (composed of water, chemicals, and materials to keep the induced fracture open) into a wellbore. Fracking has been most developed in the United States, where it has contributed to increased oil and natural gas production for several years. Shale gas in particular has been heralded as an energy revolution — shale gas has grown from 2% of U.S. gas production in 2000 to 40% in 2012, and is touted as a substantially cleaner alternative to coal.

Thomas Friedman, author of *Hot, Flat, and Crowded*, agrees that fracking should be exploited, as it is much cleaner than coal, and inexpensive to disseminate. However, he is clear about the environmental dangers of fracking, including large amounts of methane leakage. Methane is even more dangerous than carbon dioxide in terms of its atmospheric warming properties. Friedman suggests that we regulate fracking, ensuring the environment is as protected as it can be. At the same time he warns that fracking must not be relied upon in any long-term plans. It is imperative to continue developing renewable energy technologies, and providing the political and economic incentives to implement such technologies. Fracking should be used on a short-term basis only, while we quickly transition to a sustainable, renewable energy future.

Thomas Princen, Jack P. Manno, and Pamela Martin explore this possible new future in their *State of the World 2013* chapter, "Keep Them in the Ground: Ending the Fossil Fuel Era." They understand that we live in a world built by fossil fuels, and we cannot simply ignore the energy potential of fossil fuels, but in order to prevent catastrophic climate change, we must utilize that potential as a springboard towards a world where renewable energy drives society. Fossil fuels must be strictly regulated and used only when a substitute cannot be found. Instead of racing to uncover hidden reservoirs of fossil fuels, the authors argue that we must "imagine a deliberately chosen post-fossil fuel world," and then act in such a way to make that dream a reality.

However, it is difficult for many to ignore the immediate economic benefits to fracking. Boomtowns have arisen in congruence with the increased emphasis on fracking, and some of the most depressed parts of the United States now have unemployment rates below 1%, providing high-paying jobs to thousands of workers. Fracking has the potential to provide energy independence, a transition to cleaner energy, and economic prosperity to regions rich in untapped natural resources. However, it also poses dangerous risks to the environment, and may increase our dependence on fossil fuels instead of helping the transition to renewable energy and a cleaner future.

From an environmental perspective, fracking poses a number of risks. Millions of gallons of water are pumped underground, and in places that already suffer from water shortages, this will only add to the problem. Chemicals are mixed with the water, and multiple studies have shown that these chemicals may contaminate groundwater. In addition to massive water usage and groundwater contamination, fracking has also been linked to increases in seismic activity.

Indeed, many areas have banned fracking in response to public outcries and environmental concern. In 2011 France became the first country to ban fracking, and lawmakers have vowed to uphold the ban until it can be proven that fracking definitively does not lead to groundwater contamination. Quebec has also instituted a fracking moratorium, as have several states in the United States, as a result of increased public pressure. Reports of increased earthquake activity, illnesses in livestock exposed to fracking fluid, and fears of groundwater contamination have prompted protests and legal action across the globe.

But the most dangerous aspect of fracking is the perpetuation of our fossil fuel dependence. Though fracking offers access to more fuel, and increases extraction efficiency in difficult wells, it is still concerned with a finite, polluting resource. Burning natural gas releases fewer carbon emissions than does burning coal, but this benefit may be offset by high methane leakage from gas fields. Additionally, shifting from coal to natural gas simply shifts our reliance from one fossil fuel to another. Though many fracking proponents claim that natural gas can provide the United States with 100 years of energy, this claim has been slashed to only 24 years, and that assumes no huge leaps in consumption. While we have built a society on fossil fuels, it is becoming increasingly obvious that we cannot sustain such a society for very much longer—not if we hope to prevent dramatic disruptions in human society caused by temperature increases of 4 or even more degrees Celsius. Thus we're going to need strong commitments to policies that get us toward a sustainable future, one where the use of fossil fuels and their effects on the climate is considered seriously.

> "Though fracking offers access to more fuel, and increases extraction efficiency in difficult wells, it is still concerned with a finite, polluting resource"

In order to provide measurement standards and promote better policy making, the Sustainable Governance Indicators (SGI) project has evaluated 31 OECD states, many of which are among the world's top polluters, in terms of their environmental protection. The overarching question they ask is whether current policies protect and preserve resources and the quality of the environment. SGI uses six indicators to compile an overall score: policy rhetoric and implementation, energy intensity, CO_2 emissions, renewable energy, water usage, and waste management.

Overall, Nordic states scored highest, with waste management being the most pervasive problem, and proposed increases in nuclear energy causing some controversy. States with lower scores often demonstrate policy failures or political gridlock. For example, France abandoned its carbon tax and South Korea lowered its gas tax. Additionally, many states continue to have high CO_2 emissions and a lack of incentives for renewable energy. The SGI's analysis points to some serious problems in current environmental policies, and is indicative of the global difficulty to lower emissions and fossil fuel dependence. But it also offers some insight into how we might solve, or at least bypass, these problems and move towards a more renewable, sustainable society.

10

Understanding the Text

1. How does the author define fracking?
2. What do the experts have to say about the benefits and consequences of fracking?
3. What does the author claim is the most "dangerous aspect" of fracking?
4. What does the article propose as a solution to the dangers of fracking?

Reflection and Response

5. Do you believe that the benefits of fracking outweigh the consequences or vice versa?
6. Why do you think fracking is so appealing to policy makers?
7. How does fracking relate to sustainability, as you understand the term?

Making Connections

8. Conduct research on fracking-related accidents. Do you see these as serious issues or as minor side-effects? What steps were taken to remedy these mishaps and were they effective?
9. Conduct some research to compare the various methods for extracting fossil fuels, including fracking. Is fracking more or less efficient than other methods? Is it more or less harmful to the environment and to people living near the extraction?
10. The article states that the production of shale gas grew from 2% to 40% from 2000 to 2012. Has that percentage grown since 2012? Why or why not?

4 Key Impacts of the Keystone XL and Dakota Access Pipelines

Heather Brady

Heather Brady is a journalist and web producer for *National Geographic*, where her writing focuses on environmental and sustainability issues. Brady holds a Master's degree in journalism from Georgetown University, and she has published work in *Slate*, *U.S. News and World Report*, NPR, and other news outlets.

This article appeared in *National Geographic* in 2017, and it discusses the Keystone XL and Dakota Access pipelines. These oil pipelines were a polarizing topic during the 2016 presidential race. Large protests broke out in Standing Rock, North Dakota, where citizens gathered for months in an effort to stave off the development of the pipeline and stand in solidarity with the Standing Rock Indian Reservation. The article explains how the construction of these two pipelines may affect animals and the environment, the economy, and the people who live on the land where the pipelines will be built. As you read, consider how these pipelines intersect with the three pillars of sustainability: people, planet, and profit.

President Donald Trump signed executive orders [in January 2017] that restarted the effort to complete the Keystone XL pipeline across the Great Plains (see a map of the route on page 140) and the Dakota Access pipeline in the northern plains.

If the two pipeline projects that were halted during former President Barack Obama's time in office begin moving forward again, here's the impact they may have on the environment and people.

1. How The Pipelines May Affect Animals

Opponents have warned that the pipelines could endanger many animals and their habitats in the U.S. and Canada through the infrastructure's construction, maintenance, and possible failures that could lead to an oil spill.

The critically endangered whooping crane is at risk of flying into new power lines that would be constructed to keep oil pumping through the Keystone XL pipeline, the National Wildlife Federation has said. While the greater sage-grouse isn't officially an endangered species, it has already lost some of its habitat, and the Keystone XL pipeline route is close enough to areas where grouse mate that noise from roads, pumping

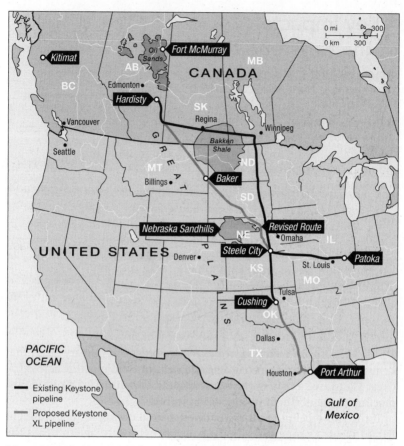

Map of the Keystone and proposed Keystone XL oil pipelines.
International Mapping

stations, and construction could impact the breeding success of this shy bird.

The Keystone XL pipeline route would go through most of the remaining locations of the swift fox, a tiny canid about the size of a house cat. The U.S. State Department's Environmental Impact Report also said that some American burying beetles will be killed and their habitats also destroyed by the pipeline, though the agency added that a monitoring and habitat-restoration program would help mitigate losses and the species wouldn't be seriously threatened.

There are nine threatened, endangered, and candidate species in the areas that the Dakota Access pipeline would run through, according to an environmental assessment by the U.S. Fish and Wildlife Service published in May 2016. The assessment concluded that the pipeline does not pose a specific threat to any of their habitats.

2. How The Pipelines May Impact Oil Production

If the Keystone XL pipeline is built, about 830,000 barrels of heavy crude oil per day will flow from Alberta, Canada, to the refineries along the U.S. Gulf Coast, which are built to handle the kind of heavy crude oil that comes out of the tar sands. Those refineries need crude oil in order to function and to support the people who work there, and places like Mexico and Venezuela, which typically export oil to the U.S., are beginning to run out of it.

> "If the Keystone XL pipeline is built, about 830,000 barrels of heavy crude oil per day will flow from Alberta, Canada, to the refineries along the U.S. Gulf Coast"

The U.S. State Department said TransCanada, the company behind the Keystone XL pipeline, has agreed to change its planned pipeline route to go around the environmentally sensitive sandhills of Nebraska, bury the pipeline deeper in the ground than they had planned, and closely monitor the pipeline's safety. These steps are intended to help minimize the harm of an oil spill if one happens.

The alternative to a pipeline also presents concerns. The State Department estimated that as of January 2014, 180,000 barrels of Canadian crude oil per day is being transported by freight trains. If no pipeline is built, that number will rise. Using trains to transport oil to refineries in the United States poses a safety concern because explosions can occur, killing people and damaging habitats nearby.

The Dakota Access pipeline project was meant to address the growing amount of oil being shipped out of North Dakota by freight trains. It's cheaper to move oil through pipelines and reduces the likelihood that explosions will happen, according to Energy Transfer Partners, the pipeline project's builder. 10

3. What The Pipelines Mean for Climate

Many climate activists have opposed the pipelines on the suspicion that they may increase our reliance on, and use, of fossil fuels, and further delay investment in more renewable technologies.

But the State Department said in a 2014 assessment that the Keystone XL pipeline would have no additional impact on greenhouse gas emissions because the oil would be extracted from tar sands in Canada at the same rate anyway, regardless of whether or not the pipeline was built.

The EPA contested that finding, saying that extracting oil from the tar sands generates more greenhouse gases than extracting oil through more conventional methods and therefore contributes to a greater amount of greenhouse gas emissions over time. If more pipelines are built, more oil could theoretically be extracted at a faster rate, meaning greenhouse gases would actually be released more quickly.

The State Department's assessment argued that the oil extracted from tar sands would find its way to market regardless of whether the Keystone XL pipeline was built or not. However, it's also true that the fate of the pipelines remains uncertain, with activists in Canada and the United States opposing the plans. The volatile market also does not guarantee that demand will make the high cost of extracting oil from the tar sands worthwhile.

The Natural Resources Defense Council and other major environmen- 15
tal groups say that, most likely, Keystone XL pipeline would accelerate the pace and expand the scale of tar sands development. Using trains slows down the process of getting the oil to refineries and ultimately to market, so it is better long-term for the environment, the groups said.

No environmental impact report has been created for the Dakota Access pipeline, though the U.S. Army Corps of Engineers said they would conduct an environmental impact survey when they halted the project in December 2016.

Ultimately, Anthony Swift, staff attorney for the Natural Resources Defense Council, told National Geographic it's a question of whether the United States will support development of "one of the most carbon-intensive sources of energy in the world, or whether we really are going to move in a direction to cut greenhouse gases."

4. How The Pipelines Will Impact People

Aside from the long-term impact that a warming climate could have on human life as a result of reliance on oil, the pipelines could pose an immediate threat to the drinking water of nearby communities and may damage areas considered sacred by Native American tribes, according to opponents.

The Dakota Access pipeline project has encountered fierce opposition in part because the threat of an oil spill and poisoned water sources could impact the Standing Rock Sioux Tribe, whose reservation is immediately downstream of the point where the pipeline will cross the Missouri River. Many tribe members are also concerned about burial grounds being disturbed during construction of the pipeline. Bulldozers have already removed some topsoil on ground that the tribe considers sacred.

Both pipelines would create jobs during their construction. The 20
State Department estimated that the Keystone XL pipeline would create
42,100 jobs over the one to two years of the pipeline's construction and
would create 50 permanent jobs. While that isn't a lot of long-term job
creation, it would keep the crude oil refineries in the Gulf Coast up and
running. If the pipeline is not built, it could eventually endanger jobs at
those refineries.

Energy Transfer Partners says the Dakota Access pipeline would create
up to 12,000 jobs during its construction. It would create around 40 permanent jobs.

Understanding the Text

1. How could animals be affected by the construction of the pipelines? What
   are the short- and long-term consequences?
2. Do these pipelines impact the global climate in any way?
3. How many jobs would the pipelines create? Are there other economic
   benefits or consequences to these oil pipelines?

Reflection and Response

4. Do the benefits of the pipelines outweigh the risks they pose to people, the
   environment, and animals?
5. After reading this article, do you believe that those protesting the construction of the pipelines are justified in their disapproval? Why or why not?
6. How would you react if an oil pipeline were being constructed in your town
   or neighborhood?
7. Does the author of this article present the facts in an unbiased manner?

Making Connections

8. Search for images of the protest at Standing Rock. What do these images
   portray regarding the opinions surrounding the Dakota Access pipeline?
9. Aldo Leopold's "Thinking Like a Mountain" from Chapter 1 discusses the
   connection that humans have to nature. What are the connections between
   Leopold's essay and this article?
10. How does this article compare to the last article in this chapter, "Fracking:
    The Solution? Or the Problem?"

The Sixth Extinction

Elizabeth Kolbert

Elizabeth Kolbert is a journalist, author, and visiting fellow at Williams College. She is best known for her Pulitzer Prize–winning book *The Sixth Extinction: An Unnatural History*, and this reading selection is an excerpt from that book. Kolbert is a frequent contributor to the *New York Times* and the *New Yorker*, where her work focuses on issues surrounding the environment and climate change. Kolbert has been awarded more than a dozen prestigious writing awards, most of them in the category of science writing and global change.

Published in 2014 in the *New York Times Upfront*, this excerpt outlines what scientists describe as "the five mass extinctions" on planet earth and describes how and why we may be entering a sixth mass extinction event. As you read the article, think about how the sixth extinction has different causes and effects than the previous five mass extinctions.

Something was killing the frogs of Central America—and it was killing them fast.

One of the first to notice was Karen Lips, an American graduate student studying amphibians in the rainforest there. In 1993, she was shocked to discover that all the frogs had vanished from her research site in Costa Rica. When she later relocated to Panama, she found that the frogs were dying there too. And no one could explain why.

Whatever was killing the frogs continued to move, like a wave, across Panama. By 2006, it had swept across the central part of the country, home to the Panamanian golden frog, famous for being so toxic that the poison on the skin of just one could kill a thousand mice. Soon afterward, the golden frog was declared extinct in the wild.

The recent demise of the frog, along with dozens of other brightly colored amphibians in Central America, is part of a much larger phenomenon that's been dubbed the Sixth Extinction. Extinction rates today are probably higher than they've been at any point since the dinosaurs disappeared 65 million years ago. Frogs and toads are the world's most threatened group of animals—nearly 40 percent are endangered—but extinction rates among pretty much all groups are soaring. A century from now, pandas, tigers, and rhinos may well exist only in zoos. And most coral reefs, home to thousands of underwater species, are threatened. Within this century, 20 to 50 percent of all living species—from plants to mammals—might be headed toward oblivion.

While the forces behind the Sixth Extinction vary, trace them back far 5
enough and you get to the same source: us. By inhabiting every corner of

the planet, razing forests, and burning fossil fuels, people are changing the world so fast that many other species can't cope.

"We're seeing right now that a mass extinction can be caused by human beings," says Walter Alvarez, a scientist at the University of California, Berkeley.

Cold Snaps & Asteroids

For most of human history, people had no idea that creatures went extinct. When Thomas Jefferson became president in 1801, he seriously expected that live mastodons would be found roaming the American West.

But around the same time, while working at the museum of natural history in Paris, a French naturalist named Georges Cuvier realized that a lot of the bones in the museum's collection belonged to animals that no longer existed.

"Life on Earth has often been disturbed by terrible events," Cuvier wrote. "Living things without number have been the victims of these catastrophes."

Over the next several decades, many scientists—including Charles 10 Darwin—helped develop the scientific concept of extinction. Today, most scientists agree that the world usually changes very slowly. In ordinary times, species rarely go extinct: Scientists estimate that under normal circumstances, one amphibian species disappears every 1,000 years or so.

The Panamanian Golden Frog is a critically endangered species.
Dante Fenolio/Getty Images.

But sometimes, the world changes very suddenly. In those rare moments of rapid change, species disappear much more quickly. These events are known as mass extinctions.

Since complex life evolved, about a half billion years ago, there have been five major mass extinctions called the Big Five. The first one took place 444 million years ago, when creatures like trilobites, which resembled horseshoe crabs, and conodonts, which looked like eels, roamed the oceans. The extinction was most likely caused by a sudden global cold snap and killed roughly 80 percent of all species in the seas.

The most recent of the Big Five was caused 65 million years ago by a six-mile-wide asteroid that was traveling at 25,000 miles per hour when it hit Earth in what is now the Gulf of Mexico. Exploding on contact, the asteroid released as much energy as a million of the most powerful nuclear bombs ever tested. Debris spread around the globe, day turned to night, and temperatures plunged.

In addition to the dinosaurs, 75 percent of the other species on Earth—everything from pterosaurs to ammonites, and also many snakes, birds, and mammals—died off. The world that we live in today is very much a product of this event. After the impact, those mammals that survived evolved to fill the niches the dinosaurs had occupied. In a very real sense, you are here today only because of that extinction.

A New Mass Extinction

Today, most scientists believe we're witnessing a new mass extinction.   15
Across all sorts of different groups, extinction rates are now up to 10,000 times higher than they were before humans appeared, according to a recent report in *Science* magazine. Among the animals threatened today are pandas, gorillas, and rhinos—and many other lesser-known species, like the kakapo, a flightless parrot in New Zealand, and the Franklin's bumblebee, in Northern California.

This time, a giant asteroid isn't to blame. We are, most scientists agree. Because of human activity, Earth is now changing very fast, probably faster than at any point since the asteroid impact.

How are we doing this? One way is by moving species around the globe. Before boats (and then planes) were invented, it was almost impossible for a land species to cross an ocean or a marine species to cross a continent, and it happened very rarely. But today, as the pace and volume of global trade have picked up, so too has the number of accidental imports. Species that couldn't survive an ocean crossing at the bottom of a canoe or the hold of a whaling ship may easily withstand the same journey on a modern cargo ship or in a tourist's suitcase. An estimated

10,000 species are being moved around every day just in the ballast water of supertankers—undoing millions of years of geographic separation.

Moving species around can have devastating consequences: New species can become invasive and, in the long run, they can drive native species into extinction.

Hawaii, for example, is acquiring a new species each month, according to the Center for Invasive Species Research. The result? Hundreds of species that existed only in Hawaii for thousands of years—including a variety of land snails, birds, ferns, and flowers—are now gone forever or disappearing because other species have taken over.

When scientists finally figured out what was killing the amphibians in Central America, it turned out to be a fungal disease that had arrived with non-native frogs. (Scientists haven't pin-pointed which species.) The disease has also killed amphibians in North and South America, Australia, and the Caribbean.

> "Homo sapiens might not only be the agent of the Sixth Extinction... but also risks being one of its victims."

Another way people are changing the planet is by cutting down forests and burning fossil fuels like oil and coal. That has led to a buildup of carbon dioxide and other gases that trap heat in the atmosphere, which is causing Earth to warm up. The changing temperatures force species to adapt to new climates or move to cooler habitats. If neither of those strategies works, they die out. For many species, the latter outcome is the more likely one.

But it's not all grim. Thousands of scientists all over the world are trying to reverse the trend. In Panama, a conservation center is filled with tanks containing endangered frogs—including Panamanian golden frogs. They're equipped with running water so the animals can breed near a facsimile of the streams that were once their home.

The U.S. Congress passed the Endangered Species Act in 1973, and since then the length to which people have gone to protect vulnerable creatures is incredible. To save the whooping crane, whose population in the wild is down to 200, volunteers fly ultralight aircraft each year to teach chicks raised in captivity how to migrate from Wisconsin to Florida for the winter. The 1,300-mile journey can take up to three months, with a dozen stops on private land that owners give over to the birds.

And millions of Americans donate to groups like the World Wildlife Fund, the National Wildlife Federation, and the Nature Conservancy.

But despite all these efforts, what matters the most is that people are changing the world—and, with it, the biodiversity we depend on to raise animals and crops, feed ourselves, and survive. Millions of years from now, the planet will be inhabited only by the descendants of those creatures that survive this new mass extinction. And it's not taken for granted that we will be among them.

"Homo sapiens might not only be the agent of the Sixth Extinc- 5 tion," says anthropologist Richard Leakey, "but also risks being one of its victims."

Understanding the Text

1. What were the causes of the five mass extinctions?
2. Why do scientists believe the earth is facing its sixth mass extinction?
3. What is different about the causes and effects of the current sixth mass extinction event?
4. Why is the "demise of the frog" troubling in terms of extinction?

Reflection and Response

5. Do you believe that humans are largely responsible for the increasing number of endangered and extinct animals? Why or why not?
6. Why does Kolbert begin her article by discussing the frogs of Central America? As a reader, did this example grab your attention?
7. How does animal extinction relate to sustainability? Does the extinction of animals pose a threat to humanity or to the earth in general?
8. Do you think people, organizations, or governments can do anything to stop the sixth extinction? What would you do if you had the power to enact a change?

Making Connections

9. Do some research and find out how many native U.S. species have become extinct in the past one hundred years. Which extinctions are the most significant? Is it possible to assess the impact of one species extinction over another?
10. Kolbert quotes anthropologist Richard Leakey, who says, "Homo sapiens might not only be the agent of the Sixth Extinction, but also risks being one of its victims." How does this quote relate to the next reading in this chapter, "The Last Americans: Environmental Collapse and the End of Civilization"?
11. The article mentions organizations such as the World Wildlife Fund, the National Wildlife Federation, and the Nature Conservancy. Pick one of the three organizations and research what they are currently doing to help endangered animals.

The Last Americans: Environmental Collapse and the End of Civilization

Jared Diamond

Jared Diamond is a scientist and an author of thirteen books, including *The Third Chimpanzee*; the Pulitzer Prize–winning *Guns, Germs, and Steel*; and *Collapse: How Societies Choose to Fail or Succeed*. He earned a BA in biochemistry from Harvard University and a PhD in physiology and membrane biophysics from the University of Cambridge. He is currently a professor of geography and physiology at University of California, Los Angeles. Diamond is equally renowned for his work in the fields of ecology and evolutionary biology as for his groundbreaking studies of the birds of Papua New Guinea.

Diamond begins this article by comparing today's society with those of previous civilizations that have crumbled. He relates overpopulation and environmental stress to governmental collapse. Diamond specifically compares our modern society to that of the Mayans, examining their lifestyles and technology regarding sustaining population. As you read the article, think about the similarities to and differences between our own society and those that have collapsed.

I met a traveler from an antique land
Who said: Two vast and trunkless legs of stone
Stand in the desert . . . Near them, on the sand,
Half sunk, a shattered visage lies, whose frown,
And wrinkled lip, and sneer of cold command,
Tell that its sculptor well those passions read
Which yet survive, stamped on these lifeless things,
The hand that mocked them, and the heart that fed.
And on the pedestal these words appear:
"My name is Ozymandias, king of kings:
Look on my works, ye Mighty, and despair!"
Nothing beside remains. Round the decay
Of that colossal wreck, boundless and bare
The lone and level sands stretch far away.

—PERCY BYSSHE SHELLEY, "OZYMANDIAS"

One of the disturbing facts of history is that so many civilizations collapse. Few people, however, least of all our politicians, realize that a primary cause of the collapse of those societies has been the destruction of the environmental resources on which they depended. Fewer still

149

appreciate that many of those civilizations share a sharp curve of decline. Indeed, a society's demise may begin only a decade or two after it reaches its peak population, wealth, and power.

Recent archaeological discoveries have revealed similar courses of collapse in such otherwise dissimilar ancient societies as the Maya in the Yucatán, the Anasazi in the American Southwest, the Cahokia mound builders outside St. Louis, the Greenland Norse, the statue builders of Easter Island, ancient Mesopotamia in the Fertile Crescent, Great Zimbabwe in Africa, and Angkor Wat in Cambodia. These civilizations, and many others, succumbed to various combinations of environmental degradation and climate change, aggression from enemies taking advantage of their resulting weakness, and declining trade with neighbors who faced their own environmental problems. Because peak population, wealth, resource consumption, and waste production are accompanied by peak environmental impact—approaching the limit at which impact outstrips resources—we can now understand why declines of societies tend to follow swiftly on their peaks.

"Few people . . . realize that a primary cause of the collapse of those societies has been the destruction of the environmental resources on which they depended."

These combinations of undermining factors were compounded by cultural attitudes preventing those in power from perceiving or resolving the crisis. That's a familiar problem today. Some of us are inclined to dismiss the importance of a healthy environment, or at least to suggest that it's just one of many problems facing us—an "issue." That dismissal is based on three dangerous misconceptions.

Foremost among these misconceptions is that we must balance the environment against human needs. That reasoning is exactly upside down. Human needs and a healthy environment are not opposing claims that must be balanced; instead, they are inexorably linked by chains of cause and effect. We need a healthy environment because we need clean water, clean air, wood, and food from the ocean, plus soil and sunlight to grow crops. We need functioning natural ecosystems, with their native species of earthworms, bees, plants, and microbes, to generate and aerate our soils, pollinate our crops, decompose our wastes, and produce our oxygen. We need to prevent toxic substances from accumulating in our water and air and soil. We need to prevent weeds, germs, and other pest species from becoming established in places where they aren't native and where they cause economic damage. Our strongest arguments for a healthy environment are selfish: we want it for ourselves, not for threatened species like snail darters, spotted owls, and Furbish louseworts.

Another popular misconception is that we can trust in technology to   5
solve our problems. Whatever environmental problem you name, you
can also name some hoped-for technological solution under discussion.
Some of us have faith that we shall solve our dependence on fossil fuels
by developing new technologies for hydrogen engines, wind energy, or
solar energy. Some of us have faith that we shall solve our food problems with new or soon-to-be-developed genetically modified crops. Some
of us have faith that new technologies will succeed in cleaning up the
toxic materials in our air, water, soil, and foods without the horrendous
cleanup expenses that we now incur.

Those with such faith assume that the new technologies will ultimately
succeed, but in fact some of them may succeed and others may not. They
assume that the new technologies will succeed quickly enough to make
a big difference soon, but all of these major technological changes will
actually take five to thirty years to develop and implement—if they
catch on at all. Most of all, those with faith assume that new technology
won't cause any new problems. In fact, technology merely constitutes
increased power, which produces changes that can be either for the
better or for the worse. All of our current environmental problems are
unanticipated harmful consequences of our existing technology. There
is no basis for believing that technology will miraculously stop causing
new and unanticipated problems while it is solving the problems that it
previously produced.

The final misconception holds that environmentalists are fear-
mongering, overreacting extremists whose predictions of impending
disaster have been proved wrong before and will be proved wrong again.
Behold, say the optimists: water still flows from our faucets, the grass is
still green, and the supermarkets are full of food. We are more prosperous
than ever before, and that's the final proof that our system works.

Well, for a few billion of the world's people who are causing us
increasing trouble, there isn't any clean water, there is less and less green
grass, and there are no supermarkets full of food. To appreciate what
the environmental problems of those billions of people mean for us
Americans, compare the following two lists of countries. First ask some
ivory-tower academic ecologist who knows a lot about the environment
but never reads a newspaper and has no interest in politics to list the
overseas countries facing some of the worst problems of environmental
stress, overpopulation, or both. The ecologist would answer, "That's a
no-brainer, it's obvious. Your list of environmentally stressed or overpopulated countries should surely include Afghanistan, Bangladesh,
Burundi, Haiti, Indonesia, Iraq, Nepal, Pakistan, the Philippines, Rwanda,
the Solomon Islands, and Somalia, plus others." Then ask a First World

politician who knows nothing, and cares less, about the environment and population problems to list the world's worst trouble spots: countries where state government has already been overwhelmed and has collapsed, or is now at risk of collapsing, or has been wracked by recent civil wars; and countries that, as a result of their problems, are also creating problems for us rich First World countries, which may be deluged by illegal immigrants, or have to provide foreign aid to those countries, or may decide to provide them with military assistance to deal with rebellions and terrorists, or may even (God forbid) have to send in our own troops. The politician would answer, "That's a no-brainer, it's obvious. Your list of political trouble spots should surely include Afghanistan, Bangladesh, Burundi, Haiti, Indonesia, Iraq, Nepal, Pakistan, the Philippines, Rwanda, the Solomon Islands, and Somalia, plus others."

The connection between the two lists is transparent. Today, just as in the past, countries that are environmentally stressed, overpopulated, or both are at risk of becoming politically stressed, and of seeing their governments collapse. When people are desperate and undernourished, they blame their government, which they see as responsible for failing to solve their problems. They try to emigrate at any cost. They start civil wars. They kill one another. They figure that they have nothing to lose, so they become terrorists, or they support or tolerate terrorism. The results are genocides such as the ones that already have exploded in Burundi, Indonesia, and Rwanda; civil wars, as in Afghanistan, Indonesia, Nepal, the Philippines, and the Solomon Islands; calls for the dispatch of First World troops, as to Afghanistan, Indonesia, Iraq, the Philippines, Rwanda, the Solomon Islands, and Somalia; the collapse of central government, as has already happened in Somalia; and overwhelming poverty, as in all of the countries on these lists.

But what about the United States? Some might argue that the environmental collapse of ancient societies is relevant to the modern decline of weak, far-off, overpopulated Rwanda and environmentally devastated Somalia, but isn't it ridiculous to suggest any possible relevance to the fate of our own society? After all, we might reason, those ancients didn't enjoy the wonders of modern environment-friendly technologies. Those ancients had the misfortune to suffer from the effects of climate change. They behaved stupidly and ruined their own environment by doing obviously dumb things, like cutting down their forests, watching their topsoil erode, and building cities in dry areas likely to run short of water. They had foolish leaders who didn't have books and so couldn't learn from history, and who embroiled them in destabilizing wars and didn't pay attention to problems at home. They were overwhelmed by desperate immigrants, as one society after another collapsed, sending floods of economic refugees to tax the resources of the societies that weren't collapsing. In all those respects, we modern Americans are fundamentally different from those primitive ancients, and there is nothing that we could learn from them.

Or so the argument goes. It's an argument so ingrained both in our subconscious and in public discourse that it has assumed the status of objective reality. We think we are different. In fact, of course, all of those powerful societies of the past thought that they too were unique, right up to the moment of their collapse. It's sobering to consider the swift decline of the ancient Maya, who 1,200 years ago were themselves the most advanced society in the Western Hemisphere, and who, like us now, were then at the apex of their own power and numbers. Two excellent recent books, David Webster's *The Fall of the Ancient Maya* and Richardson Gill's *The Great Maya Droughts*, help bring the trajectory of Maya civilization back to life for us. Their studies illustrate how even sophisticated societies like that of the Maya (and ours) can be undermined by details of rainfall, farming methods, and motives of leaders.

• • •

By now, millions of modern Americans have visited Maya ruins. To do so, one need only take a direct flight from the United States to the Yucatán capital of Mérida, jump into a rental car or minibus, and drive an hour on a paved highway. Most Maya ruins, with their great temples and monuments, lie surrounded by jungles (seasonal tropical forests), far from current human settlement. They are "pure" archaeological sites. That is, their locations became depopulated, so they were not covered up by later buildings as were so many other ancient cities, like the Aztec capital of Tenochtitlán—now buried under modern Mexico City—and Rome.

One of the reasons few people live there now is that the Maya homeland poses serious environmental challenges to would-be farmers. Although it has a somewhat unpredictable rainy season from May to October, it also has a dry season from January through April. Indeed, if one focuses on the dry months, one could describe the Yucatán as a "seasonal desert."

Complicating things, from a farmer's perspective, is that the part of the Yucatán with the most rain, the south, is also the part at the highest elevation above the water table. Most of the Yucatán consists of karst—a porous, sponge-like, limestone terrain—and so rain runs straight into the ground, leaving little or no surface water. The Maya in the lower-elevation regions of the north were able to reach the water table by way of deep sinkholes called *cenotes*, and the Maya in low coastal areas without sinkholes could reach it by digging wells up to 75 feet deep. Most Maya, however, lived in the south. How did they deal with their resulting water problem?

Technology provided an answer. The Maya plugged up leaks on karst   15 promontories by plastering the bottoms of depressions to create reservoirs, which collected rain and stored it for use in the dry season. The reservoirs at the Maya city of Tikal, for example, held enough water to meet the needs of about 10,000 people for eighteen months. If a drought lasted longer than that, though, the inhabitants of Tikal were in deep trouble.

Maya farmers grew mostly corn, which constituted the astonishingly high proportion of about 70 percent of their diet, as deduced from isotope analyses of ancient Maya skeletons. They grew corn by means of a modified version of swidden slash-and-burn agriculture, in which forest is cleared, crops are grown in the resulting clearing for a few years until the soil is exhausted, and then the field is abandoned for fifteen to twenty years until regrowth of wild vegetation restores the soil's fertility. Because most of the land under a swidden agricultural system is fallow at any given time, it can support only modest population densities. Thus, it was a surprise for archaeologists to discover that ancient Maya population densities, judging from numbers of stone foundations of farmhouses, were often far higher than what unmodified swidden agriculture could support: often 250 to 750 people per square mile. The Maya probably achieved those high populations by such means as shortening the fallow period and tilling the soil to restore soil fertility, or omitting the fallow period entirely and growing crops every year, or, in especially moist areas, growing two crops per year.

Socially stratified societies, ours included, consist of farmers who produce food, plus nonfarmers such as bureaucrats and soldiers who do not produce food and are in effect parasites on farmers. The farmers must grow enough food to meet not only their own needs but also those of everybody else. The number of nonproducing consumers who can be supported depends on the society's agricultural productivity. In the United States today, with its highly efficient agriculture, farmers make up only 2 percent of our population, and each farmer can feed, on the average, 129 other people. Ancient Egyptian agriculture was efficient enough for an Egyptian peasant to produce five times the food required for himself and his family. But a Maya peasant could produce only twice the needs of himself and his family.

Fully 80 percent of Maya society consisted of peasants. Their inability to support many nonfarmers resulted from several limitations of their agriculture. It produced little protein, because corn has a much lower protein content than wheat, and because the few edible domestic animals kept by the Maya (turkeys, ducks, and dogs) included no large animals like our cows and sheep. There was little use of terracing or irrigation to increase production. In the Maya area's humid climate, stored corn would rot or become infested after a year, so the Maya couldn't get through a longer drought by eating surplus corn accumulated in good years. And unlike Old World peoples with their horses, oxen, donkeys, and camels, the Maya had no animal-powered transport. Indeed, the Maya lacked not only pack animals and animal-drawn plows but also metal tools, wheels, and boats with sails. All of those great Maya temples were built by stone and wooden tools and human muscle power alone, and all overland transport went on the backs of human porters. Those limitations on food supply and food transport may in part explain why Maya society remained politically organized in small kingdoms that were perpetually at war with one another and that never became unified into large empires like the Aztec empire of the Valley of Mexico (fed by highly productive agriculture) or the Inca empire of the Andes (fed by diverse crops carried on llamas). Maya armies were small and unable to mount lengthy campaigns over long distances. The typical Maya kingdom held a population of only up to 50,000 people, within a radius of two or three days' walk from the king's palace. From the top of the temple of some Maya kingdoms, one could see the tops of the temples of other kingdoms.

Presiding over the temple was the king himself, who functioned both as head priest and as political leader. It was his responsibility to pray to the gods, to perform astronomical and calendrical rituals, to ensure the timely arrival of the rains on which agriculture depended, and thereby to bring prosperity. The king claimed to have the supernatural power to deliver those good things because of his asserted family relationship to the gods. Of course, that exposed him to the risk that his subjects would become disillusioned if he couldn't fulfill his boast of being able to deliver rains and prosperity. . . .

• • •

We can identify increasingly familiar strands in the Classic Maya collapse. 20
One consisted of population growth outstripping available resources: the dilemma foreseen by Thomas Malthus in 1798. As Webster succinctly puts it in *The Fall of the Ancient Maya*, "Too many farmers grew too many crops on too much of the landscape." While population was increasing, the area of usable farmland paradoxically was decreasing from the effects of deforestation and hillside erosion.

The next strand consisted of increased fighting as more and more people fought over fewer resources. Maya warfare, already endemic, peaked just before the collapse. That is not surprising when one reflects that at least 5 million people, most of them farmers, were crammed into an area smaller than the state of Colorado. That's a high population by the standards of ancient farming societies, even if it wouldn't strike modern Manhattan-dwellers as crowded.

Bringing matters to a head was a drought that, although not the first one the Maya had been through, was the most severe. At the time of previous droughts, there were still uninhabited parts of the Maya landscape, and people in a drought area or dust bowl could save themselves by moving to another site. By the time of the Classic collapse, however, there was no useful unoccupied land in the vicinity on which to begin anew, and the whole population could not be accommodated in the few areas that continued to have reliable water supplies.

The final strand is political. Why did the kings and nobles not recognize and solve these problems? A major reason was that their attention was evidently focused on the short-term concerns of enriching themselves, waging wars, erecting monuments, competing with one another, and extracting enough food from the peasants to support all those activities. Like most leaders throughout human history, the Maya kings and nobles did not have the leisure to focus on long-term problems, insofar as they perceived them.

* * *

What about those same strands today? The United States is also at the peak of its power, and it is also suffering from many environmental problems. Most of us have become aware of more crowding and stress. Most of us living in large American cities are encountering increased commuting delays, because the number of people and hence of cars is increasing faster than the number of freeway lanes. I know plenty of people who in the abstract doubt that the world has a population problem, but almost all of those same people complain to me about crowding, space issues, and traffic experienced in their personal lives.

Many parts of the United States face locally severe problems of water 25 restriction (especially southern California, Arizona, the Everglades, and, increasingly, the Northeast); forest fires resulting from logging and forest-management practices throughout the intermontane West; and losses of farmlands to salinization, drought, and climate change in the northern Great Plains. Many of us frequently experience problems of air quality, and some of us also experience problems of water quality and taste. We are losing economically valuable natural resources. We have already lost American chestnut trees, the Grand Banks cod fishery, and the Monterey sardine fishery; we are in the process of losing swordfish and tuna and Chesapeake Bay oysters and elm trees; and we are losing topsoil.

The list goes on: All of us are experiencing personal consequences of our national dependence on imported energy, which affects us not only through higher gas prices but also through the current contraction of the national economy, itself the partial result of political problems associated with our oil dependence. We are saddled with expensive toxic cleanups at many locations, most notoriously near Montana mines, on the Hudson River, and in the Chesapeake Bay. We also face expensive eradication problems resulting from hundreds of introduced pest species—including zebra mussels, Mediterranean fruit flies, Asian longhorn beetles, water hyacinth, and spotted knapweed—that now affect our agriculture, forests, waterways, and pastures.

These particular environmental problems, and many others, are enormously expensive in terms of resources lost, cleanup and restoration costs, and the cost of finding substitutes for lost resources: a billion dollars here, 10 billion there, in dozens and dozens of cases. Some of the problems, especially those of air quality and toxic substances, also exact health costs that are large, whether measured in dollars or in lost years or in quality of life. The cost of our homegrown environmental problems adds up to a large fraction of our gross national product, even without mentioning the costs that we incur from environmental problems overseas, such as the military operations that they inspire. Even the mildest of bad scenarios for our future include a gradual economic decline, as happened to the Roman and British empires. Actually, in case you didn't notice it, our economic decline is already well under way. Just check the numbers for our national debt, yearly government budget deficit, unemployment statistics, and the value of your investment and pension funds.

● ● ●

The environmental problems of the United States are still modest compared with those of the rest of the world. But the problems of environmentally devastated, overpopulated, distant countries are now our problems as well. We are accustomed to thinking of globalization in terms of us rich, advanced First Worlders sending our good things, such as the Internet and Coca-Cola, to those poor backward Third Worlders. Globalization, however, means nothing more than improved worldwide communication and transportation, which can convey many things in either direction; it is not restricted to good things carried only from the

First to the Third World. They in the Third World can now, intentionally or unintentionally, send us their bad things: terrorists; diseases such as AIDS, SARS, cholera, and West Nile fever, carried inadvertently by passengers on transcontinental airplanes; unstoppable numbers of immigrants, both legal and illegal, arriving by boat, truck, train, plane, and on foot; and other consequences of their Third World problems. We in the United States are no longer the isolated Fortress America to which some of us aspired in the 1930s; instead, we are tightly and irreversibly connected to overseas countries. The United States is the world's leading importer, and it is also the world's leading exporter. Our own society opted long ago to become interlocked with the rest of the world.

That's why political stability anywhere in the world now affects us, our trade routes, and our overseas markets and suppliers. We are so dependent on the rest of the world that if a decade ago you had asked a politician to name the countries most geopolitically irrelevant to U.S. interests because of their being so remote, poor, and weak, the list would have begun with Afghanistan and Somalia, yet these countries were subsequently considered important enough to warrant our dispatching U.S. troops. The Maya were "globalized" only within the Yucatán: the southern Yucatán Maya affected the northern Yucatán Maya and may have had some effects on the Valley of Mexico, but they had no contact with Somalia. That's because Maya transportation was slow, short-distance, on foot or else in canoes, and had low cargo capacity. Our transport today is much more rapid and has much higher cargo capacity. The Maya lived in a globalized Yucatán; we live in a globalized world.

• • •

If all of this reasoning seems straightforward when expressed so bluntly, 30 one has to wonder: Why don't those in power today get the message? Why didn't the leaders of the Maya, Anasazi, and those other societies also recognize and solve their problems? What were the Maya thinking while they watched loggers clearing the last pine forests on the hills above Copán? Here, the past really is a useful guide to the present. It turns out that there are at least a dozen reasons why past societies failed to anticipate some problems before they developed, or failed to *perceive* problems that had already developed, or failed even to try to solve problems that they did perceive. All of those dozen reasons still can be seen operating today. Let me mention just three of them.

First, it's difficult to recognize a slow trend in some quantity that fluctuates widely up and down anyway, such as seasonal temperature, annual rainfall, or economic indicators. That's surely why the Maya didn't recognize the oncoming drought until it was too late, given that rainfall in the Yucatán varies several-fold from year to year. Natural fluctuations also explain why it's only within the last few years that all climatologists have become convinced of the reality of climate change, and why our president still isn't convinced but thinks that we need more research to test for it.

Second, when a problem is recognized, those in power may not attempt to solve it because of a clash between their short-term interests and the interests of the rest of us. Pumping that oil, cutting down those trees, and catching those fish may benefit the elite by bringing them money or prestige and yet be bad for society as a whole (including the children of the elite) in the long run. Maya kings were consumed by immediate concerns for their prestige (requiring more and bigger temples) and their success in the next war (requiring more followers), rather than for the happiness of commoners or of the next generation. Those people with the greatest power to make decisions in our own society today regularly make money from activities that may be bad for society as a whole and for their own children; those decision-makers include Enron executives, many land developers, and advocates of tax cuts for the rich.

Finally, it's difficult for us to acknowledge the wisdom of policies that clash with strongly held values. For example, a belief in individual freedom and a distrust of big government are deeply ingrained in Americans, and they make sense under some circumstances and up to a certain point. But they also make it hard for us to accept big government's legitimate role in ensuring that each individual's freedom to maximize the value of his or her land holdings doesn't decrease the value of the collective land of all Americans.

● ● ●

Not all societies make fatal mistakes. There are parts of the world where societies have unfolded for thousands of years without any collapse, such as Java, Tonga, and (until 1945) Japan. Today, Germany and Japan are successfully managing their forests, which are even expanding in area rather than shrinking. The Alaskan salmon fishery and the Australian lobster fishery are being managed sustainably. The Dominican Republic, hardly a rich country, nevertheless has set aside a comprehensive system of protected areas encompassing most of the country's natural habitats.

Is there any secret to explain why some societies acquire good environ-   35
mental sense while others don't? Naturally, part of the answer depends
on accidents of individual leaders' wisdom (or lack thereof). But part also
depends upon whether a society is organized so as to minimize built-in
clashes of interest between its decision-making elites and its masses.
Given how our society is organized, the executives of Enron, Tyco, and
Adelphi correctly calculated that their own interests would be best promoted by looting the company coffers, and that they would probably get
away with most of their loot. A good example of a society that minimizes
such clashes of interest is the Netherlands, whose citizens have perhaps
the world's highest level of environmental awareness and of membership in environmental organizations. I never understood why, until on a
recent trip to the Netherlands I posed the question to three of my Dutch
friends while driving through their countryside.

Just look around you, they said. All of this farmland that you see lies
below sea level. One fifth of the total area of the Netherlands is below
sea level, as much as 22 feet below, because it used to be shallow bays,
and we reclaimed it from the sea by surrounding the bays with dikes and
then gradually pumping out the water. We call these reclaimed lands
"polders." We began draining our polders nearly a thousand years ago.
Today, we still have to keep pumping out the water that gradually seeps
in. That's what our windmills used to be for, to drive the pumps to pump
out the polders. Now we use steam, diesel, and electric pumps instead. In
each polder there are lines of them, starting with those farthest from the
sea, pumping the water in sequence until the last pump finally deposits
it into a river or the ocean. And all of us, rich or poor, live down in the
polders. It's not the case that rich people live safely up on top of the dikes
while poor people live in the polder bottoms below sea level. If the dikes
and pumps fail, we'll all drown together.

Throughout human history, all peoples have been connected to some
other peoples, living together in virtual polders. For the ancient Maya,
their polder consisted of most of the Yucatán and neighboring areas.
When the Classic Maya cities collapsed in the southern Yucatán, refugees
may have reached the northern Yucatán, but probably not the Valley of
Mexico, and certainly not Florida. Today, our whole world has become
one polder, such that events in even Afghanistan and Somalia affect
Americans. We do indeed differ from the Maya, but not in ways we might
like: we have a much larger population, we have more potent destructive technology, and we face the risk of a worldwide rather than a local
decline. Fortunately, we also differ from the Maya in that we know their
fate, and they did not. Perhaps we can learn.

Understanding the Text

1. What are the three "dangerous misconceptions" the author refers to regarding the lack of seriousness about a healthy environment?

2. What were some factors that influenced the Mayans' success? What were some of their downfalls?

3. According to Diamond, why is it important that we concern ourselves with the problems of third-world countries as well as our own?

4. Near the end of the article, Diamond lists several reasons why past societies failed to anticipate problems (pars. 30–34). What are these reasons? Which seems most damaging to a society? In what ways is our own society failing to anticipate such problems?

Reflection and Response

5. Describe the tone Diamond uses and the effect it has on your opinions.

6. This article discusses overpopulation as a major problem. Do you agree with Diamond's perspective? Do you think something should be done about the problem? Why or why not?

7. World leaders are often blamed for the problems of a society. People say, "Well, I would have done things differently." If you were a world leader, how would you address some of the problems Diamond describes in the article?

8. In what ways is Diamond's article about sustainability? How can an understanding of history help us make more sustainable decisions for the future?

Making Connections

9. Diamond writes that "those with faith assume that new technology won't cause any new problems" (par. 6). In what ways does technology help us advance as a society? In what ways does it cause problems that might affect future sustainability and our environment?

10. In 1979 China passed a law that couples were allowed to have only one child. Research this law and its current state today. Did it work? Would a law like this work in the United States? Should such a law be enforced nationally or even globally?

4

How Is Sustainability Connected to Local and Urban Environments?

S ustainability often addresses the need for preserving the natural world, recognizing the value of forests, oceans, wildlife, and natural ecosystems. As the introduction to this book explains, our current definitions of sustainability are closely tied to our historical and cultural relationship with nature. However, sustainability also focuses on creating and implementing sustainable practices in cities, suburbs, and other urban or industrial areas. Sustainability is about preserving resources and maintaining processes that are cyclical, repeatable, and enduring — the concept remains the same whether the focus is on the long-term biodiversity of a wetland or on the development of a shopping mall. Natural and urban environments are all part of the same global system; in fact, as should be clear by now, all environments are deeply enmeshed and interrelated in one way or another.

This chapter focuses on the ways sustainability is connected to local, urban, and industrial environments and processes. Many of the reading selections deal with things you encounter in your everyday life, including the food you eat, the products you use, the communities and spaces you inhabit, and even the profession you may choose. These selections draw attention to the three pillars of sustainability (social equity, environmental preservation, and economic viability) as vital interlocking components; all three factors must be considered in a sustainable human society. The People, Planet, Profit model is central to sustainability in developed cultural settings, and it can serve as a useful guide in your personal choices and decisions about your role in the world.

Kaplan helps contextualize this subject by addressing the history of consumer culture in America. Bloomberg and de Lille discuss the reasons for creating and investing in sustainable or "green" cities in the future. The next article by Smith looks at sustainability efforts in cities and suburbs, both now and in the future. Westervelt examines the issue of recycling, which is deeply tied to local and urban environments but also impacts global and natural systems. Prince Charles and the educators working with the TED

photo: Thomas Goeppert/EyeEm/Getty Images

organization both explore the important interrelations among food, health, and environments. Fritjof Capra's article also speaks to educators, arguing for an ecological, networked view of communities. Poschen and Renner examine sustainable jobs, while Carlson's article addresses sustainability on college campuses. Sutton's article finishes the chapter by examining how companies can use social media to promote environmental activism. Collectively, these articles provide a broad overview of the challenges and opportunities of sustainability in local and urban environments.

As you read the selections in this chapter, think about how sustainability affects your local environment and the ways in which you operate on a personal level. Other chapters in this book address sustainability in terms of national and global issues, but this chapter can help you consider sustainability as a subject that impacts you personally, immediately, and locally. Consequently, the reading selections have the potential to influence the choices you make in your everyday life.

The Gospel of Consumption

Jeffrey Kaplan

Jeffrey Kaplan is an activist and a writer who lives in the San Francisco Bay area. Kaplan writes regularly for *Orion* magazine, in which this article first appeared, as well as for the *Chicago Tribune* and *Yes!* magazines.

This article (2008) describes consumption in the early twentieth century, particularly the rapid rate at which goods were being produced. It goes on to explain how American consumption has changed since then in the light of consumerism. As you read, think about the idea of consumerism and what it means in modern society.

Private cars were relatively scarce in 1919 and horse-drawn conveyances were still common. In residential districts, electric streetlights had not yet replaced many of the old gaslights. And within the home, electricity remained largely a luxury item for the wealthy.

Just ten years later things looked very different. Cars dominated the streets and most urban homes had electric lights, electric flat irons, and vacuum cleaners. In upper-middle-class houses, washing machines, refrigerators, toasters, curling irons, percolators, heating pads, and popcorn poppers were becoming commonplace. And although the first commercial radio station didn't begin broadcasting until 1920, the American public, with an adult population of about 122 million people, bought 4,438,000 radios in the year 1929 alone.

But despite the apparent tidal wave of new consumer goods and what appeared to be a healthy appetite for their consumption among the well-to-do, industrialists were worried. They feared that the frugal habits maintained by most American families would be difficult to break. Perhaps even more threatening was the fact that the industrial capacity for turning out goods seemed to be increasing at a pace greater than people's sense that they needed them.

It was this latter concern that led Charles Kettering, director of General Motors Research, to write a 1929 magazine article called "Keep the Consumer Dissatisfied." He wasn't suggesting that manufacturers produce shoddy products. Along with many of his corporate cohorts, he was defining a strategic shift for American industry—from fulfilling basic human needs to creating new ones.

In a 1927 interview with the magazine *Nation's Business*, Secretary of 5 Labor James J. Davis provided some numbers to illustrate a problem that the *New York Times* called "need saturation." Davis noted that "the textile mills of this country can produce all the cloth needed in six months' operation each year" and that 14 percent of the American shoe factories could produce a year's supply of footwear. The magazine went on to suggest, "It may be that the world's needs ultimately will be produced by three days' work a week."

Business leaders were less than enthusiastic about the prospect of a society no longer centered on the production of goods. For them, the new "labor-saving" machinery presented not a vision of liberation but a threat to their position at the center of power. John E. Edgerton, president of the National Association of Manufacturers, typified their response when he declared: "I am for everything that will make work happier but against everything that will further subordinate its importance. The emphasis should be put on work—more work and better work." "Nothing," he claimed, "breeds radicalism more than unhappiness unless it is leisure."

By the late 1920s, America's business and political elite had found a way to defuse the dual threat of stagnating economic growth and a radicalized working class in what one industrial consultant called "the gospel of consumption"—the notion that people could be convinced that however much they have, it isn't enough. President Herbert Hoover's 1929 Committee on Recent Economic Changes observed in glowing terms the results: "By advertising and other promotional devices . . . a measurable pull on production has been created which releases capital otherwise tied up." They celebrated the conceptual breakthrough: "Economically we have a boundless field before us; that there are new wants which will make way endlessly for newer wants, as fast as they are satisfied."

Today "work and more work" is the accepted way of doing things. If anything, improvements to the labor-saving machinery since the 1920s have intensified the trend. Machines *can* save labor, but only if they go idle when we possess enough of what they can produce. In other words, the machinery offers us an opportunity to work less, an opportunity that as a society we have chosen not to take. Instead, we have allowed the owners of those machines to define their purpose: not reduction of labor, but "higher productivity"—and with it the imperative to consume virtually everything that the machinery can possibly produce.

• • •

From the earliest days of the Age of Consumerism there were critics. One of the most influential was Arthur Dahlberg, whose 1932 book *Jobs, Machines, and Capitalism* was well known to policymakers and elected officials in Washington. Dahlberg declared that "failure to shorten the length of the working day . . . is the primary cause of our rationing of opportunity, our excess industrial plant, our enormous wastes of competition, our high pressure advertising, [and] our economic imperialism." Since much of what industry produced was no longer aimed at satisfying human physical needs, a four-hour workday, he claimed, was necessary to prevent society from becoming disastrously materialistic. "By not shortening the working day when all the wood is in," he suggested, the profit motive becomes "both the creator and satisfier of spiritual needs." For when the profit motive can turn nowhere else, "it wraps our soap in pretty boxes and tries to convince us that that is solace to our souls."

There was, for a time, a visionary alternative. In 1930 Kellogg Company, the world's leading producer of ready-to-eat cereal, announced that all of its nearly fifteen hundred workers would move from an eight-hour to a six-hour workday. Company president Lewis Brown and owner W. K. Kellogg noted that if the company ran "Four six-hour shifts . . . instead of three eight-hour shifts, this will give work and paychecks to the heads of three hundred more families in Battle Creek."

This was welcome news to workers at a time when the country was rapidly descending into the Great Depression. But as Benjamin Hunnicutt explains in his book *Kellogg's Six-Hour Day*, Brown and Kellogg wanted to do more than save jobs. They hoped to show that the "free exchange of goods, services, and labor in the free market would not have to mean mindless consumerism or eternal exploitation of people and natural resources." Instead "workers would be liberated by increasingly higher wages and shorter hours for the final freedom promised by the Declaration of Independence—the pursuit of happiness."

To be sure, Kellogg did not intend to stop making a profit. But the company leaders argued that men and women would work more efficiently on shorter shifts, and with more people employed, the overall purchasing power of the community would increase, thus allowing for more purchases of goods, including cereals.

A shorter workday did entail a cut in overall pay for workers. But Kellogg raised the hourly rate to partially offset the loss and provided for production bonuses to encourage people to work hard. The company eliminated time off for lunch, assuming that workers would rather work their shorter shift and leave as soon as possible. In a "personal letter" to employees, Brown pointed to the "mental income" of "the enjoyment of the surroundings of your home, the place you work, your neighbors, the other pleasures you have [that are] harder to translate into dollars and cents." Greater leisure, he hoped, would lead to "higher standards in school and civic . . . life" that would benefit the company by allowing it to "draw its workers from a community where good homes predominate."

It was an attractive vision, and it worked. Not only did Kellogg prosper, but journalists from magazines such as *Forbes* and *BusinessWeek* reported that the great majority of company employees embraced the shorter workday. One reporter described "a lot of gardening and community beautification, athletics and hobbies . . . libraries well patronized and the mental background of these fortunate workers . . . becoming richer."

A U.S. Department of Labor survey taken at the time, as well as inter-   15
views Hunnicutt conducted with former workers, confirm this picture. The government interviewers noted that "little dissatisfaction with lower earnings resulting from the decrease in hours was expressed, although in the majority of cases very real decreases had resulted." One man spoke of "more time at home with the family." Another remembered: "I could go home and have time to work in my garden." A woman noted that the six-hour shift allowed her husband to "be with 4 boys at ages it was important."

Those extra hours away from work also enabled some people to accomplish things that they might never have been able to do otherwise. Hunnicutt describes how at the end of her inter-

> "If we want to save the Earth, we must also save ourselves from ourselves."

view an eighty-year-old woman began talking about ping-pong. "We'd get together. We had a ping-pong table and all my relatives would come for dinner and things and we'd all play ping-pong by the hour." Eventually she went on to win the state championship.

Many women used the extra time for housework. But even then, they often chose work that drew in the entire family, such as canning. One recalled how canning food at home became "a family project" that "we all enjoyed," including her sons, who "opened up to talk freely." As Hunnicutt puts it, canning became the "medium for something more important than preserving food. Stories, jokes, teasing, quarreling, practical instruction, songs, griefs, and problems were shared. The modern discipline of alienated work was left behind for an older . . . more convivial kind of working together."

This was the stuff of a human ecology in which thousands of small, almost invisible, interactions between family members, friends, and neighbors create an intricate structure that supports social life in much the same way as topsoil supports our biological existence. When we allow either one to become impoverished, whether out of greed or intemperance, we put our long-term survival at risk.

Our modern predicament is a case in point. By 2005 per capita household spending (in inflation-adjusted dollars) was twelve times what it had been in 1929, while per capita spending for durable goods—the big stuff such as cars and appliances—was thirty-two times higher. Meanwhile, by 2000 the average married couple with children was working almost five hundred hours a year more than in 1979. And according to reports by the Federal Reserve Bank in 2004 and 2005, over 40 percent of American families spend more than they earn. The average household carries $18,654 in debt, not including home-mortgage debt, and the ratio of household debt to income is at record levels, having roughly doubled over the last two decades. We are quite literally working ourselves into a frenzy just so we can consume all that our machines can produce.

Yet we could work and spend a lot less and still live quite comfortably. By 1991 the amount of goods and services produced for each hour of labor was double what it had been in 1948. By 2006 that figure had risen another 30 percent. In other words, if as a society we made a collective decision to get by on the amount we produced and consumed seventeen years ago, we could cut back from the standard forty-hour week to 5.3 hours per day—or 2.7 hours if we were willing to return to the 1948 level. We were already the richest country on the planet in 1948 and most of the world has not yet caught up to where we were then.

Rather than realizing the enriched social life that Kellogg's vision offered us, we have impoverished our human communities with a form of materialism that leaves us in relative isolation from family, friends, and neighbors. We simply don't have time for them. Unlike our great-grandparents who passed the time, we spend it. An outside observer might conclude that we are in the grip of some strange curse, like a modern-day King Midas whose touch turns everything into a product built around a microchip.

Of course not everybody has been able to take part in the buying spree on equal terms. Millions of Americans work long hours at poverty wages while many others can find no work at all. However, as advertisers well know, poverty does not render one immune to the gospel of consumption.

Meanwhile, the influence of the gospel has spread far beyond the land of its origin. Most of the clothes, video players, furniture, toys, and other goods Americans buy today are made in distant countries, often by underpaid people working in sweatshop conditions. The raw material for many of those products comes from clearcutting or strip mining or other disastrous means of extraction. Here at home, business activity is centered on designing those products, financing their manufacture, marketing them—and counting the profits.

• • •

Kellogg's vision, despite its popularity with his employees, had little support among his fellow business leaders. But Dahlberg's book had a major influence on Senator (and future Supreme Court justice) Hugo Black who, in 1933, introduced legislation requiring a thirty-hour workweek. Although Roosevelt at first appeared to support Black's bill, he soon sided with the majority of businessmen who opposed it. Instead, Roosevelt went on to launch a series of policy initiatives that led to the forty-hour standard that we more or less observe today.

By the time the Black bill came before Congress, the prophets of the gospel of consumption had been developing their tactics and techniques for at least a decade. However, as the Great Depression deepened, the public mood was uncertain, at best, about the proper role of the large corporation. Labor unions were gaining in both public support and legal legitimacy, and the Roosevelt administration, under its New Deal° program, was implementing government regulation of industry on an unprecedented scale. Many corporate leaders saw the New Deal as a serious threat. James A. Emery, general counsel for the National Association of Manufacturers (NAM), issued a "call to arms" against the "shackles of irrational regulation" and the "back-breaking burdens of taxation," characterizing the New Deal doctrines as "alien invaders of our national thought."

In response, the industrial elite represented by NAM, including General Motors, the big steel companies, General Foods, DuPont, and others, decided to create their own propaganda. An internal NAM memo called for "re-selling all of the individual Joe Doakes on the advantages and benefits he enjoys under a competitive economy." NAM launched a massive public relations campaign it called the "American Way." As the minutes of a NAM meeting described it, the purpose of the campaign was to link "free enterprise in the public consciousness with free speech, free press and free religion as integral parts of democracy."

Consumption was not only the linchpin of the campaign; it was also recast in political terms. A campaign booklet put out by the J. Walter Thompson advertising agency told readers that under "private capitalism, the *Consumer,* the *Citizen* is boss," and "he doesn't have to wait for election day to vote or for the Court to convene before handing down his verdict. The consumer 'votes' each time he buys one article and rejects another."

According to Edward Bernays, one of the founders of the field of public relations and a principal architect of the American Way, the choices available in the polling booth are akin to those at the department store; both should consist of a limited set of offerings that are carefully determined

25

New Deal: a recovery program enacted by the U.S. government from 1933 to 1938, designed to provide jobs and stimulate the economy during the Great Depression.

by what Bernays called an "invisible government" of public-relations experts and advertisers working on behalf of business leaders. Bernays claimed that in a "democratic society" we are and should be "governed, our minds . . . molded, our tastes formed, our ideas suggested, largely by men we have never heard of."

NAM formed a national network of groups to ensure that the booklet from J. Walter Thompson and similar material appeared in libraries and school curricula across the country. The campaign also placed favorable articles in newspapers (often citing "independent" scholars who were paid secretly) and created popular magazines and film shorts directed to children and adults with such titles as "Building Better Americans," "The Business of America's People Is Selling," and "America Marching On."

Perhaps the biggest public relations success for the American Way campaign was the 1939 New York World's Fair. The fair's director of public relations called it "the greatest public relations program in industrial history," one that would battle what he called the "New Deal propaganda." The fair's motto was "Building the World of Tomorrow," and it was indeed a forum in which American corporations literally modeled the future they were determined to create. The most famous of the exhibits was General Motors' 35,000-square-foot Futurama, where visitors toured Democracity, a metropolis of multilane highways that took its citizens from their countryside homes to their jobs in the skyscraper-packed central city.

For all of its intensity and spectacle, the campaign for the American Way did not create immediate, widespread, enthusiastic support for American corporations or the corporate vision of the future. But it did lay the ideological groundwork for changes that came after the Second World War, changes that established what is still commonly called our post-war society.

The war had put people back to work in numbers that the New Deal had never approached, and there was considerable fear that unemployment would return when the war ended. Kellogg workers had been working forty-eight-hour weeks during the war and the majority of them were ready to return to a six-hour day and thirty-hour week. Most of them were able to do so, for a while. But W. K. Kellogg and Lewis Brown had turned the company over to new managers in 1937.

The new managers saw only costs and no benefits to the six-hour day, and almost immediately after the end of the war they began a campaign to undermine shorter hours. Management offered workers a tempting set of financial incentives if they would accept an eight-hour day. Yet in a vote taken in 1946, 77 percent of the men and 87 percent of the women wanted to return to a thirty-hour week rather than a forty-hour one. In making that choice, they also chose a fairly dramatic drop in earnings from artificially high wartime levels.

The company responded with a strategy of attrition, offering special deals on a department-by-department basis where eight hours had pockets of support, typically among highly skilled male workers. In the culture of a post-war, post-Depression U.S., that strategy was largely successful. But not everyone went along. Within Kellogg there was a substantial, albeit slowly dwindling group of people Hunnicutt calls the "mavericks," who resisted longer work hours. They clustered in a few departments that had managed to preserve the six-hour day until the company eliminated it once and for all in 1985.

The mavericks rejected the claims made by the company, the union, 35 and many of their co-workers that the extra money they could earn on an eight-hour shift was worth it. Despite the enormous difference in societal wealth between the 1930s and the 1980s, the language the mavericks used to explain their preference for a six-hour workday was almost identical to that used by Kellogg workers fifty years earlier. One woman, worried about the long hours worked by her son, said, "He has no time to live, to visit and spend time with his family, and to do the other things he really loves to do."

Several people commented on the link between longer work hours and consumerism. One man said, "I was getting along real good, so there was no use in me working any more time than I had to." He added, "Everybody thought they were going to get rich when they got that eight-hour deal and it really didn't make a big difference. . . . Some went out and bought automobiles right quick and they didn't gain much on that because the car took the extra money they had."

The mavericks, well aware that longer work hours meant fewer jobs, called those who wanted eight-hour shifts plus overtime "work hogs." "Kellogg's was laying off people," one woman commented, "while some of the men were working really fantastic amounts of overtime—that's just not fair." Another quoted the historian Arnold Toynbee, who said, "We will either share the work, or take care of people who don't have work."

• • •

People in the Depression-wracked 1930s, with what seems to us today to be a very low level of material goods, readily chose fewer work hours for the same reasons as some of their children and grandchildren did in the 1980s: to have more time for themselves and their families. We could, as a society, make a similar choice today.

But we cannot do it as individuals. The mavericks at Kellogg held out against company and social pressure for years, but in the end the marketplace didn't offer them a choice to work less and consume less. The reason is simple: that choice is at odds with the foundations of the marketplace itself—at least as it is currently constructed. The men and women who masterminded the creation of the consumerist society understood that theirs was a political undertaking, and it will take a powerful political movement to change course today.

Bernays's version of a "democratic society," in which political decisions are marketed to consumers, has many modern proponents. Consider a comment by Andrew Card, George W. Bush's former chief of staff. When asked why the administration waited several months before making its case for war against Iraq, Card replied, "You don't roll out a new product in August." And in 2004, one of the leading legal theorists in the United States, federal judge Richard Posner, declared that "representative democracy . . . involves a division between rulers and ruled," with the former being "a governing class," and the rest of us exercising a form of "consumer sovereignty" in the political sphere with "the power not to buy a particular product, a power to choose though not to create."

Sometimes an even more blatant antidemocratic stance appears in the working papers of elite think tanks. One such example is the prominent Harvard political scientist Samuel Huntington's 1975 contribution to a Trilateral Commission report on "The Crisis of Democracy." Huntington warns against an "excess of democracy," declaring that "a democratic political system usually requires some measure of apathy and noninvolvement on the part of some individuals and groups." Huntington notes that "marginal social groups, as in the case of the blacks, are now becoming full participants in the political system" and thus present the "danger of overloading the political system" and undermining its authority.

According to this elite view, the people are too unstable and ignorant for self-rule. "Commoners," who are viewed as factors of production at work and as consumers at home, must adhere to their proper roles in order to maintain social stability. Posner, for example, disparaged a proposal for a national day of deliberation as "a small but not trivial reduction in the amount of productive work." Thus he appears to be an ideological descendant of the business leader who warned that relaxing the imperative for "more work and better work" breeds "radicalism."

As far back as 1835, Boston workingmen striking for shorter hours declared that they needed time away from work to be good citizens: "We have rights, and we have duties to perform as American citizens and members of society." As those workers well understood, any meaningful democracy requires citizens who are empowered to create and re-create their government, rather than a mass of marginalized voters who merely choose from what is offered by an "invisible" government. Citizenship requires a commitment of time and attention, a commitment people cannot make if they are lost to themselves in an ever-accelerating cycle of work and consumption.

We can break that cycle by turning off our machines when they have created enough of what we need. Doing so will give us an opportunity to re-create the kind of healthy communities that were beginning to emerge with Kellogg's six-hour day, communities in which human welfare is the overriding concern rather than subservience to machines and those who own them. We can create a society where people have time to play together as well as work together, time to act politically in their common interests, and time even to argue over what those common interests might be. That fertile mix of human relationships is necessary for healthy human societies, which in turn are necessary for sustaining a healthy planet.

If we want to save the Earth, we must also save ourselves from our-   45 selves. We can start by sharing the work *and* the wealth. We may just find that there is plenty of both to go around.

Understanding the Text

1. Why did some 1920s industrialists view saving and frugality as threats? What did they do to change this?

2. What happened when the Kellogg Company shortened the work day in 1930? Why and how did this practice stop?

3. What is the "gospel of consumption" that Kaplan refers to in the title of this essay?

Reflection and Response

4. This article suggests that people would be happier with a shorter work schedule. Do you agree? What are the arguments for and against a six-hour work day?

5. What is the relationship between working and democracy? Do you think that Americans would be more involved in politics if they spent less time working and spending money? Would this be a good thing or a bad thing?

6. How are working and consumption tied to issues of sustainability?

Making Connections

7. Do some research on the debates surrounding a shorter work week. Is this debate still active today? What are the arguments for and against it?

8. In what ways is consumption tied to the other concerns in this chapter? For instance, how are recycling, green jobs, personal electronics, and other issues essentially based on the ways in which we produce and consume things? How is consumption a sustainability issue? Compare and contrast the articles in this chapter based on the notion of consumption.

Green Cities: Why Invest in Sustainable Cities?

Michael Bloomberg and Patricia de Lille

Michael Bloomberg is a businessman, philanthropist, and the former mayor of New York City, where he served three terms from 2002 to 2013. Throughout his career, Bloomberg has initiated programs and backed businesses that support change through innovation. He is the founder of Bloomberg Philanthropy, which focuses on public health, arts and culture, the environment, education, and government innovation.

Patricia de Lille is a South African politician and the current mayor of Cape Town. She has contributed to campaigns targeting issues such as health, minerals and energy, trade and industry, and communications. In 2004, de Lille was honored as one of the Top 5 Women in Government and Government Agencies and is one of four South Africans to be presented with Birmingham, Alabama's Freedom of the City Award.

This article discusses the reasons for creating and investing in sustainable or "green" cities in the future. As you read the piece, think about the major issues facing a city in your area, and how sustainable solutions might help mitigate those issues.

More than two-thirds of total investment in infrastructure in the next 15 years will be made in cities. It's no wonder, as people are flocking to cities around the world. By 2050, around 66% of the global population likely will live in urban areas. In Africa alone, there will be nearly 800 million more people living in cities than today.

To provide for all these new urban dwellers, we need more buildings, more bridges, more public transport and more energy—and all of that requires money.

City governments often struggle to raise the funds they need for urban mobility projects such as rail or bus rapid transit. There is a significant gap between the supply and demand for urban infrastructure—some estimates suggest it is upward of $1 trillion per year to 2030.

"Despite the challenges, the economic and environmental arguments for increasing investments in cities are clear."

Despite the challenges, the economic and environmental arguments for increasing investments in cities are

Sustainable building can have positive effects for residents and the environment.
Jeffrey Penalosa/EyeEM/Getty Images

clear. Investing in more compact, connected, efficient cities with modern public transport systems can spur economic growth while also having positive effects for the well-being of residents and for the climate.

Investing in Sustainable Infrastructure

Research from the New Climate Economy has found that investing in sustainable urban infrastructure such as public transport, building efficiency and waste management could generate energy savings with a current value of $16.6 trillion by 2050. Meanwhile, sustainable cities have cleaner air, less traffic congestion and fewer greenhouse gas emissions.

Devising ways to scale financing for urban infrastructure, and to shift capital flows to make sure new projects are sustainable, is the next great challenge facing cities. To meet it, cities must have the authority and resources they need to make bold investments. Mayors and local policymakers are eager to take on the challenge, but they must have the authority and resources to do so.

The first step is to improve cities' access to private finance by improving their creditworthiness. Right now, only 4% of the 500 largest cities in developing countries are considered creditworthy, hampering their ability to raise capital.

Turning to the Private Sector for Investment

Estimates suggest that with the right policies, private sector investment could fill up to half of the infrastructure-financing gap.

For example, Kampala, Uganda, recently set out a plan to improve its governance and financial management, and has gained a reputation as an effective, reform-minded and innovative authority. This improved the city's creditworthiness to an "A" rating at the national scale for long-term debt instruments.

The improved rating almost doubled its borrowing allowance for 10 large-scale sustainable urban infrastructure.

Municipal green bonds are another way to attract capital. The municipal green bond market is relatively small, valued at about $6 billion in 2015, but fast growing.

Last year, in the biggest issuance yet, Seattle's Sound Transit sold nearly $1 billion of green bonds that will help fund voter-approved regional transit projects, including construction of more than 30 miles of light rail extensions.

Johannesburg recently issued a green municipal bond with a target value of $136 million. The bond was oversubscribed. Another South African city, Cape Town, is looking to use its "AAA" credit rating and pipeline of climate action projects to issue a green bond that it intends to have certified through the Climate Bonds Initiative.

These measures, coupled with increasing pressure on the market to invest in instruments that support and deliver sustainable objectives, mean that Cape Town is hopeful that this bond will attract a favorable investor response when it goes to market.

Public-private partnerships can also be an effective way for cities to 15 improve access to private finance for urban infrastructure.

Bangkok's Skytrain and Bogota's Bus Rapid Transit were both financed in part through such partnerships.

Cities, especially in the developing world, can also tap into multilateral development banks and international climate funds.

For example, the Global Environment Facility has a new $140 million program in 22 pilot cities expected to leverage $1.4 billion for smart urban development.

New Heart of Economic Development

City-level action works best when supported by national policies that place urban infrastructure at the heart of economic development. A new global initiative—the Coalition for Urban Transitions, with experts from more than 20 of the world's leading urban-focused institutions—will help support national governments to develop these strategies.

But even if national action stalls, as some worry may happen after the 20 US election, city-level action will continue to blaze forward. As part of the new Global Covenant of Mayors for Climate & Energy, more than 7,000 cities and urban areas have committed to developing energy and climate action plans, a good starting point for identifying city infrastructure needs.

In addition, city networks such as the C40 Cities Climate Leadership Group, ICLEI-Local Governments for Sustainability, and United Cities and Local Governments can share best practices, spread new technologies, facilitate new forms of finance and support project preparation.

As both a co-chair and member of the Global Covenant's mayoral board, we will ensure investors see the data cities are reporting on significant actions they are taking as evidence for increasing funding.

Building the sustainable cities of the future will be challenging, and we have a long way to go to close the urban financing gap. The good news is that cities are finding innovative solutions to do it, and we are already seeing results.

Understanding the Text

1. How do the authors define sustainable urban infrastructure?
2. What examples of green cities do the authors provide and how have they made sustainable choices?
3. What are some of the challenges cities face when developing sustainability initiatives?

Reflection and Response

1. How could you initiate or participate in sustainable change in your community?
2. Would sustainability efforts made by a city impact your decision to live there? Why or why not?

Making Connections

1. Has the area you live in made any efforts to make the area more sustainable? How have the changes impacted the quality of life of those who live in the town, city, or neighborhood?
2. Many climate change researchers, as well as some of the authors included in this book, maintain that technology is the key to combatting climate change. How could technology be used to create greener cities?
3. Research one of the sustainable changes made by a city mentioned in the article. What were the benefits and drawbacks of the change?

The Cities of the Future Will Be Smart, Sustainable, and Efficient

Kendra L. Smith

Kendra L. Smith earned her PhD at the School of Community Resources and Development at Arizona State University. Smith previously worked for the Morrison Institute for Public Policy as a policy analyst working on tasks surrounding civic engagement, science and technology, and economic development. Currently, she works as the Associate Director for Community Engaged Research in the Center for Population Health Sciences at the School of Medicine at Stanford University.

This article appeared on Futurism.com, an online news source devoted to science, technology, and the future of humanity. Smith discusses a growing topic in sustainability conversations: smart cities. The author proposes that rather than planning smart cities around the necessary technology, cities should be adapting their plans to fit the lives of the people who live there so the city will be "intelligently adapted to their residents' needs." Smith maintains that when done correctly, smart cities should make residents' lives more efficient, healthy, and equal. As you read the article, think about what a "smart" city should include, from the standpoint of sustainability.

By 2030, 60 percent of the world's population is expected to live in mega-cities. How all those people live, and what their lives are like, will depend on important choices leaders make today and in the coming years.

Technology has the power to help people live in communities that are more responsive to their needs and that can actually improve their lives. For example, Beijing, notorious for air pollution, is testing a 23-foot-tall air purifier that vacuums up smog, filters the bad particles and releases clear air.

This isn't a vision of life like on "The Jetsons." It's real urban communities responding in real-time to changing weather, times of day and citizen needs. These efforts can span entire communities. They can vary from monitoring traffic to keep cars moving efficiently or measuring air quality to warn residents (or turn on massive air purifiers) when pollution levels climb.

Using data and electronic sensors in this way is often referred to as building "smart cities," which are the subject of a major global push to improve how cities function. In part a response to incoherent infrastructure design and urban planning of the past, smart cities promise real-time monitoring, analysis and improvement of city decision-making. The results, proponents say, will improve efficiency, environmental sustainability and citizen engagement.

> "By 2030, 60 percent of the world's population is expected to live in mega-cities."

Smart city projects are big investments that are supposed to drive 5 social transformation. Decisions made early in the process determine what exactly will change. But most research and planning regarding smart cities is driven by the technology, rather than the needs of the citizens. Little attention is given to the social, policy and organizational changes that will be required to ensure smart cities are not just technologically savvy but intelligently adaptive to their residents' needs. Design will make the difference between smart city projects offering great promise or actually reinforcing or even widening the existing gaps in unequal ways their cities serve residents.

City Benefits from Efficiency

A key feature of smart cities is that they create efficiency. Well-designed technology tools can benefit government agencies, the environment and residents. Smart cities can improve the efficiency of city services by eliminating redundancies, finding ways to save money and streamlining workers' responsibilities. The results can provide higher-quality services at lower cost.

For instance, in 2014, the Transport for London transit agency deployed a system that lets residents and London's 19 million visitors pay for bus and subway fares more quickly and safely than in the past. When riders touch or tap their phone or other mobile device on a reader when entering and exiting the bus and subway system, a wireless transaction deducts the appropriate amount from a user's bank account.

The city benefits by reducing the cost of administering its fare payment system, including avoiding issuing and distributing special smartcards for use at fareboxes. Transit users benefit from the efficiency through convenience, quick service and capped fares that calculate the best value for their contactless travel in a day or across a seven-day period.

Environmental Effects

Another way to save money involves real-time monitoring of energy use, which can also identify opportunities for environmental improvement.

The city of Chicago has begun implementing an "Array of Things" 10 initiative by installing boxes on municipal light poles with sensors and cameras that can capture air quality, sound levels, temperature, water levels on streets and gutters, and traffic.

The data collected are expected to serve as a sort of "fitness tracker for the city," by identifying ways to save energy, to address urban flooding and improve living conditions.

Helping Residents

Perhaps the largest potential benefit from smart cities will come from enhancing residents' quality of life. The opportunities cover a broad range of issues, including housing and transportation, happiness and optimism, educational services, environmental conditions and community relationships.

Efforts along this line can include tracking and mapping residents' health, using data to fight neighborhood blight, identifying instances of discrimination and deploying autonomous vehicles to increase residents' safety and mobility.

Ensuring Focus on Service, Not Administration

Many of the efficiencies touted as resulting from smart city efforts relate to government functions. The benefits, therefore, are most immediate for government agencies and employees. The assumption, of course, is that what benefits government will in turn benefit the public.

However, focus on direct improvements for the public can become an 15 afterthought. It can also be subverted for other reasons.

For instance, global market projections for smart cities are huge. Companies see big opportunities for selling technology to cities, and local leaders are eager to find new investors who will improve their communities. That can make smart cities appear to be a win-win situation.

City leaders may also use smart city discussions as a vague "self-congratulatory" method to emphasize their forward thinking, and to reinforce a broadly positive—if undefined—view of the city. By talking about greater connectivity and improved technical capabilities, city leaders can market the city to future residents and businesses alike.

But if leaders focus on smart city projects as helping government, that won't necessarily improve residents' lives. In fact, it can reinforce existing problems, or even make them worse.

Who Wins from Smart City Projects?

When governments decide on smart city projects, they necessarily choose whom those efforts will benefit—and whom they will neglect.

Songdo City is a new "smart city" built on reclaimed land in South Korea.
Joern Pollex/FIFA/Getty Images

Even when it's unintentional—which it often is—the results are the same: Not all areas of a smart city will be exactly equally "smart." Some neighborhoods will have a greater density of air-quality sensors or traffic cameras, for example.

And not all smart city projects are having completely positive effects.   20 In India, for example, Prime Minister Narendra Modi pledged to build 100 smart cities as a way to manage the needs of his country's rapidly urbanizing population. Yet the efforts are bumping up against challenges new and old. These include longstanding problems with land ownership documentation, developing policies to accommodate new markets and limit the old, and conflicts with vulnerable populations pushed out to make room for new smart city initiatives.

In Philadelphia, a program intended to provide the city's low-income, underemployed residents with job training on their smartphones didn't address widespread socioeconomic inequality, among other problems. As one researcher put it, the program was "empty policy rhetoric" designed to attract business.

The much-ballyhooed Songdo City development in South Korea involved enormous investment from the public and private sectors to create a smart city billed as an urban hub of innovation and commerce.

And yet, 10 years after it began, its highest praise has been from those who call it a "work in progress." Others, less charitable, have called it an outright failure. The reason should give us pause when designing other smart cities: Songdo was designed and built as a top-down, "high-tech utopia" with no history and, crucially, without people at its center.

To avoid these troubled fates, officials, business leaders and residents alike must keep a critical eye on smart city efforts in their communities. Projects must be both transparent and aimed at publicly desirable improvements in society. Technology cannot become the focal point, nor the end goal. Smart city innovation, like all urban development and redevelopment, is a very political process. Residents must hold city leaders accountable for their efforts and their implications—which must be to improve everyone's lives, not just ease government functions.

Understanding the Text

1. How does the author define "smart cities"?
2. Why is efficiency an important aspect of a potential smart city?
3. The author discusses one of Chicago's smart city initiatives. Why does she cite this as an example of the environmental effects of smart cities?

Reflection and Response

4. In what ways do smart cities correspond with sustainability?
5. Do the examples provided by the author effectively support her argument? Why or why not?
6. As a child, what did you imagine cities would look like in the future? Do smart cities align with that mental image?

Making Connections

7. Research what residents of cities have to say about smart cities or the efforts made by their city to become more sustainable. Are their words positive or negative?
8. What are some other cities that have taken steps toward technology-focused sustainability? Were there any complications with the initiative?

Can Recycling Be Bad for the Environment?

Amy Westervelt

Amy Westervelt is a freelance journalist based in Oakland, California, who writes about environmental issues. She is a contributing editor to *Forbes* magazine and won the prestigious Folio Eddie award in 2007. Westervelt has written for *Condé Nast Traveler*, *BusinessWeek*, *Travel + Leisure* magazine, *Sustainable Industries*, and other publications.

This article, first published in *Forbes* in 2012, discusses the potential ramifications of recycling. Westervelt explains how public opinion about recycling has changed over the past decades and how that is tied to government recycling programs. As you read, think about how recycling is perceived in today's culture and whether you think this will change in the coming years.

It could be argued that the U.S. environmental movement started with recycling. For old-school environmentalists, recycling is such an integral part of the movement that it's difficult to separate the two. And in those early days, back in the 1980s, the cause was noble and pure: Why throw away products that could be new again? Why not turn trash into raw materials?

At a certain point, though, recycling developed something of a dark side from an environmental perspective. On the surface, it's still a good idea both to recycle waste and to design products and packaging with the idea of recycling them in a closed loop. Unfortunately, in its modern-day incarnation, recycling has also given the manufacturers of disposable items a way to essentially market overconsumption as environmentalism. Every year, reports come out touting rising recycling rates and neglecting to mention the soaring consumption that goes along with them. American consumers assuage any guilt they might feel about consuming mass quantities of unnecessary, disposable goods by dutifully tossing those items into their recycling bins and hauling them out to the curb each week.

Trade groups representing various packaging interests — plastic, paper, glass — have become the largest proponents and financial sponsors of recycling. If you go to the Environmental Protection Agency's° website looking for statistics on packaging recycling, the stats on plastics

---

Environmental Protection Agency: an agency of the U.S. government that protects human health and the environment by writing and enforcing laws.

A recycling station in Quebec, Canada.
Design Pics/David Chapman/Getty Images

recycling come from the American Plastics Council and the Society of the Plastics Industries, Inc. (SPI), both trade associations representing the plastics industry.

The plastics industry's interest in recycling is two-fold of course — on the one hand, by supporting recycling and helping to establish infrastructure for plastic recycling, the industry ensures a steady supply of new materials. On the other, it helps consumers to justify the consumption of more disposable plastic goods and packaged items if they can comfort themselves with the idea that whatever they toss in the bin will be recycled.

The thing is, recycling isn't the small operation it once was, it's a com- 5
modity business that fluctuates with supply and demand. It's also a global market, with recyclables collected in the United States being shipped to wherever demand is highest (often China). A few years ago, when demand for recycled paper products dropped, recyclers all over the country were warehousing stacks of cardboard, waiting for the prices to turn around. "The hope is that eventually the markets turn around and that the material is sold, but I have heard of instances where it gets landfilled, because a

community doesn't have the demand or the space or the company to deal with it," says Gene Jones, executive director of Southern Waste Information Exchange—a nonprofit center for information about recycling waste.

"Recycling has . . . given the manufacturers of disposable items a way to essentially market overconsumption as environmentalism."

Moreover, not everything that's "recyclable" actually gets recycled. Even when you're dealing with easily recycled items like PET or HDPE plastic (the plastics commonly used for bottles), or glass or cardboard, first you've got to get consumers to dispose of the items properly, then you've got to have a collection system in place (just over half of U.S. cities have curbside recycling, keep in mind), and then recyclers typically need to have a buyer lined up to justify recycling anything.

"There's a difference between things being recyclable and actually being recycled," says Gerry Fishbeck, vice president of United Resource Recovery Corporation (URRC), one of the largest recyclers in the country. "It's centered around critical mass—is there enough of the material out there? And even if there is, is it worth it for recyclers to create a whole separate stream?"

Fishbeck cites PVC as a perfect example: Technically it's recyclable, but most recyclers don't handle the stuff. It can mimic PET and thus easily get into a PET recycling stream, but when it's melted down it will create brown particles in the resin, creating color problems with the resulting material. "So even though it's recyclable, that material will get separated out and disposed of as waste at the recycling facility," Fishbeck explains.

Bioplastics° are another example. With the exception of bio-based PET and HDPE, bioplastics fall into the recyclable but not recycled category. They are treated as contaminants of the recycling stream by most recyclers and separated out as waste. "If PLA (polylactic acid, the most common bioplastic today) gets into the recycling stream, it will cause contamination, it will be a defect, and that means we'll do everything we can to keep it out of the stream and it will become waste," Fishbeck says. "There's just not enough of it around to have the critical mass to justify getting it separated and recycled. It can be done, but it isn't."

Emissions are another sticky subject for recycling. In the case of some 10 materials—aluminum, corrugated cardboard, newspaper, dimensional lumber, and medium-density fiberboard—the net greenhouse gas emissions reductions enabled by recycling are actually greater than they

---

bioplastics: a form of plastics made from renewable biomass sources, such as vegetable fats and oils.

would be if the waste source was simply reduced, according to the EPA. For others—glass, plastic—while in some cases the energy required to recycle versus making virgin material is lower, there are concerns about the particulates emitted by recycling factories. In recent studies of air quality in Oakland [California], recycling centers were, perhaps surprisingly, included amongst the city's polluters.

One metal recycling plant in West Oakland has been protested so much by local residents that it was set to close its doors and move out of the city until a local group came up with the idea of helping the plant move to a more industrial part of town. The city wanted to keep the plant within its limits not just to maintain its tax base and keep jobs, but to support the so-called hidden economy, wherein some local residents make a living collecting and redeeming recyclable materials.

It's a perfect illustration of the state of recycling today: Like any other business, it's neither altruistic nor completely self-serving; it comes with clear societal and environmental benefits—perhaps more so than many other businesses—but it also comes with some costs and cannot be considered a perfect solution to the United States' large and ever-growing consumption and waste problems.

Understanding the Text

1. What are the downsides to recycling as described in this article?
2. Why is the plastics industry so interested in recycling?
3. Are bioplastics and emissions recyclable or nonrecyclable? Why or why not?

Reflection and Response

4. Do you believe that recycling could have a negative impact on the environment? Back up your opinion with examples from the text or from other sources.
5. How do you think recycling will continue to change over the next decade?
6. Do you believe that recycling is an important sustainability issue? In what ways does the recycling debate depend on the concept and philosophy of sustainability?

Making Connections

7. Westervelt begins the article by describing the "early days" of recycling in the 1980s. Do some research to find out the similarities and differences between recycling then and now. What do we do differently today?
8. What sort of recycling efforts are taking place on your campus or in your community? Do you think that these efforts are entirely beneficial, or do you see negative impacts that are not accounted for? Explain your response.

On the Future of Food

Prince Charles of Wales

Prince Charles of Wales is the eldest child of Queen Elizabeth II and the heir to the throne of England. He is involved in many humanitarian and social concerns, and he is especially focused on promoting environmental awareness. A strong proponent of organic farming, Prince Charles launched his own organic food brand, Duchy Originals, in 1990; it sells sustainably produced goods, including many food products. He also wrote *Highgrove: An Experiment in Organic Gardening and Farming* (with *The Daily Telegraph* environment editor Charles Clover) and *The Elements of Organic Gardening* (with Stephanie Donaldson).

Prince Charles is recognized as a leading voice in the fight for sustainable agriculture. In his May 4, 2011, keynote speech (excerpted here) at the Future of Food conference at Georgetown University in Washington, D.C., Prince Charles argued that feeding the world's population using sustainable methods is one of our most important challenges. As you read this excerpt from his speech, think about the ways in which food production, politics, and sustainability intersect.

Over the past 30 years I have been venturing into extremely dangerous territory by speaking about the future of food. I have all the scars to prove it . . . ! Questioning the conventional world view is a risky business. And the only reason I have done so is for the sake of your generation and for the integrity of Nature herself. It is your future that concerns me and that of your grandchildren, and theirs too. That is how far we should be looking ahead. I have no intention of being confronted by my grandchildren, demanding to know why on Earth we didn't do something about the many problems that existed, when we knew what was going wrong. The threat of that question, the responsibility of it, is precisely why I have gone on challenging the assumptions of our day. And I would urge you to do the same, because we need to face up to asking whether how we produce our food is actually fit for purpose in the very challenging circumstances of the twenty-first century. We simply cannot ignore that question any longer.

Very nearly 30 years ago I began by talking about the issue, but I realized in the end I had to go further. I had to put my concern into action, to demonstrate how else we might do things so that we secure food production for the future, but also, crucially, to take care of the Earth that sustains us. Because if we don't do that, if we do not work within Nature's system, then Nature will fail to be the durable, continuously sustaining force she has always been. Only by safeguarding Nature's resilience can we hope to have a resilient form of food production and ensure food security in the long term.

This is the challenge facing us. We have to maintain a supply of healthy food at affordable prices when there is mounting pressure on nearly every element affecting the process. In some cases we are pushing Nature's life-support systems so far, they are struggling to cope with what we ask of them. Soils are being depleted, demand for water is growing ever more voracious, and the entire system is at the mercy of an increasingly fluctuating price of oil.

Remember that when we talk about agriculture and food production, we are talking about a complex and interrelated system and it is simply not possible to single out just one objective, like maximizing production, without also ensuring that the system which delivers those increased yields meets society's other needs. As Eric Schlosser° has highlighted, these should include the maintenance of public health, the safeguarding of rural employment, the protection of the environment, and contributing to overall quality of life.

So I trust that this conference will not shy away from the big 5 questions. Chiefly, how can we create a more sustainable approach to agriculture while recognizing those wider and important social and economic parameters — an approach that is capable of feeding the world with a global population rapidly heading for nine billion? And can we do so amid so many competing demands on land, in an increasingly volatile climate, and when levels of the planet's biodiversity are under such threat or in serious decline?

As I see it, these pressures mean we haven't much choice in the matter. We are going to have to take some very brave steps. We will have to develop much more sustainable, or durable forms of food production because the way we have done things up to now are no longer as viable as they once appeared to be. The more I talk with people about this issue, the more I realize how vague the general picture remains of the perilous state we are in. So, just to be absolutely clear, I feel I should offer you a quick pen sketch of just some of the evidence that this is so.

Certainly, internationally, food insecurity is a growing problem. There are also many now who consider that global food systems are well on the way to being in crisis. Yield increases for staple food crops are declining. They have dropped from 3 percent in the 1960s to 1 percent today — and that is really worrying because, for the first time, that rate is less than

Eric Schlosser: Eric Schlosser also spoke at the conference, http://www.georgetown. edu/story/futureoffoodgallery.html

the rate of population growth. And all of this, of course, has to be set against the ravages caused by climate change. Already yields are suffering in Africa and India where crops are failing to cope with ever-increasing temperatures and fluctuating rainfall. We all remember the failure of last year's wheat harvest in Russia and droughts in China. They have caused the cost of food to rocket and, with it, inflation around the world, stoking social discontent in many countries, notably in the Middle East. It is a situation I fear will only become more volatile as we suffer yet more natural disasters. . . .

Set against these threats to yields is the ever-growing demand for food. The United Nations Food and Agriculture Organization estimates that the demand will rise by 70 percent between now and 2050. The curve is quite astonishing. The world somehow has to find the means of feeding a staggering 219,000 new mouths every day. That's about 450 since I started talking! What is more, with incomes rising in places like China and India, there will also be more people wealthy enough to consume more, so the demand for meat and dairy products may well increase yet further. And all that extra livestock will compete for feed more and more with an energy sector that has massively expanded its demand for biofuels. Here in the U.S., I am told, four out of every ten bushels of corn are now grown to fuel motor vehicles.

This is the context we find ourselves in and it is set against the backdrop of a system heavily dependent upon fossil fuels and other forms of diminishing natural capital—mineral fertilizers and so on. Most forms of industrialized agriculture now have an umbilical dependency on oil, natural gas, and other non-renewable resources. One study I have read estimates that a person today on a typical Western diet is, in effect, consuming nearly a U.S. gallon of diesel every day! And when you consider that in the past decade the cost of artificial nitrogen fertilizers has gone up fourfold and the cost of potash three times, you start to see how uncomfortable the future could become if we do not wean ourselves off our dependency. And that's not even counting the impact of higher fuel prices on the other costs of production—transport and processing—all of which are passed on to the consumer. It is indeed a vicious circle.

Then add the supply of land into the equation—where do we grow all   10 of the extra plants or graze all that extra stock when urban expansion is such a pressure? Here in the United States I am told that one acre is lost to development every minute of every day—which means that since 1982 an area the size of Indiana has been built over—though that is small fry compared with what is happening in places like India where, somehow, they have to find a way of housing another 300 million people in the next 30 years. But on top of this is the very real problem of soil erosion.

Again, in the U.S., soil is being washed away 10 times faster than the Earth can replenish it, and it is happening 40 times faster in China and India. Twenty-two thousand square miles of arable land is turning into desert every year and, all told, it appears a quarter of the world's farmland, two billion acres, is degraded.

Given these pressures, it seems likely we will have to grow plants in more difficult terrain. But the only sustainable way to do that will be by increasing the long-term fertility of the soil, because, as I say, achieving increased production using imported, non-renewable inputs is simply not sustainable.

There are many other pressures on the way we produce our food, but I just need to highlight one more, if I may, before I move on to the possible solutions, because it is so important. It is that magical substance we have taken for granted for so long—water.

In a country like the United States a fifth of all your grain production is dependent upon irrigation. For every pound of beef produced in the industrial system, it takes 2,000 gallons of water. That is a lot of water and there is plenty of evidence that the Earth cannot keep up with the demand. The Ogallala Aquifer on the Great Plains, for instance, is depleting by 1.3 trillion gallons faster than rainfall can replenish it. And when you consider that of all the water in the world, only 5 percent of it is fresh and a quarter of that sits in Lake Baikal in Siberia, there is not a lot left. Of the remaining 4 percent, nearly three quarters of it is used in agriculture, but 30 percent of that water is wasted. If you set that figure against future predictions, then the picture gets even worse. By 2030 it is estimated that the world's farmers will need 45 percent more water than today. And yet already, because of irrigation, many of the world's largest rivers no longer reach the sea for part of the year—including, I am afraid, the Colorado and Rio Grande.

Forgive me for laboring these points, but the impact of all of this has 15 already been immense. Over a billion people—one-seventh of the world's population—are hungry and another billion suffer from what is called "hidden hunger," which is the lack of essential vitamins and nutrients in their diets. And on the reverse side of the coin, let us not forget the other tragic fact—that over a billion people in the world are now considered overweight or obese. It is an increasingly insane picture. In one way or another, half the world finds itself on the wrong side of the food equation.

You can see, I hope, that in a global ecosystem that is, to say the least, under stress, our apparently unbridled demands for energy, land, and water put overwhelming pressure on our food systems. I am not alone in thinking that the current model is simply not durable in the long term. It is not "keeping everything going continuously" and it is, therefore, not sustainable.

So what is a "sustainable food production" system? We should be very clear about it, or else we will end up with the same system that we have now, but dipped in "green wash." For me, it has to be a form of agriculture that does not exceed the carrying capacity of its local ecosystem and which recognizes that the soil is the planet's most vital renewable resource. Topsoil is the cornerstone of the prosperity of nations. It acts as a buffer against drought and as a carbon sink and it is the primary source of the health of all animals, plants, and people. If we degrade it, as we are doing, then Nature's capital will lose its innate resilience and it won't be very long, believe you me, before our human economic capital and economic systems also begin to lose their resilience.

Let's, then, try and look for a moment at what very probably is not a genuinely sustainable form of agriculture—for the long term, and by that I mean generations as yet unborn. In my own view it is surely not dependent upon the use of chemical pesticides, fungicides, and insecticides; nor, for that matter, upon artificial fertilizers and growth-promoters or G.M. You would have perhaps thought it unlikely to create vast monocultures and to treat animals like machines by using industrial rearing systems. Nor would you expect it to drink the Earth dry, deplete the soil, clog streams with nutrient-rich run-off and create, out of sight and out of mind, enormous dead zones in the oceans. You would also think, wouldn't you, that it might not lead to the destruction of whole cultures or the removal of many of the remaining small farmers around the world? Nor, presumably, would it destroy biodiversity at the same time as cultural and social diversity.

On the contrary, genuinely sustainable farming maintains the resilience of the entire ecosystem by encouraging a rich level of biodiversity in the soil, in its water supply, and in the wildlife—the birds, insects, and bees that maintain the health of the whole system. Sustainable farming also recognizes the importance to the soil of planting trees; of protecting and enhancing water-catchment systems; of mitigating, rather than adding to, climate change. To do this it must be a mixed approach. One where animal waste is recycled and organic waste is composted to build the soil's fertility. One where antibiotics are only used on animals to treat illnesses, not deployed in prophylactic doses to prevent them; and where those animals are fed on grass-based regimes as Nature intended.

You may think this an idealized definition—that it isn't possible in   20 "the real world"—but if you consider this the gold standard, then for food production to become more "sustainable" it has to reduce the use of those substances that are dangerous and harmful not only to human health, but also to the health of those natural systems, such as the oceans, forests, and wetlands, that provide us with the services essential to life on this planet—but which we rashly take for granted. At the same time, it has to minimize the use of non-renewable external inputs. Fertilizers that do not come from renewable sources do not enable a sustainable approach which, ultimately, comes down to giving back to Nature as much as it

Prince Charles tours Penbedw Farm in Nannerch, Wales.
Tim Graham/Getty Images

takes out and recognizing that there are necessary limits to what the Earth can do. Equally, it includes the need for producers to receive a reasonable price for their labors above the price of production. And that, ladies and gentlemen, leads me to the nub of what I would like you to consider.

Having myself tried to farm as sustainably as possible for some 26 years in England, which is not as long as other people here I know, I certainly know of plenty of current evidence that adopting an approach which mirrors the miraculous ingenuity of Nature can produce surprisingly high yields of a wide range of vegetables, arable crops, beef, lamb, and milk. And yet we are told ceaselessly that sustainable or organic agriculture cannot feed the world. I find this claim very hard to understand. Especially when you consider the findings of an impeccably well-researched International Assessment of Agricultural Knowledge, Science and Technology for Development, conducted in 2008 by the U.N. I am very pleased, by the way, to see that the co-chair of that report, Professor Hans Herren, will be taking part in the International Panel discussion towards the end of the conference. His report drew on evidence from more than 400 scientists worldwide and concluded that small-scale, family-based farming systems, adopting so-called agro-ecological approaches, were among the most productive systems in developing countries. This was a major study and a very explicit statement. And yet, for some strange reason, the conclusions of this exhaustive report seem to have vanished without trace.

"This is the heart of the problem, it seems to me— why it is that an industrialized system, deeply dependent on fossil fuels and chemical treatments, is promoted as viable, while a much less damaging one is rubbished and condemned as unfit for purpose."

This is the heart of the problem, it seems to me—why it is that an industrialized system, deeply dependent on fossil fuels and chemical treatments, is promoted as viable, while a much less damaging one is rubbished and condemned as unfit for purpose. The reasons lie in the anomalies that exist behind the scenes.

I would certainly urge you, first, to look at the slack in the system. Under the current, inherently unsustainable system, in the developed world we actually throw away approximately 40 percent of the food we have bought.

Food is now much cheaper than it was and one of the unexpected consequences of this is, perhaps, that we do not value it as once we did. I cannot help feeling some of this problem could be avoided with better food education. You only have to consider the progress your First Lady, Mrs. Obama, has achieved lately by launching her "Let's Move" campaign—a wonderful initiative, if I may say so. With manufacturers making their "Healthy Weight Commitment" and pledging to cut 1.5 trillion calories a year from their products; with Walmart promising to sell products with less sugar, salt, and trans-fats, and to reduce their prices on healthy items like fresh fruits and vegetables; and with the first lady's big drive to improve healthy eating in schools and the excellent thought of urging doctors to write out prescriptions for exercise; these are marvelous ideas that I am sure will make a major difference.

Alas, in developing countries approximately 40 percent of food is lost between farm and market. Could that be remedied too, this time by better on-farm storage? And we should also remember that many, if not most, of the farmers in the developing world are achieving a fraction of the yields they might do if the soil was nurtured more with an eye to organic matter content and improved water management.

However, the really big issue we need to consider is how conventional, agri-industrial techniques are able to achieve the success they do, and how we measure that success. And here I come to the aspect of food production that troubles me most.

The well-known commentator in this country on food matters, Michael Pollan, pointed out recently that, so far, the combined market for local and organic food, both in the U.S. and Europe, has only reached around 2 or 3 percent of total sales. And the reason, he says, is quite simple. It is the difficulty in making sustainable farming more profitable for producers and sustainable food more affordable for consumers. With so much growing concern about this, my International Sustainability Unit carried out a study into why sustainable food production systems struggle to make a profit, and how it is that intensively produced food costs less. The answer to that last question may seem obvious, but my I.S.U. study reveals a less apparent reason.

It looked at five case studies and discovered two things: firstly, that the system of farm subsidies is geared in such a way that it favors overwhelmingly those kinds of agricultural techniques that are responsible for the many problems I have just outlined. And secondly, that the cost of that damage is not factored into the price of food production. Consider, for example, what happens when pesticides get into the water supply. At the moment, the water has to be cleaned up at enormous cost to consumer water bills; the primary polluter is not charged. Or take the emissions from the manufacture and application of nitrogen fertilizer, which are potent greenhouse gases. They, too, are not costed at source into the equation.

This has led to a situation where farmers are better off using intensive methods and where consumers who would prefer to buy sustainably produced food are unable to do so because of the price. There are many producers and consumers who want to do the right thing but, as things stand, "doing the right thing" is penalized. And so this raises an admittedly difficult question—has the time arrived when a long, hard look is needed at the way public subsidies are generally geared? And should the recalibration of that gearing be considered so that it helps healthier approaches and "techniques"? Could there be benefits if public finance were redirected so that subsidies are linked specifically to farming practices that are more sustainable, less polluting, and of wide benefit to the public interest, rather than what many environmental experts have called the curiously "perverse" economic incentive system that too frequently directs food production?

The point, surely, is to achieve a situation where the production of health- 30 ier food is rewarded and becomes more affordable and that the Earth's capital is not so eroded. Nobody wants food prices to go up, but if it is the case that the present low price of intensively produced food in developed countries is actually an illusion, only made possible by transferring the costs of cleaning up pollution or dealing with human health problems onto other agencies, then could correcting these anomalies result in a more beneficial arena where nobody is actually worse off in net terms? It would simply be a more honest form of accounting that may make it more desirable for producers to operate more sustainably—particularly if subsidies were redirected to benefit sustainable systems of production. It is a question worth considering, and I only ask it because my concern is simply that we seek to produce the healthiest food possible from the healthiest environment possible—for the long term—and to ensure that it is affordable for ordinary consumers. . . .

I am a historian, not an economist, but what I am hinting at here is that it is surely time to grasp one of the biggest nettles of all and re-assess what has become a fundamental aspect of our entire economic model. As far as I can see, responding to the problems we have with a "business as usual" approach towards the way in which we measure G.D.P. offers us only short-term relief. It does not promise a long-term cure. Why? Because we cannot possibly maintain the approach in the long term if we continue to consume our planet as rapaciously as we are doing. Capitalism depends upon capital, but our capital ultimately depends upon the health of Nature's capital. Whether we like it or not, the two are in fact inseparable.

There are alternative ways to growing our food which, if used with new technology—things like precision irrigation, for instance—would go a very long way to resolving some of the problems we face. If they are underpinned by smarter financial ways of supporting them, they could strengthen the resilience of our agriculture, marine, and energy systems. We could ensure a means of supply that is capable of withstanding the sorts of sudden fluctuations on international markets which are bound to come our way, as the price of oil goes up and the impact of our accelerating disruption of entire natural systems becomes greater.

In essence what I am suggesting here is something very simple. We need to include in the bottom line the true costs of food production— the true financial costs and the true costs to the Earth. It is what I suppose you could call "Accounting for Sustainability," a name I gave to a project I set up six years ago, initially to encourage businesses to expand their accounting process so that it incorporates the interconnected impact of financial, environmental, and social elements on their long-term performance. What if Accounting for Sustainability was applied to the agricultural sector? This was certainly the implicit suggestion in a recent and very important study by the U.N. The Economics of Ecosystems and Biodiversity, or T.E.E.B., assessed the multi-trillion-dollar importance to the world's economy of the natural world and concluded that the present system of national accounts needs to be upgraded rapidly so they include the health of natural capital, and thereby accurately reflect how the services offered by natural ecosystems are performing—let alone are paid for. Incidentally, to create a genuine market for such services—in the same way as a carbon market has been created—could conceivably make a substantial contribution to reducing poverty in the developing world.

This is very important. If we hope to redress the market failure that will otherwise blight the lives of future generations, we have to see that there is a direct relationship between the resilience of the planet's ecosystems and the resilience of our national economies. . . .

It is, I feel, our apparent reluctance to recognize the interrelated nature 35 of the problems and therefore the solutions, that lies at the heart of our predicament and certainly of our ability to determine the future of food. How we deal with this systemic failure in our thinking will define us as a civilization and determine our survival. Ladies and gentlemen, let me end by reminding you of the words of one of your own founding fathers and visionaries. It was George Washington who entreated your forebears to "Raise a standard to which the wise and honest can repair; the rest is in the hands of God"—and, indeed, as so often in the past, in the hands of your great country, the United States of America.

Understanding the Text

1. What do you know about Prince Charles, and how does his personal history give him a unique platform to speak about the future of food?

2. According to Prince Charles, what issues will affect the future of food?

3. Why is Prince Charles committed to making positive impacts on the future of food? What impact does he hope to make?

Response and Reflection

4. Prince Charles argues that the central problem with industrialized food production is a failure of values, which he blames on "anomalies that exist behind the scenes." What does he mean by anomalies? What anomalies is he talking about?

5. What was the International Assessment of Agricultural Knowledge, Science and Technology for Development study conducted by the United Nations in 2008? What were its findings? Why is Prince Charles so pleased with them?

Making Connections

6. What does Prince Charles say about Michelle Obama's "Let's Move" program? Why does he think ideas like hers are sure to make a difference? What kind of difference? Do you agree? Why or why not?

7. Prince Charles critiques some of Blake Hurst's ("The Omnivore's Delusion") conclusions about the difference between the industrialized food system and sustainable food systems. What arguments made by Hurst does Prince Charles reject? How? What counter-evidence does he offer? Which position do you find more compelling? Why?

8. Prince Charles states that his main hope is that "we seek to produce the healthiest food possible from the healthiest environment possible — for the long term — and to ensure that it is affordable for ordinary consumers." Which authors in this chapter make suggestions for the future of food that would help Prince Charles achieve his goals? Describe how their suggestions would help make Prince Charles's desired end a reality.

9. "Nature" plays an important role in Prince Charles's conception of the future of food. How does Prince Charles cast Nature? Compare his depiction to the depiction of Nature offered by at least two other authors.

Ecology and Community

Fritjof Capra

Fritjof Capra is an Austrian-born physicist, writer, and systems theorist. He is a founding director of the Center for Ecoliteracy in Berkeley, California, and is on the faculty of Schumacher College, an international center for ecological studies in London, England. Capra is the author of several best-selling books, including *The Tao of Physics*, *Steering Business Toward Sustainability*, edited with Gunter Pauli, and *The Web of Life*.

Capra's work focuses on the networked relationships of living systems, and he speaks regularly on holistic and systems thinking to professional and academic audiences. The following essay was first delivered to a group of school administrators in 1994, and it provides an overview of the basic principles of ecology. As you read the essay, think about what Capra is saying about life, communities, and the ways we think about our place in the world.

The understanding of community is extremely important today, not only for our emotional and spiritual well-being, but for the future of our children and, in fact, for the survival of humanity.

As you well know, we are faced with a whole series of global environmental problems which are harming the biosphere and human life in alarming ways that may soon become irreversible. The great challenge of our time is to create sustainable communities; that is, social and cultural environments in which we can satisfy our needs without diminishing the chances of future generations.

In our attempts to build and nurture sustainable communities we can learn valuable lessons from ecosystems, which *are* sustainable communities of plants, animals, and microorganisms. In over four billion years of evolution, ecosystems have developed the most intricate and subtle ways of organizing themselves so as to maximize sustainability.

There are laws of sustainability which are natural laws, just as the law of gravity is a natural law. In our science in past centuries, we have learned a lot about the law of gravity and similar laws of physics, but we have not learned very much about the laws of sustainability. If you go up to a high cliff and step off it, disregarding the laws of gravity, you will surely die. If we live in a community, disregarding the laws of sustainability, as a community we will just as surely die in the long run. These laws are just as stringent as the laws of physics, but until recently they have not been studied.

The law of gravity, as you know, was formalized by Galileo° and 5
Newton,° but people knew about stepping off cliffs long before Galileo
and Newton. Similarly, people knew about the laws of sustainability long
before ecologists in the twentieth century began to discover them. In
fact, what I'm going to talk about today is nothing that a ten-year-old
Navajo boy or Hopi girl who grew up in a traditional Native American
community would not understand and know. In preparing this presentation, I discovered that if you really try to distill the essence of the laws
of sustainability, it's very simple. The more you go to the essence, the
simpler it is.

What I want you to understand is the essence of how ecosystems organize themselves. You can abstract certain principles of organization and
call them the principles of ecology; but
it is not a list of principles that I want
you to learn. It's a pattern of organization I want you to understand. You
will see that whenever you formalize
it and say, "This is a key principle, and
this is a key principle," you don't really
know where to start, because they all
hang together. You have to understand
all of them at the same time. So, when
you teach the principles of ecology in
school, you can't say, "In third grade
we do interdependence and then in fourth grade we do diversity." One
cannot be taught or practiced without the others.

> "The great challenge of our time is to create sustainable communities; that is, social and cultural environments in which we can satisfy our needs without diminishing the chances of future generations."

What I'm going to do, then, is describe how ecosystems organize
themselves. I'll present to you the very essence of their principles of
organization.

Relationships

When you look at an ecosystem—say at a meadow or a forest—and you
try to understand what it is, the first thing you recognize is that there are
many species there. There are many plants, many animals, many micro-
organisms. And they're not just an assemblage or collection of species.
They are a community, which means that they are interdependent; they
depend on one another. They depend on one another in many ways, but
the most important way in which they depend on one another is a very

Galileo: (1564–1642), Italian physicist and astronomer.
Newton: Sir Isaac Newton (1642–1727), English philosopher and mathematician;
formulator of the law of gravity.

existential way—they eat one another. That's the most existential interdependence you can imagine.

Indeed, when ecology was developed in the 1920s, one of the first things people studied were feeding relationships. At first, ecologists formulated the concept of food chains. They studied big fish eating smaller fish, which eat still smaller fish, and so on. Soon these scientists discovered that these are not linear chains but cycles, because when the big animals die, they in turn are eaten by insects and bacteria. The concept shifted from food chains to food cycles.

And then they found that various food cycles are actually interlinked, so the focus again shifted, from food cycles to food webs or networks. In ecology, this is what people are now talking about. They're talking about food webs, networks of feeding relationships. 10

These are not the only examples of interdependence. The members of an ecological community, for example, also give shelter to one another. Birds nest in trees and fleas nest in dogs and bacteria attach themselves to the roots of plants. Shelter is another important kind of interdependent relationship.

To understand ecosystems, then, we need to understand relationships. That's a key aspect of the new thinking. Also, always keep in the back of your minds that when I talk about ecosystems I'm talking about communities. The reason we're studying ecosystems here is so that we can learn about building sustainable human communities.

So we need to understand relationships, and this is something that runs counter to the traditional scientific enterprise in Western culture. Traditionally in science, we have tried to measure and weigh things, but relationships cannot be measured and weighed. Relationships need to be mapped. You can draw a map of relationships that shows the connections between different elements or different members of the community. When you do that, you discover that certain configurations of relationships appear again and again. These are what we call patterns. The study of relationships leads us to the study of patterns. A pattern is a configuration of relationships appearing repeatedly.

The Study of Form and Pattern

So this study of ecosystems leads us to the study of relationships, which leads us to the notion of pattern. And here we discover a tension that has been characteristic in Western science and philosophy throughout the ages. It is a tension between the study of substance and the study of form. The study of substance starts with the question, What is it made of? The study of form starts with the question, What is its pattern? Those are two very different approaches. Both of them have existed throughout our scientific and philosophical tradition. The study of pattern began with the Pythagoreans° in Greek antiquity, and the study of substance began at the same time with Parmenides, Democritus, and with various philosophers who asked: What is matter made of? What is reality made of? What are its ultimate constituents? What is its essence?

In asking this question, the Greeks came up with the idea of four fundamental elements: earth, fire, air, and water. In modern times, these were recast into the chemical elements; many more than four, but still the basic elements of which all matter consists. In the nineteenth century, Dalton° identified the chemical elements with atoms, and with the rise of atomic physics in our century the atoms were reduced to nuclei and electrons, and the nuclei to other subatomic particles. 15

Similarly, in biology the basic elements first were organisms, or species. In the eighteenth and nineteenth centuries there were very complex classification schemes of species. Then, with the discovery of cells as the common elements in all organisms, the focus shifted from organisms to cells. Cellular biology was at the forefront of biology. Then the cell was broken down into its macromolecules, into the enzymes and proteins and amino acids and so on, and molecular biology was the new frontier. In all of this endeavor, the question always was: What is it made of? What is its ultimate substance?

At the same time, throughout the same history of science, the study of pattern was always there, and at various times it came to the forefront, but most times it was neglected, suppressed, or sidelined by the study of substance. As I said, when you study pattern, you need to map the pattern, whereas the study of substance is the study of quantities that can be measured. The study of pattern, or of form, is the study of quality, which requires visualizing and mapping. Form and pattern must be visualized.

This is a very important aspect of studying patterns, and it is the reason why, every time the study of pattern was in the forefront, artists contributed significantly to the advancement of science. Perhaps the two most famous examples are Leonardo da Vinci, whose scientific life was a study of pattern, and the German poet Goethe in the eighteenth century, who made significant contributions to biology through his study of pattern.

This is very important to us as parents and educators, because the study of pattern comes naturally to children; to visualize pattern, to draw pattern, is natural. In traditional schooling this has not been encouraged.

Pythagoreans: pertaining to Pythagoras (ca. 570–490 BCE), an ancient Greek philosopher and mathematician.
Dalton: John Dalton (1766–1844), English chemist and physicist.

Art has been sort of on the side. We can make this a central feature of ecoliteracy: the visualization and study of pattern through the arts.

Now, recognizing that the study of pattern is central to ecology, we can 20 then ask the crucial question: What is the pattern of life? At all levels of life—organisms, parts of organisms, and communities of organisms—we have patterns, and we can ask: What is the characteristic pattern of life? . . . I could give you a fairly technical description of the characteristics of the pattern of life; but here I want to concentrate on its very essence.

Networks

The first step in answering this question, and perhaps the most important step, is a very easy and obvious one: the pattern of life is a network pattern. Wherever you see the phenomenon of life, you observe networks. Again, this was brought into science with ecology in the 1920s when people studied food webs—networks of feeding relationships. They began to concentrate on the network pattern. Later on, in mathematics, a whole set of tools was developed to study networks. Then scientists realized that the network pattern is not only characteristic of ecological communities as a whole, but of every member of that community. Every organism is a network of organs, of cells, of various components; and every cell is a network of similar components. So what you have is networks within networks. Whenever you look at life you look at networks.

Then you can ask: What is a network and what can we say about networks? The first thing you see when you draw a network is that it is nonlinear; it goes in all directions. So the relationships in a network pattern are nonlinear relationships. Because of this nonlinearity, an influence or message may travel around a cyclical path and come back to its origin.

In a network you have cycles and you have closed loops; these loops are feedback loops. The important concept of feedback, which was discovered in the 1940s, in cybernetics, is intimately connected with the network pattern. Because you have feedback in networks, because an influence travels around a loop and comes back, you can have self-regulation; and not only self-regulation but self-organization. When you have a network—for instance, a community—it can regulate itself. The community can learn from its mistakes, because the mistakes travel and come back along these feedback loops. Then you can learn, and next time around you can do it differently. Then the effect will come back again and you can learn again, in steps.

So the community can organize itself and can learn. It does not need an outside authority to tell it "You guys did something wrong." A community has its own intelligence, its own learning capability.

In fact, every living community is always a learning community. Development and learning are always part of the very essence of life because of this network pattern.

Self-Organization

As soon as you understand that life is networks, you understand that the 25 key characteristic of life is self-organization, so if somebody asks you, "What is the essence of life? What is a living organism all about?" you could say, "It is a network and because it is a network it can organize itself." This answer is simple, but it's at the very forefront of science today. And it is not generally known. When you go around in academic departments, this is not the answer you will hear. What you will hear is "Amino Acids," "Enzymes," and things like that; very complex information, because that is the inquiry into substance: What is it made of?

It is important to understand that, in spite of the great triumphs of molecular biology, biologists still know very little about how we breathe or how a wound heals or how an embryo develops into an organism. All of the coordinating activities of life can only be grasped when life is understood as a self-organizing network. So self-organization is the very essence of life, and it's connected with the network pattern.

When you look at the network of an ecosystem, at all these feedback loops, another way of seeing it, of course, is as recycling. Energy and matter are passed along in cyclical flows. The cyclical flows of energy and matter—that's another principle of ecology. In fact, you can define an ecosystem as a community where there is no waste.

Of course, this is an extremely important lesson we must learn from nature. This is what I focus on when I talk to business people about introducing ecoliteracy into business. Our businesses are now designed in a linear way—to consume resources, produce goods, and throw them away. We need to redesign our businesses to imitate the cyclical processes of nature rather than to create waste. Paul Hawken° has recently written about this very eloquently in his book *The Ecology of Commerce.*

So we have interdependence, network relationships, feedback loops; we have cyclical flows; and we have many species in a community. All of this together implies cooperation and partnership. As various nutrients are passed along through the ecosystem, the relationships we observe are many forms of partnership, of cooperation. In the nineteenth century, the Darwinists and Social Darwinists talked about the competition in nature, the fight—"Nature, red in tooth and claw." In the twentieth

Paul Hawken: (b. 1946), environmentalist, entrepreneur, journalist, and best-selling author.

century, ecologists have discovered that in the self-organization of ecosystems cooperation is actually much more important than competition.
We constantly observe partnerships, linkages, associations, species living
inside one another depending on one another for survival. Partnership
is a key characteristic of life. Self-organization is a collective enterprise.

We see that these principles—interdependence, network patterns, 30
feedback loops, the cyclical flows of energy and matter, recycling, cooperation, partnership—are all different aspects, different perspectives on
one and the same phenomenon. This is how ecosystems organize themselves in a sustainable way.

Understanding the Text

1. In paragraph 2, Capra offers a short definition of *sustainable communities.*
   What is this definition? Do you agree with how he's defined the concept?

2. How does Capra compare ecosystems in nature to human communities?
   Why does he make this comparison? In what ways are the ecosystems and
   the human communities connected?

3. Capra uses four subheads in the article: "Relationships," "The Study of Form
   and Pattern," "Networks," and "Self-Organization." How do these four sections explain the essence of ecosystems?

Reflection and Response

4. What is Capra's goal with this essay? How does his writing style help him
   accomplish this goal? Who is his audience?

5. In paragraph 23, under Networks, Capra talks about self-regulation and
   self-organization. How do these two terms relate to sustainability?

6. What does Capra suggest about Western culture and Western ways of thinking? In what ways would Capra suggest we change our conceptions of life
   and communities?

Making Connections

7. Find other definitions of sustainability, either in this book or through online
   research. How are these definitions similar to or different from what Capra
   presents?

8. Capra mentions two artists who contributed significantly to the advancement
   of science: Leonardo da Vinci and Johann Wolfgang von Goethe. Do a little
   research on one or both of these men. How did they combine art and science? What can we learn about the patterns of life through their work?

9. This essay argues for a nontraditional approach to education — one focusing
   on ecology, interconnections, and sustainable thinking. What do you think
   about such an approach? Can you find examples of it being used in education today?

Green Jobs

Peter Poschen and Michael Renner

Peter Poschen is the Director for the Job Creation and Enterprise Development Department of the International Labor Office, or ILO, where he leads a global program on green jobs. Poschen is a visiting professor at the University of Freiburg, teaching classes in Socio-Economic Sustainability. He has written over twenty articles about environmental issues and sustainability and is the author of *Decent Work, Green Jobs and the Sustainable Economy: Solutions for Climate Change and Sustainable Development* (2015).

Michael Renner studies the connections between the environment and employment as a Senior Researcher for the World Watch Institute. In 2007, Renner became the lead author of a United Nations Environment Programme report on green jobs. He is also a Senior Advisor to the Institute for Environmental Security and a member of the Netherlands Organization for Scientific Research.

In this report published by the International Monetary Fund (IMF), Poschen and Renner define exactly what a green job is, as well as explaining the debate surrounding the term. The authors argue that given the evidence, combatting climate change will not limit the growth of the job market. In fact, they argue that job opportunities will increase due to the manufacturing of environmental goods. As you read, consider whether you would be interested in working a green job.

Protecting the environment can go hand in hand with economic prosperity and job opportunities

U.S. President Barack Obama's 2013 climate action plan and 2015 clean power plan triggered fierce debate. Senate Republican Leader Mitch McConnell denounced the proposals. "Declaring a 'War on Coal' is tantamount to declaring a 'War on Jobs,'" McConnell told the Senate. "It's tantamount to kicking the ladder out from beneath the feet of any Americans struggling in today's economy."

The perception that there is a trade-off—an intrinsic contradiction between protecting the climate and the environment on one hand and economic prosperity and job opportunities on the other—is common among government decision makers north and south, as well as among business leaders.

Doubt also lingers among voters. An annual poll of U.S. voters' top concerns conducted by the Pew Research Center showed a clear pattern over the past decade. During years of high growth with ample employment opportunities, environmental sustainability and jobs and family incomes were tied as the two top concerns of the American public, at 57 percent each. But when the Great Recession started to sting in 2009, fear of job losses became a top concern of 82 percent of the U.S. public; the environment worried only 41 percent, and climate change was all but eclipsed at 30 percent (Pew Research Center, 2009).

When jobs are the priority and environmental protection is perceived as causing job losses, political will is hard to muster.

But do we really have to choose between protecting the environment 5 and generating enough good jobs?

The answer has profound implications in a world where more than 200 million people are unemployed and almost half of those who are working have unstable and often low-paying jobs (ILO, 2015). An additional 400 million jobs will be needed to counter the unemployment that surged in the wake of the Great Recession and to offer opportunity for the young job seekers who will enter the labor market over the next decade, mostly in developing economies (ILO, 2014).

Is There a Dilemma?

On the face of it, those who worry seem to have a point. The sectors that most directly contribute to climate change and other environmental degradation are agriculture, the fishing industry, forestry, energy, resource-intensive manufacturing, waste management, construction, and transportation. These sectors are the targets of policies designed to mitigate climate change, and together they employ more than 1.5 billion people, or about half the global workforce (see ILO, 2012).

But evidence accumulated over the past decade suggests that combating climate change does not preclude the growth of a healthy job market.

Green jobs — those that reduce the environmental impact of economic activity — are critical to shifting to a more environmentally sustainable economy. They fall into two broad categories: production of environmental goods such as windmills and energy-efficient buildings, and services such as recycling and work related to reducing emissions and energy and resource consumption, such as environmental and work safety and facilities and logistics management.

> "Green jobs — those that reduce the environmental impact of economic activity — are critical to shifting to a more environmentally sustainable economy."

Two key measures for reducing greenhouse gas emissions are imple- 10 mentation of low-carbon energy production and lowering emissions from land use as a result of deforestation.

Cleaner energy production requires cutting back on fossil fuels, which release carbon dioxide when used to generate electricity or for heating and transportation. Substituting less-polluting fossil fuels such as natural gas for big polluters like coal and heavy oil offers temporary help. But ultimately, renewable energy such as power from water, wind, and sun and from sustainable biomass are what it will take to keep emissions from exceeding the ability of carbon sinks in the atmosphere and oceans to absorb them.

Industries producing renewable energy have started to generate a significant number of jobs. One of the first global assessments estimated direct and indirect employment in the renewable industry at 2.3 million as of 2006 (UNEP and others, 2008). Comparable assessments subsequently raised that figure to 7.7 million in 2014 (IRENA, 2015) (see chart). Well over half of these jobs are in emerging market economies such as Brazil, China, and India, which play a major role in the move toward renewable energy sources such as solar heat and power, biogas, and biofuels.

Investment in renewable energy has grown fast (though it slowed somewhat after 2011) and installed capacity has soared (UNEP, 2015; REN21, 2015). So far, however, renewables have not expanded at the expense of fossil fuels. Will there be job losses when that happens? Aren't renewables costing jobs because they are often more expensive than the fossil alternative? And does it make a difference if the equipment for renewable energy needs to be imported? These questions flag an important point: the full economic and employment impact of a switch to low-carbon energy must be assessed for the economy as a whole.

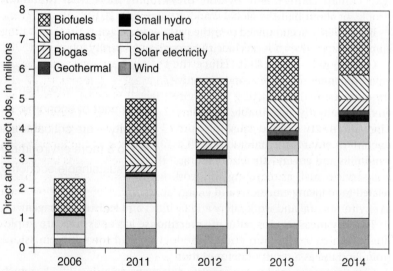

Data from UNEP and others (2008) for 2006 data; ILO (2012) for 2011 data; and IRENA (2013, 2015) for 2012–2014 data. Information from International Monetary Fund.

Millions of jobs have been lost in the fossil fuel industry over recent decades, in particular in coal, where only 9.8 million jobs remained in 2014 (Greenpeace International and others, 2015). These losses are not the result of climate policies, however, but of productivity gains in coal mines and international trade. When renewables start to displace fossil fuels, the direct comparison suggests a net gain, which is confirmed by a look at the broader economy. Filling up a car's gas tank and use of electricity in a fossil-fuel- or nuclear-based power grid do not generate many jobs, either in the energy sector or among its suppliers. These sectors generate far fewer jobs than average consumption spending does. By contrast, renewables and investment in energy efficiency generate more jobs than demand for other goods and services.

How do the cost of renewables and the prospect of equipment imports 15 affect net jobs? The cost of renewable energy has dropped unexpectedly quickly over the past decade. The International Renewable Energy Agency reckons renewables are already the cheapest way to provide electricity to the 1.3 billion people who lack access to clean energy, mostly in Africa and south Asia (IRENA, 2013). And power from wind is commercially viable in a growing number of countries—such as Brazil and the United States and in Europe—with extensive and diversified power grids.

While much of the debate on climate change and employment has focused on renewables, another and more significant source of jobs from decarbonization has received much less attention. Substantial efficiency gains are technically feasible and economically viable in industry, housing, transportation, and services. Businesses can make a profit and households can enjoy real savings. And spending the surplus on things other than fossil energy will boost an economy's employment.

For example, the United States is a diversified economy that imports substantial amounts of equipment for renewables. A recent study carefully considered economy-wide effects of reducing emissions by 40 percent by 2030 through a mix of clean energy and energy efficiency (Pollin and others, 2014). It concluded that $200 billion a year in investment would generate a net gain of about 2.7 million jobs: 4.2 million in environmental goods and service sectors and their supply chains but 1.5 million lost in the shrinking fossil- and energy-intensive sectors. The net gain of 2.7 million jobs would reduce the unemployment rate in the 2030 U.S. labor market by about 1.5 percentage points—for example, from 6.5 percent to 5 percent. The authors consider this a conservative estimate; for example, it does not take into account the 1.2 to 1.8 million jobs likely gained from reinvested savings.

Other studies show similar results. A review of 30 studies covering 15 countries and the European Union as a whole found appreciable actual or potential net gains in employment (Poschen, 2015). Most studies considering emission targets in line with the ambitions announced for a Paris agreement in December find net gains on the order of 0.5 to 2.0 percent of total employment, or 15 million to 60 million additional jobs. In emerging market economies such as Brazil, China, Mauritius, and South Africa, green investment was found to accelerate economic growth and employment generation when compared with business as usual. Several studies suggest that more ambitious climate targets would generate greater gains in employment (for a discussion of particular countries, see Poschen, 2015).

In addition to new jobs, active climate policies offer other potential employment and social gains. Increasing productivity and sustainability in sectors that are critical for the climate, such as agriculture, construction, and waste management, could, for example, lift hundreds of millions of small-scale farmers out of poverty (ILO, 2012).

Policies Matter

There is an important caveat, however. In addition to the emission- 20 reduction targets themselves and the technology deployed to meet them, policy plays a crucial role in determining economic and employment outcomes. Price has long dominated economists' debate on the right instruments for effective climate and other environmental policies. Getting the prices to speak the truth—that is, to communicate the full economic cost of consuming a good or service, including the negative impact on climate—has long been seen as the key to changing economies without destabilizing the planet's climate system in unmanageable ways.

While few would question that correct pricing is a necessary component of an effective climate policy, it may not be sufficient. In terms of employment outcomes, how the right prices are achieved also matters. Studies consistently show that environmental tax reform ("eco-tax") that shifts the burden away from labor and income—by reducing payroll and income levies—and toward emissions and resource consumption, through instruments such as carbon taxes, can both reduce emissions and create jobs (see ILO, 2011).

The proceeds from an eco-tax can also help defuse three negative effects of the transition to a climate-friendly economy.

The *first* blow is the loss of jobs in some sectors—such as coal mining, coal-fired power generation, heavy industry, and transportation—as a result of restructuring of the economy. Thanks to the lower cost of labor achieved through the reduction of payroll taxes and social protection charges, even sectors that are resource intensive can maintain employment when energy and raw material costs increase. While the limited available evidence suggests only moderate job losses from restructuring, losses do tend to occur in areas already damaged by globalization and where there are few alternatives to the mining or energy sector. In such cases, investment in social security, worker retraining, and diversification of the local economy are needed to discourage workers and politicians from the affected regions from blocking decarbonization.

A *second* worry concerns income rather than jobs. Increases in energy prices—whether from eco-taxes or the elimination of energy subsidies—are socially regressive. Wealthier households benefit the most from subsidies because they consume more energy, while poorer households spend a disproportionate share of their income on energy and on goods and services that are energy hogs, such as food and transportation. Efforts to end subsidies that encourage consumption and waste have been successful only when a portion of the savings has compensated those excessively affected.

The *third* downside is the need to adapt to climate change itself. 25 International Labour Organization research estimates the cost of unmitigated climate change will be 7 percent of world output in 2050 (ILO, 2011); the Organisation for Economic Co-operation and Development and the World Bank expect it to be even higher. Even if there is agreement in Paris and ambitious reductions of emissions are achieved in coming decades, the greenhouse gases already in the atmosphere will do increasing damage. Even with the current less than 1 degree Celsius increase over pre-industrial temperatures, erratic weather patterns and extreme weather have begun to alter ecosystems, erode infrastructure, disrupt business activity, destroy jobs and livelihoods, and kill people on an unprecedented scale (Poschen, 2015). Climate change has also become a main driver of forced migration.

To cope with these climate stresses, investment is urgently needed to fortify affected sectors, communities, and businesses. Social protection is vital to help the poor weather the storms and droughts brought on by climate change. Employment-intensive investment can build infrastructure for adaptation and bring jobs to deprived communities in the process. Watersheds can be rehabilitated by planting trees and conserving soil to prevent floods downstream, and small dams and reservoirs can harvest water for the dry season. South Africa's Expanded Public Works Programme pursues a mix of poverty reduction and community-led development through investment in economic, social, and environmental infrastructure, including water management, wetlands protection, and forest rehabilitation. It generates several hundred thousand jobs for local communities and vulnerable groups. India's Rural Employment Guarantee Act provides at least 100 days of wage employment a fiscal year to every rural household whose adult members volunteer for unskilled manual work in projects such as soil and water conservation, reforestation, and flood protection. In fiscal year 2012/13, this program put 50 million rural households to work (Poschen, 2015).

Managing change

Some of the greatest opportunities to reduce emissions come from improvements in production processes and operations. Unlike changes in hardware, which take time, substantial reductions in emissions and resource consumption can be achieved in the short and medium term. The Pollution Prevention Pays program run by manufacturing conglomerate 3M since the 1970s shows what is possible. The company asks workers to identify opportunities to save resources and reduce emissions and implements those deemed viable. Between 1990 and 2011, 3M reduced its greenhouse gas emissions by 72 percent: it reduced its emission of pollutants by 1.4 million tons and saved $1.4 billion in the process (3M, 2011).

This is just one example of the many ways businesses and employer organizations, workers, and trade unions—the so-called world of work—can help achieve the transition to a low-carbon, sustainable economy. Green businesses can save through more energy- and resource-efficient processes. Managers and workers can deploy energy- and resource-efficient technology. When businesses and workers are not prepared and lack the skills to install and use new technology, the economic and environmental gains are diminished or lost altogether. Skills shortages have been a bottleneck for green growth in almost all economic sectors and virtually all countries around the world.

Ministries of labor, employer organizations, and trade unions have also made major contributions to climate change adaptation. In Germany, these three actors launched the largest program to improve energy efficiency in the world, with more than €120 billion invested to date. In Brazil, these key players have integrated renewable energy into large-scale social housing programs. In India and South Africa, they pioneered the use of social protection systems—ensuring social security and adequate working conditions—for the purpose of rehabilitation work and increased resilience to climate change. And in Bangladesh, the Ministry of Labour and Employment scaled up training for renewable energy installers, which brought solar home systems to more than 4 million rural homes.

The environmental and social challenges the world is now facing are 30 closely linked. We have neither the time nor the money to deal with them separately or consecutively. Mobilizing employers, workers, and trade unions will be critical to putting a climate agreement into practice and garnering the needed political support. And that's one ladder that can mean a step up for rich and poor alike.

References

1. 3M Company, 2011, *Sustainability Report* (Maplewood, Minnesota).

2. Greenpeace International, Global Wind Energy Council, and SolarPowerEurope, 2015, *Energy [R]evolution: A Sustainable World Energy Outlook 2015* (Amsterdam and Brussels).

3. International Labour Organization (ILO), 2011, "Economic Transition following an Emission Tax in a RBC Model with Endogenous Growth," EC-IILS Joint Discussion Paper Series No. 17 (Geneva).

4. ———, 2012, *Working Towards Sustainable Development: Opportunities for Decent Work and Social Inclusion in a Green Economy* (Geneva).

5. ———, 2014, *Global Employment Trends 2014* (Geneva).

6. ———, 2015, *World Employment and Social Outlook—Trends 2015* (Geneva).

7. International Renewable Energy Agency (IRENA), 2013, IOREC 2012: International Off-Grid Renewable Energy Conference. Key Findings and Recommendations (Abu Dhabi).

8. ———, 2015, *Renewable Energy and Jobs: Annual Review 2015* (Abu Dhabi).

9. Pollin, Robert, Heidi Garrett-Peltier, James Heintz, and Bracken Hendricks, 2014, "Green Growth: A U.S. Program for Controlling Climate Change and Expanding Job Opportunities," Center for American Progress and Political Economy Research Institute report (Washington).

10. Poschen, Peter, 2015, *Decent Work, Green Jobs and the Sustainable Economy* (Sheffield, United Kingdom: Greenleaf).

11. Quirion, Philippe, and Damien Demailly, 2008, *–30% de CO2 = + 684000 emplois: L'équation gagnante pour la France*, World Wildlife France report (Paris).

12. REN21, 2015, *Renewables 2015 Global Status Report* (Paris).

13. United Nations Environment Programme (UNEP), 2015, *Global Trends in Renewable Energy Investment 2015*, Frankfurt School-UNEP Collaborating Centre report (Frankfurt).

14. ———, and others, 2008, *Green Jobs: Towards Decent Work in a Sustainable, Low-Carbon World* (Nairobi).

Understanding the Text

1. What exactly is a green job?

2. Identify the employment sectors the authors claim most heavily impact climate change and explain why they might oppose green jobs.

3. What are the three negative effects from the transition to a "climate-friendly economy"?

Reflection and Response

4. In your opinion, do the authors effectively demonstrate their point about the potential growth of green jobs? What did they do well and what could have been added for better clarity?

5. Do you believe green jobs will become more popular in the future? Why or why not?

6. Would you be interested in a green job? If so, in what sector of the green economy would you like to work?

Making Connections

7. Find the website for Green Careers or some other green company. List the things you find on the website that would encourage you to work for them. How do they market and promote their "green" perspective?

8. Research whether there are any green jobs in your local community. How does this company impact your community through their work?

Whatever Happened to the Drive for Campus Sustainability?

Scott Carlson

Scott Carlson is a Senior Writer for the *Chronicle of Higher Education*, where he covers issues surrounding the cost and value of higher education, campus planning, energy, and sustainability. Carlson has contributed to publications such as the *Baltimore Sun*, *Urbanite*, and Grist, a website for environmental news.

"Whatever Happened to the Drive for Campus Sustainability?" discusses the slow shift away from college campuses being a site of activism for sustainability. The author proposes that campus sustainability has hit a plateau and that rewriting curriculum, among other things, may be the key to revamping environmental activism. As you read the article, think about what campus sustainability should look like, whether you see it happening on your campus, and how you can get involved.

Indonesia is on fire. Greenland is melting. The strongest tropical cyclone on record hit Mexico last month. Scientists and policy makers are worried about energy security, drought, the health of ocean life, the implications of global urbanization, and what it all means for a socioeconomically divided world.

This is the future student environmentalists saw coming, and higher education was supposed to lead the way to take on those challenges.

A decade ago, campus sustainability emerged as the big activist movement at many colleges. Students, with allies on the faculty and staff, pushed their colleges to reduce waste, construct green buildings, buy local food, and run on renewable energy.

By 2010, nearly 700 leaders had signed the American College & University Presidents' Climate Commitment, which bound them to reduce greenhouse-gas emissions to zero. The Association for the Advancement of Sustainability in Higher Education was one of the sector's fastest-growing organizations, and there was buzz everywhere about new bike-sharing programs, campus gardens and farms, even green sports teams.

In the past few years, that buzz has become more like a low background hum. Sustainability no longer gets as much campus attention as sexual assault, affordability, or institutional viability. Among the top results of a Google search for "the sustainable university" now are links to articles about financially troubled institutions. 5

"Sustainability no longer gets as much campus attention as sexual assault, affordability, or institutional viability."

What happened? It's not as if students stopped caring. Nearly 70 percent of them believe that responding to climate change should be a federal priority, according to the most recent Freshman Survey by the Higher Education Research Institute at the University of California at Los Angeles. Pushing colleges to divest holdings in fossil-fuel companies has gained traction. And the sustainability association is still going: Its annual conference in Minneapolis last month was the biggest ever, with more than 2,300 attendees, many of them students or recent graduates.

But a question permeated discussions there: Now that campus sustainability has been talked about for 10 years, what do the next 10 hold? Advocates see the movement at a precarious moment. It has been largely confined to operations—highly visible projects in green power, recycling, or local food—and needs now to be infused into missions and curricula.

"Sustainability in higher ed is at such a critical point, such a threshold, and we are all collectively holding our breath," says Denice H. Wardrop, a professor of geography and ecology and the director of Pennsylvania State University's Sustainability Institute. She has started working with a group of sustainability directors from major research universities—a club dubbed the "Big 10 and Friends"—to outline how sustainability principles contribute to their educational priorities.

Penn State took a potentially significant step last month: In a public draft of its new strategic plan, the university included "ensuring a sustainable future" as one of six values that will guide its educational mission. Fund raisers are pitching the university's sustainability efforts to donors.

At other colleges, projects chug along, but there are broad worries 10 about the future of institutional commitments. Stephenie Presseller, sustainability manager at Moraine Valley Community College, near Chicago, says green efforts started small there, with the formation of a "green team" of faculty and staff members and students in 2007. Eventually the scale grew, as Moraine Valley signed the presidents' climate commitment and pursued climate neutrality.

Broader Proposition

But lately momentum has stalled, says Ms. Presseller. At many colleges, sustainability has gone from being an ambitious campaign pursued by enthusiasts to just another office, just another staff member. The administration at Moraine Valley still strongly supports sustainability, she says, but it competes for attention: "The biggest conversation right now is budget."

Colleagues at other colleges, she says, worry that leaders will cut sustainability programs, thinking of them as just a fad of the new millennium.

Those were heady days for the sustainability movement. In 2006, *An Inconvenient Truth* hit movie screens, and *The Omnivore's Dilemma* lined shelves at the bookstore, jump-starting popular conversations about climate change and local food. In 2007, high gas prices got people talking about energy and limits on natural resources. After the recession hit, in 2008, pundits like Thomas L. Friedman called for a "green revolution," while the activist Van Jones outlined a "green new deal" that would put people to work retrofitting buildings with insulation and solar panels.

The enthusiasm was dampened after Republicans won decisive victories in the 2010 elections, and climate-change skeptics took control in Washington. Leading environmental causes—like the Keystone XL pipeline and campaigns to divest from fossil-fuel companies—became slogs with incremental victories. And in the wake of the recession, survival was the main focus for many colleges.

That was also true for the main sustainability groups—the sus-   15
tainability association and Second Nature, which runs the climate commitment—amid stumbles and leadership transitions. Anthony Cortese, Second Nature's co-founder and longtime president, who had been a key figure in the sustainability movement, retired in 2012.

The Association for the Advancement of Sustainability in Higher Education, meanwhile, has had three executive directors since then. Meghan Fay Zahniser, who has been with the group since 2009 and took over as executive director in December, says that during those tumultuous years, the organization had overestimated its membership and had budget deficits. Many employees were laid off or quit, making it hard to forge ahead.

"Instead of being able to advance sustainability in higher education, which is what we're here to do, it was crisis management," Ms. Zahniser says. "It's disheartening that we lost momentum."

Now the group is ramping back up. It plans to connect more campus-based sustainability programs, allowing directors to collaborate on projects and to share resources and information, and to help them make the case for sustainability. In partnership with a consulting firm, it is providing free help to colleges looking to set up big green-power deals. The goal is to get one gigawatt—or 1,000 megawatts—of energy in higher education from renewable rather than fossil-fuel sources.

The climate commitment, too, is getting a reboot. Second Nature has added a "resilience commitment," encouraging colleges to work with local communities to adapt to climate change. The group says it will also drop colleges from the signatory list because many have not kept up progress on going "climate neutral." Integrity, says Timothy Carter, the group's new president, is more important than numbers.

It makes sense for colleges to take the lead on sustainability because 20 of their longevity, nonprofit status, and educational missions, says Blaine Collison, managing director of network services at Altenex, the consulting firm working with the sustainability association on the green-gigawatt goal. Corporations are not going to take up climate neutrality, he says. That and many other sustainability efforts, he says, colleges are uniquely positioned to pursue.

The big challenge for the campus-sustainability movement, as Mr. Collison sees it, is finding the right way to present its agenda. "Some of these people have done a fabulous job talking about the broader value proposition," he says, pointing to students and sustainability directors moving around the exhibit hall at the last month's sustainability conference. "Some of them have not."

Advocates should be able to make the case for how green programs can reduce costs and risks in energy prices, appeal to prospective students and forward-thinking businesses, or keep educational programs relevant for the future.

"Some of them are still talking about rescuing a polar bear on an iceberg," says Mr. Collison. "If they don't get to the next level, we're doomed."

Understanding the Text

1. Why does the author discuss the "Freshman Survey" from the University of California and the sustainability association's annual conference? What do the numbers he cites say about campus sustainability or sustainability in general?

2. What is the "biggest conversation" surrounding campus sustainability right now, and how does it pose a threat to sustainability efforts on college campuses?

3. What does Blaine Collison have to say about why college campuses are the right setting for sustainability activism?

Reflection and Response

4. Do you believe that college campuses should lead the effort in sustainability causes? Why or why not?

5. What are some things colleges could do to become more sustainable without having to increase the budget?

6. Based on your experience at your campus, what might be the potential challenges for a sustainability activist group?

Making Connections

7. Does your campus have a sustainability club or have they made any changes to be more sustainable? How do these changes impact the students and the outside community?

8. Research another university's sustainability efforts. Do they have a mission statement regarding sustainability? Is their budget available to view, and how do they use the budget to develop sustainability initiatives?

9. The American Association of Sustainability in Higher Education (AASHE) is the largest organization for sustainability in U.S. colleges and universities. Spend some time browsing the AASHE website, and report to your instructor on what you find.

Why Social Media and Sustainability Should Go Hand in Hand

Jeff Sutton

Jeff Sutton is the vice president of Parallax, a brand-building company with the goal of helping businesses market their company through sustainable means. Sutton has previously been the director of business development at London's Salterbaxter MSLGROUP, a premier sustainability creative communications agency.

Initially published on triplepundit.com in 2016, this article explores the effectiveness of using social media to promote sustainability. The author examines brands like H&M, Toms, and SAP to provide an example of how companies can use their large social media platforms to promote environmental activism. As you read, consider which brands you shop have participated in sustainability movements and how they use social media to their advantage.

Over the last decade, we have seen social media and sustainability play an increasingly important role in the way that businesses conduct and talk about themselves. Together they've helped push corporations to new levels of transparency, opened up avenues for greater engagement, forced organizations to rethink their role in society, and aligned individuals, businesses and communities around shared purpose.

Unfortunately, for all the common benefits, many companies still haven't quite figured out how to put the two together effectively. This article[1] puts it bluntly: "Brands are blowing a major opportunity to communicate their sustainability initiatives to millions of consumers with social media updates that are 'inane, safe and saccharinely artificial in their bonhomie.'"

[A study] by the Pew Research Center in association with the John S. and James L. Knight Foundation found that "clear majorities of Twitter (63 percent) and Facebook users (63 percent) now say each platform serves as a source for news about events and issues outside the realm of friends and family." Social media has quickly taken a front seat to other, more traditional ways of receiving information—and the trend shows no sign of slowing down. If sustainability messages seek to reach specific audiences, it stands to reason that those messages should be communicated through the audiences' preferred channels.

---

[1] https://www.foodnavigator-usa.com/Article/2015/12/11/Big-food-firms-are-climate-smart-but-social-media-stupid?utm_content=buffere9381&utm_medium=social&utm_source=twitter.com&utm_campaign=buffer#

But identifying proper channels is only one part of the equation. Organizations must then engage audiences—no short order in light of the amount of messaging vying for users' attention. According to cio .com, Facebook's 1.44 billion monthly active users sent out an average of 31.25 million messages *every minute*—and that's only one network. That figure doesn't even begin to account for LinkedIn, Twitter, Snapchat, Instagram, Medium or any of the host of other social media apps available to users. Making sustainability messages stand out in an ocean of noise means doing more than posting links to a report PDF.

What follows are a few examples of companies that have risen above the social media fracas to effectively engage with audiences on their sustainability initiatives.

H&M

In April, H&M utilized a strong social media push to raise awareness for the brand's sustainability programs and reduce the environmental footprint of the fast fashion industry. Using the hashtag #WorldRecycleWeek, H&M encouraged customers to "close the loop in fashion" by recycling unwanted clothes at their stores.

While many people have questioned the fast fashion giant's agenda or decried it as corporate greenwashing, leveraging the power of social media provided H&M the platform to engage with these critics and respond publicly through exposure and awareness of their sustainability efforts. No matter what you thought, if you interacted with the brand at all, it was there, in your face, and difficult not to notice.

The social media rollout surrounding #WorldRecycleWeek is especially noteworthy in the way that it catered directly to audiences and demographics that might not normally spend much time thinking about issues of sustainability. Rather than using social media to call out facts and data about the environmental ills of non-recycled clothing (very little of which would likely have resonated with an average fast-fashion consumer), an online music video by musician M.I.A. urging H&M's customers to "rewear it" and be part of H&M's sustainability initiative. Through their efforts, H&M used social media to "dress up" its sustainability story.

Toms

Outside the realm of environmental sustainability, Toms shoes regularly uses social media to promote initiatives in the arena of social good. Once a year, Toms promotes One Day Without Shoes using the hashtag #withoutshoes on social media to raise awareness about children's health. Last year, they gave shoes to over 27,000 children based on the results of the one-day campaign.

[. . .] Consistency is a key part of building a corporate social responsibility (CSR) message that resonates, and Toms provides a compelling example of how effective this can be. Last year marked the ninth year that Toms has run the campaign—and it's already planning for 2017. This consistency demonstrates that the brand is dedicated to their initiative for the long term. And, more importantly, it gives the campaign a chance to grow. Next year will likely be bigger than ever.

SAP

Outside the realm of consumer-facing brands, the software corporation SAP has also found success in communicating its sustainability efforts through social media. The company created its own separate Twitter account (@sap4good) for its sustainability and corporate responsibility initiatives and posts enough compelling content to gain over 15,000 followers. Much of the company's success rests in the fact that SAP posts more than what it is doing for sustainability on its own end; it also utilizes social media by engaging with users, collaborating with peers and sharing interesting posts from other organizations—creating a truly social community.

As sustainability professionals, we regularly have the opportunity to interact with organizations that are doing amazing things to benefit our planet. Some of these organizations have become quite adept at interweaving sustainability initiatives into their social media—and they've begun to reap the benefits. Unfortunately, we've also seen examples of initiatives that go largely unnoticed, simply because they aren't communicated effectively.

"For many of these corporations, the challenge is understanding how to effectively engage their audiences on these topics using language and media that may be foreign to the boardroom."

For many of these corporations, the challenge is understanding how to effectively engage their audiences on these topics using language and media that may be foreign to the boardroom.

For brands and marketers, social media channels have been a mainstay for years, but many corporate communications and sustainability teams have been much slower to adapt. Which is a shame, because social media is more than just a marketing tool, it's a powerful platform for driving engagement on critical issues with your core audiences (and ones that historically may have been unheard). In today's world, if you're not talking about these issues on the channels where your audience lives, the message may be interpreted that they aren't important enough to discuss.

There is no debating that both social media and sustainability have proven to be a tremendous force for positive change. Now as sustainability practitioners, we just have to find the creativity and desire to learn how to use them together.

Understanding the Text

1. What does the Pew Research Center say about how social media users interact with different platforms? Why does the author include that information?
2. What is greenwashing and why might some people accuse H&M of being guilty of it?
3. Why is consistency key in social media activism?

Reflection and Response

1. Does a brand's sustainability beliefs impact your decision to buy their product? Why or why not?
2. If you ran a company with sustainability as one of its core values, how would you use social media to promote your brand's sustainability efforts?

Making Connections

1. How do environmental organizations or institutions like the Sierra Club or the Environmental Protection Agency use social media to further their causes? Examine an organization or institution's social media accounts. How do they use each platform? Is one platform more effective than another?
2. Look up the two hashtags the author mentions in the article. What are some of the images/post associated with the hashtag? What types of responses did they receive?
3. "Whatever Happened to the Drive for Campus Sustainability?" pointed out that economics is the largest challenge in promoting and furthering campus sustainability. Social media is free. Devise a social media plan that could help a campus promote their sustainability initiatives.

Thomas Goeppert/EyeEm/Getty Images

5 | How Is Sustainability a Transnational Issue?

Sustainability is a global, transnational issue, although that may not be obvious to readers of this textbook who live in the United States. The world we live in is increasingly interconnected, and the challenges of sustainability are not limited by geographic, cultural, or political boundaries. Choices about how to manage resources, facilitate social equity, and address environmental degradation affect all of us, no matter where those choices and the resulting actions originate or are centralized. Though some of the subjects addressed in this chapter may seem far removed from your daily life, it is important to remember that we are all part of the same global system. Sustainability is not just a local, regional, and a national issue — it is a global issue as well.

This chapter highlights sustainability and environmental challenges as global, transnational subjects. It begins with a report written by the UN Panel on Global Sustainability entitled "Resilient People, Resilient Planet," which has been described as "a second Brundtland report" because it provides a twenty-five-year update on progress toward international sustainability. You may wish to read the two UN reports together — see Chapter 2 for the first report. The next two articles (by McKibben and Galloway) examine climate change and its relationship to the fuel sources we use; compare the ways in which these two articles address fossil fuels and the integration of renewable energy sources as both global and local concerns. The three articles that follow examine the "other" 70% of the earth's surface that is often forgotten in discussions of sustainability — the oceans and seas. Smith's article looks at ocean fisheries and speculates on various methods to better use oceanic food sources, while Frischkorn explains the threat of coral bleaching and the possibilities of genetic manipulation to save the world's reefs. Similarly, Evans-Pughe looks at scientific and technological options to reduce the giant floating vortex of plastic known as the Great Pacific Garbage Patch. The next two pieces examine sustainability issues on continents beyond North America. Hay's article touches on the devastating impact of Japan's Fukushima nuclear disaster five years after it occurred, as well as debates surrounding Japan's nuclear future. Kameri-Mbote's article addresses the challenges of sustainability on the African continent. The last piece in the chapter looks more broadly at the limits of global resources (Moyer and Storrs), providing a speculative view of the Earth's future.

These nine readings provide just a glimpse into the many transnational issues involving sustainability. Many other sustainability-related topics are worth considering, and you may encounter some of them through your research and writing. As you read the selections in this chapter, consider the ways in which the issues they address transcend various borders, the ways in which these seemingly remote topics influence and affect you, and the degree to which your choices can impact global sustainability.

Resilient People, Resilient Planet: A Future Worth Choosing

The United Nations Panel on Global Sustainability

In January 2012, the United Nations Panel on Global Sustainability released a report containing recommendations for world leaders to put sustainable development into practice and to mainstream sustainability into global economic policy. The report, titled "Resilient People, Resilient Planet: A Future Worth Choosing," was coauthored by more than twenty global political figures led by Tarja Halonen, president of the Republic of Finland, and Jacob Zuma, president of the Republic of South Africa.

The report has been referred to as "a second Brundtland report," designed to be visionary and describe a future twenty years from now. This excerpt serves as the panel's introduction to the ninety-five-page report. As you read this introduction, consider what it suggests about our future and what world leaders could do to shape it.

The Panel's Vision

Today our planet and our world are experiencing the best of times, and the worst of times. The world is experiencing unprecedented prosperity, while the planet is under unprecedented stress. Inequality between the world's rich and poor is growing, and more than a billion people still live in poverty. In many countries, there are rising waves of protest reflecting universal aspirations for a more prosperous, just and sustainable world.

Every day, millions of choices are made by individuals, businesses and governments. Our common future lies in all those choices. Because of the array of overlapping challenges the world faces, it is more urgent than ever that we take action to embrace the principles of the sustainable development agenda. It is time that genuine global action is taken to enable people, markets and governments to make sustainable choices.

The need to integrate the economic, social and environmental dimensions of development so as to achieve sustainability was clearly defined a quarter of a century ago. It is time to make it happen. The opportunities for change are vast. We are not passive, helpless victims of the impersonal, determinist forces of history. And the exciting thing is that we can choose our future.

The challenges we face are great, but so too are the new possibilities that appear when we look at old problems with new and fresh eyes. These possibilities include technologies capable of pulling us back from the planetary brink; new markets, new growth and new jobs emanating from game-changing products and services; and new approaches to public and private finance that can truly lift people out of the poverty trap.

The truth is that sustainable development is fundamentally a question 5 of people's opportunities to influence their future, claim their rights and voice their concerns. Democratic governance and full respect for human rights are key prerequisites for empowering people to make sustainable choices. The peoples of the world will simply not tolerate continued environmental devastation or the persistent inequality which offends deeply held universal principles of social justice. Citizens will no longer accept governments and corporations breaching their compact with them as custodians of a sustainable future for all. More generally, international, national and local governance across the world must fully embrace the requirements of a sustainable development future, as must civil society and the private sector. At the same time, local communities must be encouraged to participate actively and consistently in conceptualizing, planning and executing sustainability policies. Central to this is including young people in society, in politics and in the economy.

> "Sustainable development is fundamentally a question of people's opportunities to influence their future, claim their rights and voice their concerns."

Therefore, the long-term vision of the High-level Panel on Global Sustainability is to eradicate poverty, reduce inequality and make growth inclusive, and production and consumption more sustainable, while combating climate change and respecting a range of other planetary boundaries. This reaffirms the landmark 1987 report by the World Commission on Environment and Development, "Our Common Future" (United Nations document A/42/427, annex), known to all as the Brundtland° report.

But what, then, is to be done if we are to make a real difference for the world's people and the planet? We must grasp the dimensions of the challenge. We must recognize that the drivers of that challenge include unsustainable lifestyles, production and consumption patterns and the impact of population growth. As the global population grows from 7 billion to almost 9 billion by 2040, and the number of middle-class consumers increases by 3 billion over the next 20 years, the demand for resources will rise exponentially. By 2030, the world will need at least 50 percent more food, 45 percent more energy and 30 percent more water—all at

---

Brundtland: the Brundtland Commission, a UN organization of world leaders formed in 1983 whose mission was to unite countries to pursue sustainable development together. See the Brundtland report in Chapter 2, page 74.

a time when environmental boundaries are throwing up new limits to supply. This is true not least for climate change, which affects all aspects of human and planetary health.

The current global development model is unsustainable. We can no longer assume that our collective actions will not trigger tipping points as environmental thresholds are breached, risking irreversible damage to both ecosystems and human communities. At the same time, such thresholds should not be used to impose arbitrary growth ceilings on developing countries seeking to lift their people out of poverty. Indeed, if we fail to resolve the sustainable development dilemma, we run the risk of condemning up to 3 billion members of our human family to a life of endemic poverty. Neither of these outcomes is acceptable, and we must find a new way forward.

A quarter of a century ago, the Brundtland report introduced the concept of sustainable development to the international community as a new paradigm for economic growth, social equality and environmental sustainability. The report argued that sustainable development could be achieved by an integrated policy framework embracing all three of those pillars. The Brundtland report was right then, and it remains right today. The problem is that, 25 years later, sustainable development remains a generally agreed concept, rather than a day-to-day, on-the-ground, practical reality. The Panel has asked itself why this is the case, and what can now be done to change that.

The Panel has concluded that there are two possible answers. They 10 are both correct, and they are interrelated. Sustainable development has undoubtedly suffered from a failure of political will. It is difficult to argue against the principle of sustainable development, but there are few incentives to put it into practice when our policies, politics and institutions disproportionately reward the short term. In other words, the policy dividend is long-term, often intergenerational, but the political challenge is often immediate.

There is another answer to this question of why sustainable development has not been put into practice. It is an answer that we argue with real passion: the concept of sustainable development has not yet been incorporated into the mainstream national and international economic policy debate. Most economic decision makers still regard sustainable development as extraneous to their core responsibilities for macroeconomic management and other branches of economic policy. Yet integrating environmental and social issues into economic decisions is vital to success.

For too long, economists, social activists and environmental scientists have simply talked past each other—almost speaking different languages, or at least different dialects. The time has come to unify the disciplines, to develop a common language for sustainable development that transcends the warring camps; in other words, to bring the sustainable development paradigm into mainstream economics. That way, politicians and policymakers will find it much harder to ignore.

That is why the Panel argues that the international community needs what some have called "a new political economy" for sustainable development. This means, for example: radically improving the interface between environmental science and policy; recognizing that in certain environmental domains, such as climate change, there is "market failure," which requires both regulation and what the economists would recognize as the pricing of "environmental externalities," while making explicit the economic, social and environmental costs of action and inaction; recognizing the importance of innovation, new technologies, international cooperation and investments responding to these problems and generating further prosperity; recognizing that an approach should be agreed [on] to quantify the economic cost of sustained social exclusion—for example, the cost of excluding women from the workforce; recognizing that private markets alone may be incapable of generating at the scale necessary to bring about a proper response to the food security crisis; and requiring international agencies, national governments and private corporations to report on their annual sustainable development performance against agreed sustainability measures. We must also recognize that this is a core challenge for politics itself. Unless the political process is equally capable of embracing the sustainable development paradigm, there can be no progress.

The scale of investment, innovation, technological development and employment creation required for sustainable development and poverty eradication is beyond the range of the public sector. The Panel therefore argues for using the power of the economy to forge inclusive and sustainable growth and create value beyond narrow concepts of wealth. Markets and entrepreneurship will be a prime driver of decision-making and economic change. And the Panel lays down a challenge for our governments and international institutions: to work better together in solving common problems and advancing shared interests. Quantum change is possible when willing actors join hands in forward-looking coalitions and take the lead in contributing to sustainable development.

The Panel argues that by embracing a new approach to the political economy of sustainable development, we will bring the sustainable development paradigm from the margins to the mainstream of the global economic debate. Thus, both the cost of action and the cost of inaction will become transparent. Only then will the political process be able to summon both the arguments and the political will necessary to act for a sustainable future.

The Panel calls for this new approach to the political economy of sustainable development so as to address the sustainable development challenge in a fresh and operational way. That sustainable development is right is self-evident. Our challenge is to demonstrate that it is also rational—and that the cost of inaction far outweighs the cost of action.

The Panel's report makes a range of concrete recommendations to take forward our vision for a sustainable planet, a just society and a growing economy:

- It is critical that we embrace a new nexus between food, water and energy rather than treating them in different "silos." All three need to be fully integrated, not treated separately if we are to deal with the global food security crisis. It is time to embrace a second green revolution—an "ever-green revolution"—that doubles yields but builds on sustainability principles;

- It is time for bold global efforts, including launching a major global scientific initiative, to strengthen the interface between science and policy. We must define, through science, what scientists refer to as "planetary boundaries," "environmental thresholds" and "tipping points." Priority should be given to challenges now facing the marine environment and the "blue economy";

- Most goods and services sold today fail to bear the full environmental and social cost of production and consumption. Based on the science, we need to reach consensus, over time, on methodologies to price them properly. Costing environmental externalities could open new opportunities for green growth and green jobs;

- Addressing social exclusion and widening social inequity, too, requires measuring them, costing them and taking responsibility for them. The next step is exploring how we can deal with these critical issues to bring about better outcomes for all;

- Equity needs to be at the forefront. Developing countries need time, as well as financial and technological support, to transition to sustainable development. We must empower all of society—especially women, young people, the unemployed and the most vulnerable and weakest sections of society. Properly reaping the demographic dividend calls on us to include young people in society, in politics, in the labor market and in business development;

- Any serious shift towards sustainable development requires gender equality. Half of humankind's collective intelligence and capacity is a resource we must nurture and develop, for the sake of multiple generations to come. The next increment of global growth could well come from the full economic empowerment of women;

- Many argue that if it cannot be measured, it cannot be managed. The international community should measure development beyond gross domestic product (GDP) and develop a new sustainable development index or set of indicators;

- Financing sustainable development requires vast new sources of capital from both private and public sources. It requires both mobilizing more public funds and using global and national capital to leverage global private capital through the development of incentives. Official development assistance will also remain critical for the sustainable development needs of low-income countries;

- Governments at all levels must move from a silo mentality to integrated thinking and policymaking. They must bring sustainable development to the forefront of their agendas and budgets and look at innovative models of international cooperation. Cities and local communities have a major role to play in advancing a real sustainable development agenda on the ground;

- International institutions have a critical role. International governance for sustainable development must be strengthened by using existing institutions more dynamically and by considering the creation of a global sustainable development council and the adoption of sustainable development goals;

- Governments and international organizations should increase the resources allocated to adaptation and disaster risk reduction and integrate resilience planning into their development budgets and strategies;

- Governments, markets and people need to look beyond short-term transactional agendas and short-term political cycles. Incentives that currently favor short-termism in decision-making should be changed. Sustainable choices often have higher up-front costs than business as usual. They need to become more easily available, affordable and attractive to both poor consumers and low-income countries.

This Panel believes it is within the wit and will of our common humanity to choose for the future. This Panel therefore is on the side of hope. All great achievements in human history began as a vision before becoming a reality. The vision for global sustainability, producing both a resilient people and a resilient planet, is no different.

In 2030, a child born in 2012—the year our report is published—will turn 18. Will we have done enough in the intervening years to give her the sustainable, fair and resilient future that all of our children deserve? This report is an effort to give her an answer.

Understanding the Text

1. What are the key issues identified in this report?
2. What is the relationship between this report and the Brundtland report, published twenty-five years earlier? See the excerpt on page 74.
3. How does this excerpt from "Resilient People, Resilient Planet" define "sustainable development"?

Reflection and Response

4. Who do you see as the primary audience for this report? Who are the secondary audiences?
5. In what ways does this selection portray sustainability as a social issue, involving human rights and social justice? Do you think this is an important aspect of sustainability?
6. What is the relationship between science and policy? Why is there often a breakdown between these two arenas? What can be done to bring them closer together?

Making Connections

7. This report ties racial and gender equality into sustainability. Do some research on race, gender, and sustainability, and report on your findings.
8. Find the complete report online by searching for "Resilient People, Resilient Planet: A Future Worth Choosing." Choose one excerpt from the report and analyze it.
9. Compare and contrast the focus, tone, recommendations, or any other aspect of this report with its predecessor, the Brundtland report. What similarities and differences do you see?

A Moral Atmosphere

Bill McKibben

Bill McKibben is an environmentalist, author, and founder of 350.org, a global grassroots climate movement. His organization has conducted over 20,000 rallies in every country except for North Korea. In 2014, McKibben was awarded the Right Livelihood Prize, an international award given to those whose work addresses the world's most pressing challenges. McKibben is the author of fifteen books, including *The End of Nature*, one of the first books published to address climate change. He has contributed to publications such as the *New Yorker*, *National Geographic*, and *Rolling Stone*.

Originally published in *Orion* magazine in 2013, this article poses the question: What is the right amount of action one person can take to combat climate change? McKibben points out that even though our society currently depends on fossil fuels, fighting against climate change is not a hypocritical issue. Instead, McKibben points out that the problem lies not with the individual but with the system as a whole. As you read, consider the impact you as an individual might have on the earth as well as your ties to larger systems.

The list of reasons for not acting on climate change is long and ever-shifting. First it was "there's no problem"; then it was "the problem's so large there's no hope." There's "China burns stuff too," and "it would hurt the economy," and, of course, "it would hurt the economy." The excuses are getting tired, though. Post Sandy (which hurt the economy to the tune of $100 billion) and the drought ($150 billion), 74 percent of Americans have decided they're very concerned about climate change and want something to happen.

But still, there's one reason that never goes away, one evergreen excuse not to act: "you're a hypocrite." I've heard it ten thousand times myself—how can you complain about climate change and drive a car/have a house/turn on a light/raise a child? This past fall, as I headed across the country on a bus tour to push for divestment from fossil fuels, local newspapers covered each stop. I could predict, with great confidence, what the first online comment from a reader following each account would be: "Do these morons not know that their bus takes gasoline?" In fact, our bus took biodiesel—as we headed down the East Coast, one job was watching the web app that showed the nearest station pumping the good stuff. But it didn't matter, because the next comment would be: "Don't these morons know that the plastic fittings on their bus, and the tires, and the seats are all made from fossil fuels?"

Bill McKibben speaking against the Keystone XL pipeline in Washington, D.C., in 2013.
Ken Cedeno/Getty Images

Actually, I do know—even a moron like me. I'm fully aware that we're embedded in the world that fossil fuel has made, that from the moment I wake up, almost every action I take somehow burns coal and gas and oil. I've done my best, at my house, to curtail it: we've got solar electricity, and solar hot water, and my new car runs on electricity—I can plug it into the roof and thus into the sun. But I try not to confuse myself into thinking that's helping all that much: it took energy to make the car, and to make everything else that streams into my life. I'm still using far more than any responsible share of the world's vital stuff.

And, in a sense, that's the point. If those of us who are trying really hard are still fully enmeshed in the fossil fuel system, it makes it even clearer that what needs to change are not individuals but precisely that system. We simply can't move fast enough, one by one, to make any real difference in how the atmosphere comes out. Here's the math, obviously imprecise: maybe 10 percent of the population cares enough to make strenuous efforts to change—maybe 15 percent. If they all do all they can, in their homes and offices and so forth, then, well . . . nothing much shifts. The trajectory of our climate horror stays about the same.

But if 10 percent of people, once they've changed the light bulbs, work 5
all-out to change the system? That's enough. That's more than enough. It would be enough to match the power of the fossil fuel industry, enough

to convince our legislators to put a price on carbon. At which point none of us would be required to be saints. We could all be morons, as long as we paid attention to, say, the price of gas and the balance in our checking accounts. Which even dummies like me can manage.

I think more and more people are coming to realize this essential truth. Ten years ago, half the people calling out

> "If those of us who are trying really hard are still fully enmeshed in the fossil fuel system, it makes it even clearer that what needs to change are not individuals but precisely that system."

hypocrites like me were doing it from the left, demanding that we do better. I hear much less of that now, mostly, I think, because everyone who's pursued those changes in good faith has come to realize both their importance and their limitations. Now I hear it mostly from people who have no intention of changing but are starting to feel some psychic tension. They feel a little guilty, and so they dump their guilt on Al Gore because he has two houses. Or they find even lamer targets.

For instance, as college presidents begin to feel the heat about divestment, I've heard from several who say, privately, "I'd be more inclined to listen to kids if they didn't show up at college with cars." Which in one sense is fair enough. But in another sense it's avoidance at its most extreme. Young people are asking college presidents to stand up to oil companies. (And the ones doing the loudest asking are often the most painfully idealistic, not to mention the hardest on themselves.) If as a college president you do stand up to oil companies, then you stand some chance of changing the outcome of the debate, of weakening the industry that has poured billions into climate denial and lobbying against science. The action you're demanding of your students—less driving—can't rationally be expected to change the outcome. The action they're demanding of you has at least some chance. That makes you immoral, not them.

Yes, they should definitely take the train to school instead of drive. But unless you're the president of Hogwarts, there's a pretty good chance there's no train that goes there. Your students, in other words, by advocating divestment, have gotten way closer to the heart of the problem than you have. They've taken the lessons they've learned in physics class and political science and sociology and economics and put them to good use. And you—because it would be uncomfortable to act, because you don't want to get crosswise with the board of trustees—have summoned a basically bogus response. If you're a college president making the argument that you won't act until your students stop driving cars, then clearly you've failed morally, but you've also failed intellectually. Even if you just built an energy-efficient fine arts center, and installed a bike path, and dedicated an acre of land to a college garden, you've failed. Even if you drive a Prius, you've failed.

Maybe especially if you drive a Prius. Because there's a certain sense in which Prius-driving can become an out, an excuse for inaction, the twenty-first-century equivalent of "I have a lot of black friends." It's nice to walk/drive the talk; it's much smarter than driving a semi-military vehicle to get your groceries. But it's become utterly clear that doing the right thing in your personal life, or even on your campus, isn't going to get the job done in time; and it may be providing you with sufficient psychic comfort that you don't feel the need to do the hard things it will take to get the job done. It's in our role as citizens—of campuses, of nations, of the planet—that we're going to have to solve this problem. We each have our jobs, and none of them is easy.

Understanding the Text

1. Why does the author say that one person's sustainable actions do not have much of an effect of the environment?

2. What percentage of people would it take to make an actual difference and why?

3. How is a college president immoral, in McKibben's view, if he/she doesn't divest from fossil fuel companies?

Reflection and Response

4. Where do you stand on the issues McKibben brings up? Do you believe that a real change can be made by people alone? Or do you believe that since the world we live in is powered by fossil fuels, the effort is in vain?

5. How does the author's tone support his argument?

6. What fossil fuels have you used today? Is there a way that you could cut back on your use or find an alternative method?

Making Connections

7. There are dozens of comments, in varying perspectives, on this piece on OrionMagazine.org, where this article was originally published. Find a comment you agree with and expand on their argument.

8. Research Bill McKibben's organization, 350.org. Does this site support the argument he makes in this article? Why or why not?

Renewable Energy for a Sustainable Future

Nanette Galloway

Nanette Galloway is a staff writer for *Downbeach Current*, which is a part of Shore News Today, a local news source for coastal towns in New Jersey. Her articles cover local government, community, and school news. Galloway has been the recipient of two New Jersey Press Association journalism awards.

This blog posting provides a brief overview of our dependence on fossil fuels and the efforts to move toward renewable energy sources. As you read the article, think about the advantages of renewable energy, as well as the challenges we face in integrating them into society.

In 2015, the United States invested $44.1 billion in renewable energy. Yet for every dollar spent developing renewables, nearly $4 was spent to maintain the country's dependence on fossil fuels.

Oil, coal and natural gas are derived from the accumulated remains of ancient plants and animals. Burning these fuels releases the carbon from these ancient organisms into the atmosphere. This increases the amount of greenhouse gas and is considered to be one of the principal causes of global warming.

NASA, NOAA and other scientific agencies insist it is fact, not an opinion, that the burning of fossil fuels has increased global temperatures over the last century.

When we talk about renewable energy, we are talking about harnessing energy sources that are more or less consistent and will not be depleted.

The advantages of using renewables are obvious. Resources like the 5 sun, wind, hydroelectric, geothermal and biopower will not run out and do not release any damaging material.

Conversely, fossil fuels are nonrenewable. When burned, they release carbon dioxide and other particulates that are damaging to human health. Sulfur released through the burning of these fuels produces acid rain. As a result, coral reefs are dying through ocean acidification.

> "When we talk about renewable energy, we are talking about harnessing energy sources that are more or less consistent and will not be depleted."

The Renewable Electricity Futures Study found that an 80 percent renewable future is feasible with current available technology. This includes wind turbines, solar photovoltaic, biopower, geothermal and hydropower. A comprehensive study by the Department of Energy's

National Renewable Energy Laboratory shows that the United States could generate most of its electricity from renewable sources by 2050.

Countries around the world are embracing renewable technology. China is investing $361 billion into renewable energy to meet its long-term energy needs. Other countries like Sweden, Germany, Scotland and Ireland are racing toward being the first countries to be free of producing electricity from fossil fuels. Kenya, Uganda, Tanzania, India, Nepal, Brazil and Guyana are seeing rapid expansion of small-scale renewable systems. Countries with few resources are opting for renewables because they are not only the most environmentally sound, but also the cheapest options.

Developing renewable energy systems that will carry us far into the future is a better choice than propping up outdated systems where the fuel required will eventually run out. It is better to keep the carbon that is locked in fossil fuels in the ground, rather than releasing it back in the atmosphere. Investing in renewable energy is a far better choice for ensuring a sustainable future.

Understanding the Text

1. How do oil, coal, and natural gas increase greenhouse gases?
2. What are renewable and nonrenewable resources?
3. The author quotes The Renewable Electricity Futures Study. What does the study claim and why does the author believe their findings are important or noteworthy?

Reflection and Response

4. The author states that "for every dollar spent developing renewables, nearly $4 was spent to maintain the country's dependence on fossil fuels." Why is this significant?

5. If you had the choice, would you consider building a home or a business that used only renewable resources as a mode of electricity? Would you have any concerns about this choice?

Making Connections

6. Many scientists assert that burning fossil fuels has increased global temperatures. Is there a consensus on this topic? Do some research to find other opinions on this subject. Who makes these other arguments, and are they qualified to speak on the issue?

7. Research the prices of renewable resource technology, like solar panels and wind turbines. What do the prices suggest about the popularity of renewable energy?

The Coming Green Wave: Ocean Farming to Fight Climate Change

Brendan Smith

Brendan Smith is an oysterman and the cofounder of Voices for a Sustainable Future, a group that promotes sustainable living. Smith is also a senior fellow at the Progressive Technology Project. He has written for the *Los Angeles Times*, *The Guardian*, CBS News, and other publications.

This article originally appeared in 2011 in the *Atlantic*, a magazine that offers commentary on contemporary issues. In the article, Smith raises an important question: how can we use the oceans to save us from environmental problems? Smith also introduces the idea of seaweed farms and how they can grow large amounts of nutrient-rich food. As you read, think about the benefits of ocean farming and how this practice could impact climate change in the future.

For decades environmentalists have fought to save our oceans from the perils of overfishing, climate change, and pollution. All noble efforts—but what if environmentalists have it backward? What if the question is not how to save the oceans, but how the oceans can save us?

That is what a growing network of scientists, ocean farmers, and environmentalists around the world is trying to figure out. With nearly 90 percent of large fish stocks threatened by overfishing and 3.5 billion people dependent on the seas as their primary food source, these ocean farming advocates have concluded that aquaculture is here to stay.

But rather than monolithic factory fish farms, they see the oceans as the home of small-scale farms where complementary species are cultivated to provide food and fuel—and to clean up the environment and fight climate change. Governed by an ethic of sustainability, they are re-imagining our oceans with the hope of saving us from the grip of the ever-escalating climate, energy, and food crises.

The Death and Rebirth of the Ocean Farm

Ocean farming is not a modern innovation. For thousands of years cultures as diverse as the ancient Egyptians, Romans, Aztecs, and Chinese have farmed finfish, shellfish, and aquatic plants. Atlantic salmon have been farmed in Scotland since the early 1600s; seaweed was a staple food for American settlers.

Unfortunately, what was once a sustainable fishery has been mod- 5
ernized into large-scale industrial-style farming. Modeled on land-based
factory livestock farms, aquaculture operations are infamous for their
low-quality, tasteless fish pumped full of antibiotics and polluting local
waterways. According to a recent *New York Times* editorial, aquaculture
"has repeated too many of the mistakes of industrial farming—including
the shrinking of genetic diversity, a disregard for conservation, and the
global spread of intensive farming methods before their consequences
are completely understood."

> "Governed by an ethic of sustainability, [ocean farmers] are re-imagining our oceans with the hope of saving us from the grip of the ever-escalating climate, energy, and food crises."

Unsurprisingly, once information got out among the general public, "aquaculture" quickly became a dirty word. Industry responded with a strategy of mislabeling seafood and upping their marketing budgets, rather than investing in more sustainable and environmentally benign farming techniques.

But a small group of ocean farmers and scientists decided to chart a different course. Rather than relying on mono-aquaculture operations, these new ocean farms are pioneering multi-trophic° and sea-vegetable aquaculture, whereby ocean farmers grow abundant, high-quality seafood while improving, rather than damaging, the environment.

One example is Ocean Approved° in Maine, which cultivates seaweed that doubles as a nutrient-rich food source and a sponge for organic pollutants. Farmers in Long Island Sound are exploring diversifying small-scale organic shellfish farms with various species of seaweed to filter out the pollutants, mitigate oxygen depletion, and develop a sustainable source for fertilizer and fish meal. In southern Spain Veta La Palma designed its farm to restore wetlands, and in the process created the largest bird sanctuary in Spain, with over 220 species of birds.

Seaweed farms alone have the capacity to grow massive amounts of nutrient-rich food. Professor Ronald Osinga at Wageningen University in the Netherlands has calculated that a global network of "sea-vegetable" farms totaling 180,000 square kilometers—roughly the size of Washington state—could provide enough protein for the entire world population.

multi-trophic: multi-trophic aquaculture is a form of marine farming in which different plants and animals are raised together in a mutually beneficial environment.
Ocean Approved: an organization that produces vegetables from the sea with minimal impact to the environment.

Seaweed farms have the capacity to grow large amounts of nutrient-rich food, and oysters can act as an efficient carbon and nitrogen sink.

Vladislav Gajic/Shutterstock

The goal, according to chef Dan Barber—named one of the world's 10 most influential people by *Time* and a hero of the organic food movement—is to create a world where "farms restore instead of deplete" and allow "every community to feed itself."

But here is the real kicker: Because they require no fresh water, no deforestation, and no fertilizer—all significant downsides to land-based farming—these ocean farms promise to be more sustainable than even the most environmentally sensitive traditional farms.

Ramping up food production without increasing greenhouse gas emissions is vital if we are to survive the coming decades. But land-based food production is entering an era of crisis. The UN estimates that global grain production will plummet by 63 million metric tons this year alone mainly because of weather-related calamities like the Russian heat wave and the floods in Pakistan.

Bun Lai, world-renowned sustainable seafood chef, believes that:

If done right, this new generation of green aquaculture is poised to become the most sustainable form of farming on the planet. We need healthy food that protects rather than harms our climate and Earth. It is a key piece of the puzzle for building a sustainable future.

Nature's Climate Warriors: Seaweed and Shellfish

Rather than finfish, the anchor crops of the emerging green ocean farms are seaweed and shellfish—two gifted organisms that might well be mother nature's secret weapons to fight climate change.

Considered the "tree" of coastal ecosystems, seaweed uses photosyn- 15 thesis to pull massive amounts of carbon from the atmosphere—with some varieties capable of absorbing five times more carbon dioxide than land-based plants.

Seaweed is one of the fastest growing plants in the world; kelp, for example, grows up to 9–12 feet long in a mere three months. This tur-bo-charged growth cycle enables farmers to scale up their carbon sinks quickly. Of course, the seaweed grown to mitigate emissions would need to be harvested to produce carbon-neutral biofuels to ensure that the carbon is not simply recycled back into the air as it would be if the seaweed is eaten. The Philippines, China, and other Asian countries, which have long farmed seaweed as a staple food source, now view seaweed farms as an essential ingredient for reducing their carbon emissions.

Oysters also absorb carbon, but their real talent is filtering nitrogen out of the water column. Nitrogen is the greenhouse gas you don't pay attention to—it is nearly 300 times as potent as carbon dioxide, and according to the journal *Nature*, the second worst in terms of having already exceeded a maximum "planetary boundary." Like carbon, nitrogen is an essential part of life—plants, animals, and bacteria all need it to survive—but too much has a devastating effect on our land and ocean ecosystems.

The main nitrogen polluter is agricultural fertilizer runoff. All told, the production of synthetic fertilizers and pesticides contributes more than one trillion pounds of greenhouse gas emissions to the atmosphere globally each year. That's the same amount of emissions that are generated by 88 million passenger cars each year.

Much of this nitrogen from fertilizers ends up in our oceans, where nitrogen is now 50 percent above normal levels. According to the journal *Science*, excess nitrogen "depletes essential oxygen levels in the water and has significant effects on climate, food production, and ecosystems all over the world."

Oysters to the rescue. One oyster filters 30–50 gallons of water a 20 day—and in the process filters nitrogen out of the water column. Recent work done by Roger Newell of the University of Maryland shows that a healthy oyster habitat can reduce total added nitrogen by up to 20 percent. A three-acre oyster farm filters out the equivalent nitrogen load produced by 35 coastal inhabitants.

There is an array of projects sprouting up that use a mix of seaweed and shellfish to clean up polluted urban waterways and help communities prepare for the effects of climate change. One initiative, spearheaded by Dr. Charles Yarish of the University of Connecticut, is growing kelp and shellfish on floating lines in New York's Bronx River to filter nitrogen, mercury, and other pollutants out of the city's toxic waterways, with the goal of making them healthier, more productive, and more economically viable.

Then there is the emerging field of "oyster-tecture," dedicated to building artificial oyster reefs and floating gardens to help protect coastal communities from future hurricanes, sea level rise, and storm surges. Architect Kate Orff from the design firm SCAPE is developing urban aquaculture parks that use floating rafts and suspended shellfish long-lines to build more urban green space while improving the environment. She envisions the new urban ocean farmer as part shell fisherman tending to oyster reefs, and part landscaper, tending the above-surface floating parks.

In Connecticut, advocates are pushing for an expansion of the state's existing nitrogen credit trading program to include shellfish farms, thereby reimbursing oystermen for the nitrogen they filter from Long Island Sound each year. With new oyster operations sprouting up all around the country, rewarding "green fishermen" for the positive effect their farms have on the environment could be a model for how to stimulate job growth while saving the planet.

Farm Your Fuel, Power the Planet

Finding a clean replacement for existing biofuels is becoming increasingly urgent. A report commissioned by the European Union found biofuels from soy beans can create up to four times more climate-warming emissions than equivalent fossil fuels. Biofuels have also forced global food prices up by 75 percent—far more than previously estimated—according to a confidential World Bank study. And a recent report from the International Food Policy and Research Institute warned that U.S. government support for corn ethanol was a major factor behind this year's food price spikes.

Seaweed and other algae is increasingly looking like a viable substi- 25 tute. About 50 percent of seaweed's weight is oil, which can be used to make biodiesel for cars, trucks, and airplanes. Scientists at the University of Indiana recently figured out how to turn seaweed into biodiesel four times faster than other biofuels, and researchers at the Georgia Institute of Technology have discovered a way to use alginate extracted from kelp to ramp up the storage power of lithium-ion batteries by a factor of ten.

But unlike land-based biofuel crops, seaweed farming does not require fertilizers, forest clearing, water, or heavy use of fuel-burning machinery—and, as a result, according to the World Bank, has a negative carbon footprint. While the technology is still in development, farmers are eager to begin growing their own fuel and create some of the first closed energy loop farms on the planet.

The U.S. Navy has already developed the Riverine Combat ship and Seahawk helicopters powered by seaweed-based bio-diesel. The Pentagon views seaweed and other algae as a key component in their efforts to reduce their carbon footprint. According to Alan Shaffer, the Pentagon's principal deputy director of defense research and engineering:

The beauty with algae is that you can grow it anywhere and to grow it needs to absorb carbon dioxide, so it's not only a very effective fuel, in theory it's also a carbon sink. That's a pretty good deal.

The DOE estimates that seaweed biofuel can yield up to 30 times more energy per acre than land crops such as soybeans. According to *Biofuels Digest,*

Given the high oil yield from algae, some 10 million acres would be sufficient . . . to replace the total petro-diesel fuel in the United States today. This is about 1 percent of the total amount of acreage used in the United States today for grazing and farming.

The world's energy needs could be met by setting aside 3 percent of the world's oceans for seaweed farming. "I guess it's the equivalent of striking oil," says University of California, Berkeley, microbial biology professor Tasios Melis.

The Bitter Reality of Climate Change

These are urgent times, demanding creative and bold solutions. In his 30 best-selling book *Eaarth: Making Life on a Tough New Planet*, Bill McKibben breaks the news that climate change is no longer a future threat—it is here and now and we had better get our affairs in order.

Our oceans are already locked in a death spiral. According to the International Program on the State of the Ocean (IPSO)—a consortium of 27 of the top ocean experts in the world—the effects of climate change, ocean acidification, and oxygen depletion have already triggered a "phase of extinction of marine species unprecedented in human history." Simultaneously, greenhouse gas emissions are breaking records, exceeding even the worst-case scenario envisioned by scientists four years ago.

We face a bitter new reality: Mitigating the effects of climate change may force us to develop our seas to save them—and [our] planet. This re-imaging of the oceans will be heart-wrenching and controversial. Our waters are revered as some of the last wild spaces on Earth—ungoverned and untouched by human hands. If we develop our oceans, farms will someday dot coastlines, mirroring our agricultural landscape. But in the face of the escalating climate crisis, we have little choice but to explore new ways of sustaining humanity while protecting the planet.

As we search for new solutions, we cannot afford to repeat the errors made on land, subsidizing industrial-scale factory farms at the expense of environmental and food quality. Simply substituting destructive fishing fleets with destructive fish farms will only hasten the demise of our oceans.

Instead, we can learn from our mistakes and chart a new course guided by principles of sustainability and meeting social needs. This means dedicating portions of ocean to farming—while reserving large swaths for marine conservation parks. And rather than building sprawling ocean factories, we need [to] create decentralized networks of small-scale food and energy farms growing food, generating power, and creating jobs for local communities. While no panacea, ocean farming—carefully conceived—could be a vital part of reversing course and building a greener future.

All of us who hold dear the deep blue sea need to confront the brutal reality that if we ignore the largest environmental crisis of our generation, our wild oceans will be dead oceans. 35

Understanding the Text

1. What are some ways environmentalists suggest that the ocean could help us?
2. Which other cultures have used ocean farming? Why is it important to recognize its history?
3. How can seaweed farms help the environment? What is seaweed's relationship to atmospheric carbon?

Reflection and Response

4. Do you think ocean farming is a good way to combat environmental problems and protect our oceans? Explain why or why not.
5. This article makes some comparisons between industrial land-based farming and aquaculture. What are the negative aspects of these two methods of food production? How could they be improved?

Making Connections

6. This article mentions "overfishing." Do some research to find out exactly what this is and why it is detrimental to the environment. What are the major problems caused by overfishing?
7. Do some research on ocean farms. What are the possibilities and challenges of ocean farming? Which type of ocean farming seems most logical or beneficial?

A Blueprint for Genetically Engineering a Super Coral

Kyle Frischkorn

Kyle Frischkorn is a National Science Foundation Graduate Research Fellow at Columbia University, where he studies oceanography. His research specifically focuses on how micro-organisms interact with each other and their environment. Frischkorn is a frequent contributor to publications such as *GQ*, *Scientific American*, and *Atlas Obscura*. In 2017, Frischkorn was awarded an AAAS Mass Media Fellowship at *Smithsonian Magazine*, where this article first appeared.

"A Blueprint for Genetically Engineering a Super Coral" begins by providing a brief overview on "coral bleaching" before discussing molecular biologist Rachel Levin's breakthrough study in genetically modified coral. By studying the coral's genome, Levin and her team were able to manipulate and increase the coral's heat resistant gene, making them less susceptible to damage caused by increasing water temperatures. Throughout the article, other biologists weigh in on the impact, both positive and negative, of the study. As you read, consider their responses and try to form an opinion on whether or not the genetic modification is significant enough, or too much of a change, to make a difference in the coral's danger.

A coral reef takes thousands of years to build, yet can vanish in an instant.

The culprit is usually coral bleaching, a disease exacerbated by warming waters that today threatens reefs around the globe. The worst recorded bleaching event struck the South Pacific between 2014 and 2016, when rising ocean temperatures followed by a sudden influx of warm El Niño waters traumatized the Great Barrier Reef. In just one season bleaching decimated nearly a quarter of the vast ecosystem, which once sprawled nearly 150,000 square miles through the Coral Sea.

"As awful as it was, that bleaching event was a wake-up call," says Rachel Levin, a molecular biologist who recently proposed a bold technique to save these key ecosystems. Her idea, published in the journal *Frontiers in Microbiology*, is simple: Rather than finding healthy symbionts to repopulate bleached coral in nature, engineer them in the lab instead. Given that this would require tampering with nature in a significant way, the proposal is likely to stir controversial waters.

But Levin argues that with time running out for reefs worldwide, the potential value could well be worth the risk.

Levin studied cancer pharmacology as an undergraduate, but became fascinated by the threats facing aquatic life while dabbling in marine science courses.

"A coral reef takes thousands of years to build, yet can vanish in an instant." 5

She was struck by the fact that, unlike in human disease research, there were far fewer researchers fighting to restore ocean health. After she graduated, she moved from California to Sydney, Australia to pursue a Ph.D. at the Center for Marine Bio-Innovation in the University of New South Wales, with the hope of applying her expertise in human disease research to corals.

In medicine, it often takes the threat of a serious disease for researchers to try a new and controversial treatment (i.e., merging two women's healthy eggs with one man's sperm to make a "three-parent baby"). The same holds in environmental science—to an extent. "Like a terrible disease [in] humans, when people realize how dire the situation is becoming researchers start trying to propose much more," Levin says. When it comes to saving the environment, however, there are fewer advocates willing to implement risky, groundbreaking techniques.

When it comes to reefs—crucial marine regions that harbor an astonishing amount of diversity as well as protect land masses from storm surges, floods and erosion—that hesitation could be fatal.

Coral bleaching is often presented as the death of coral, which is a little misleading. Actually, it's the breakdown of the symbiotic union that enables a coral to thrive. The coral animal itself is like a building developer who constructs the scaffolding of a high rise apartment complex. The developer rents out each of the billions of rooms to single-celled, photosynthetic microbes called Symbiodinium.

But in this case, in exchange for a safe place to live, Symbiodinium makes food for the coral using photosynthesis. A bleached coral, by contrast, is like a deserted building. With no tenants to make their meals, the coral eventually dies.

Though bleaching can be deadly, it's actually a clever evolutionary 10 strategy of the coral. The Symbiodinium are expected to uphold their end of the bargain. But when the water gets too warm, they stop photosynthesizing. When that food goes scarce, the coral sends an eviction notice. "It's like having a bad tenant—you're going to get rid of what you have and see if you can find better," Levin says.

But as the oceans continue to warm, it's harder and harder to find good tenants. That means evictions can be risky. In a warming ocean, the coral animal might die before it can find any better renters—a scenario that has decimated reef ecosystems around the planet.

Levin wanted to solve this problem, by creating a straightforward recipe for building a super-symbiont that could repopulate bleached

A healthy coral reef (left) can be quickly devastated by coral bleaching (right) just a few hundred yards away.
David Liittschwager/National Geographic Creative/Getty Images

corals and help them to persist through climate change — essentially, the perfect tenants. But she had to start small. At the time, "there were so many holes and gaps that prevented us from going forward," she says. "All I wanted to do was show that we could genetically engineer [Symbiodinium]."

Even that would prove to be a tall order. The first challenge was that, despite being a single-celled organism, Symbiodinium has an unwieldy genome. Usually symbiotic organisms have streamlined genomes, since they rely on their hosts for most of their needs. Yet while other species have genomes of around 2 million base pairs, Symbiodinium's genome is 3 orders of magnitude larger.

"They're humongous," Levin says. In fact, the entire human genome is only slightly less than 3 times as big as Symbiodinium's.

Even after advances in DNA sequencing made deciphering these 15 genomes possible, scientists still had no idea what 80 percent of the genes were for. "We needed to backtrack and piece together which gene was doing what in this organism," Levin says. A member of a group of phytoplankton called dinoflagellates, Symbiodinium are incredibly diverse. Levin turned her attention to two key Symbiodinium strains she could grow in her lab.

The first strain, like most Symbiodinium, was vulnerable to the high temperatures that cause coral bleaching. Turn up the heat dial a few notches, and this critter was toast. But the other strain, which had been isolated from the rare corals that live in the warmest environments, seemed to be impervious to heat. If she could figure out how these two strains wielded their genes during bleaching conditions, then she might find the genetic keys to engineering a new super-strain.

When Levin turned up the heat, she saw that the hardy Symbiodinium escalated its production of antioxidants and heat shock proteins, which help repair cellular damage caused by heat. Unsurprisingly, the normal Symbiodinium didn't. Levin then turned her attention to figuring out a way to insert more copies of these crucial heat tolerating genes into the weaker Symbiodinium, thereby creating a strain adapted to live with corals from temperate regions—but with the tools to survive warming oceans.

Getting new DNA into a dinoflagellate cell is no easy task. While tiny, these cells are protected by armored plates, two cell membranes, and a cell wall. "You can get through if you push hard enough," Levin says. But then again, you might end up killing the cells. So Levin solicited help from an unlikely collaborator: a virus. After all, viruses "have evolved to be able to put their genes into their host's genome—that's how they survive and reproduce," she says.

Levin isolated a virus that infected Symbiodinium, and molecularly altered it it so that it no longer killed the cells. Instead, she engineered it to be a benign delivery system for those heat tolerating genes. In her paper, Levin argues that the virus's payload could use CRISPR, the breakthrough gene editing technique that relies on a natural process used by bacteria, to cut and paste those extra genes into a region of the Symbiodinium's genome where they would be highly expressed.

It sounds straightforward enough. But messing with a living ecosystem 20 is never simple, says Dustin Kemp, professor of biology at the University of Alabama at Birmingham who studies the ecological impacts of climate change on coral reefs. "I'm very much in favor of these solutions to conserve and genetically help," says Kemp. But "rebuilding reefs that have taken thousands of years to form is going to be a very daunting task."

Considering the staggering diversity of the Symbiodinium strains that live within just one coral species, even if there was a robust system for genetic modification, Kemp wonders if it would ever be possible to engineer enough different super-Symbiodinium to restore that diversity. "If you clear cut an old growth forest and then go out and plant a few pine trees, is that really saving or rebuilding the forest?" asks Kemp, who was not involved with the study.

But Kemp agrees that reefs are dying at an alarming rate, too fast for the natural evolution of Symbiodinium to keep up. "If corals were rapidly evolving to handle [warming waters], you'd think we would have seen it by now," he says.

Thomas Mock, a marine microbiologist at the University of East Anglia in the UK and a pioneer in genetically modifying phytoplankton, also points out that dinoflagellate biology is still largely enshrouded in mystery. "To me this is messing around," he says. "But this is how it starts usually. Provocative argument is always good—it's very very challenging, but let's get started somewhere and see what we can achieve." Recently, CSIRO, the Australian government's science division, has announced that it will fund laboratories to continue researching genetic modifications in coral symbionts.

When it comes to human health—for instance, protecting humans from devastating diseases like malaria or Zika—scientists have been willing to try more drastic techniques, such as releasing mosquitoes genetically programmed to pass on lethal genes. The genetic modifications needed to save corals, Levin argues, would not be nearly as extreme. She adds that much more controlled lab testing is required before genetically modified Symbiodinium could be released into the environment to repopulate dying corals reefs.

"When we're talking 'genetically engineered,' we're not significantly   25 altering these species," she says. "We're not making hugely mutant things. All we're trying to do is give them an extra copy of a gene they already have to help them out . . . we're not trying to be crazy scientists."

Understanding the Text

1. How does the author describe "coral bleaching" and why is it a danger to coral reefs?

2. What are symbionts? Remember, if you can't find the definition in the text, look up the word to understand the article better.

3. How is Levin making the coral's DNA more resistant to heat? What is her delivery method?

4. What are the difficulties Levin and her research team face when genetically modifying coral genes?

Reflection and Response

5. Why does the author provide Rachel Levin's medical background? What is the importance of that connection?

6. Where do you stand on gene modification? Do you see it as a potential danger or a medical breakthrough?

Making Connections

7. Research some of the other ways scientists are trying to combat coral reef bleaching and extinction. What methods are they using? What are the positive and negative aspects of their method?

8. Based on the other articles you have read from this book, what can we discern about people's opinions on using science to combat environmental issues?

Cleaning up the Great Pacific Garbage Patch

Christine Evans-Pughe

Christine Evans-Pughe is a feature writer for *Engineering and Technology Magazine* and the news editor of *Compound Semiconductor*, a specialized scientific journal. Evans-Pughe holds a degree in Physics from Cardiff University in Wales. She specializes in science and technology writing, and her work has appeared in publications such as the *Economist*, the *Guardian*, and BBC *Focus*.

This article, published in *Engineering and Technology Magazine*, explores the proposed plan to clean up the "Great Pacific Garbage Patch." The author discusses The Ocean Cleanup, a crowd-funding organization whose new plan, despite limitations, may hold the key to ridding the ocean of years' worth of plastic garbage build-up. Before you read, search for images of the garbage patch. While reading, think about the effect the plastic has on the ocean life that surrounds it.

What do six decades of a throwaway culture look like? Welcome to the Great Pacific Garbage Patch—a trash vortex between California and Hawaii thought to contain over 140,000 tons of floating plastic (the contents of around 12,000 [garbage] trucks) washed into the sea from dumps, sewers and rivers.

Of the five major concentrations of "garbage-soup" in the world's oceans, the Pacific Garbage Patch is the largest (estimates range from twice the size of Britain to as big as Texas). It is also the focus of a controversial engineering project called The Ocean Cleanup (TOC), whose successful crowdfunding may point to a new way of tackling global environmental problems.

TOC hopes to remove half the Pacific Patch plastic in 10 years using a 100km array of floating barriers moored to the seabed at an estimated cost of £265m (£3.80 per kilogram of collected debris).

Resembling temporary booms for containing oil spills, TOC's barriers will concentrate the rubbish on to platforms using the same large-scale offshore circular sea currents (gyres) responsible for pulling plastic rubbish into ocean patches in the first place. In this case, the North Pacific gyre, which rotates clockwise around an area of 20,000,000km², will be doing the work. Boats will pick up the plastic for recycling.

Most ocean-cleaning initiatives target "turning off the taps," i.e., stopping the flow of plastic litter—over eight million tons a year—from 5

253

the land. Packaging is the main culprit. Without such measures, plastic in the sea will outweigh fish by 2050, according to the Ellen MacArthur Foundation's January 2016 report, "The New Plastics Economy: Rethinking the Future of Plastics." Even by 2025, projected increases in plastic production indicate the plastic-to-fish ratio will reach one-to-three, as plastic stocks in the sea grow from 150 million tons today to 250 million. While the USA, Europe and Asia jointly manufacture 85 per cent of plastic, the report says Asia is responsible for 80 percent of leakage into the sea.

"Bailing out the bath while the taps are still running," as the TOC project plans to do, is viewed by many experts as a distraction. "It's a different philosophy," says Richard Thompson, professor of marine biology and head of the International Marine Litter Research Unit at Plymouth University. "Only a small proportion of the plastic that has entered the ocean is still floating on the surface. The rest is on beaches, on the sea floor, or in animals. The best investment is in preventing litter entering the environment."

Turning Off the Taps

One way to keep plastic out of the sea is to confine it to a circular economy and the New Plastics Economy is working towards this goal. It is a global initiative formed in May 2016 by the World Economic Forum, the Ellen MacArthur Foundation and McKinsey & Company, and more than 40 plastics makers, users and recyclers including Coca-Cola, Dow, DuPont, Mars, Unilever and Veolia are on board.

UK start-up Recycling Technologies is one of the newest members. It is industrializing a form of pyrolysis (decomposing plastics at high temperatures without oxygen) to turn the random mix of waste plastics in our dustbins into a synthetic crude oil called Plaxx.

"Plastic comes from oil, so you can return it to oil, so it can become more plastic again," explains Recycling Technologies CEO Adrian Griffiths. "We remove all the extra elements such as fluorine, chlorine, flame retardants, and fillers found in a mix of plastics, but not wanted in oil."

Central to the process, which originated at Warwick University, is 10 a machine called the RT7000, housed in 20ft shipping containers so it can be easily shipped and installed on waste sites. Recycling Technologies will own and operate the machines, turning "end-of-life" plastics with no residual value into oil for less cost than discarding or incinerating them.

The vision is to have hundreds of machines dotted around the world. "The output comes back to the big centers, i.e., the polymer producers, for them to turn it back into virgin quality polymers. For islands, say in the Caribbean, Plaxx could be used locally for whatever fuel oil is used in that context," says Griffiths.

Heavy Fuel Oil (HFO) is the first market. Trials with Ricardo and Lloyd's Register Marine are underway to certify it as a marine fuel to meet new low-sulfur IMO fuel standards. Components of Plaxx are also developed as a paraffin wax and the company is engaged with plastics manufacturers to develop the "back to plastics" route.

"Taking plastics that can't be mechanically recycled and breaking them down into smaller molecules is an important way forward," says Adrian Whyle, senior manager for resource efficiency at PlasticsEurope, the trade organization for European plastics manufacturers. "We want to see an end to landfilling of plastics. You need clever chemistry and the right economics. The UK landfill tax is a driver for such technology."

Boyan Slat, TOC's charismatic young founder, came up with his array design while studying aerospace engineering at Delft University of Technology. No one would take the technology forward until Slat gave a TEDx Delft talk in 2012, "How the Oceans Can Clean Themselves." Since then, he has raised over $2m in crowdfunding from more than 38,000 funders

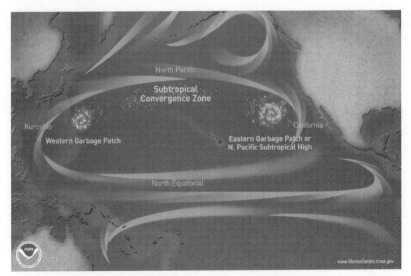

A map of the Great Pacific Garbage Patch.
Courtesy of NOAA

in 160 countries. Four years on, TOC has installed its first prototype, a 100m barrier, in the North Sea, 23km off the Dutch coast. It will remain there for a year, with sensors tracking motion and the loads it is subjected to. A pilot for the Great Pacific Garbage Patch is planned for late 2017, prior to starting the big Pacific clean-up in 2020.

Slat's initiative is idealistic. The funding is novel. Yet it is a professional 15 engineering project. Between April 2013 and May 2014, TOC investigated the technical and financial viability of the array concept with costs covered by crowdfunding. The feasibility study covered everything from fluid dynamics to preliminary testing in a 45x36m tank with wind, wave and current generators at Marin (the Maritime Research Institute Netherlands).

The North Sea prototype is testing whether the design can stand up to worst-case conditions in the Great Pacific Garbage Patch, where it will be moored far offshore in deep water, and expected to collect plastic for years with minimum maintenance. That is no walk in the park. Designing offshore structures is almost as tough as spacecraft engineering, says Cranfield University's Dr. Maurizio Collu, expert in the conceptual and preliminary design and coupled dynamics of offshore support structures for renewable energy devices.

Collu is one of a number of specialists TOC approached in April 2014 to review the feasibility report. "Sometimes a novel solution is presented as a silver bullet, but these guys took a very down-to-earth approach," he says. "TOC brought in commercial offshore engineering professionals, and they looked at a range of aspects, including ocean engineering, oceanography and environmental impact. Everything is based on theoretical and numerical methodologies, but they have pushed those analyses to the state-of-the-art. At the same time, they do not claim to have solved all the problems or have a perfect solution. They have said clearly they need to do experiments to analyze weaknesses. It's admirable."

At the launch of the prototype late in June 2016, Slat noted that a successful North Sea test would not necessarily mean the prototype would survive. "I estimate there is a 30 percent chance the system will break, but either way it will be a good test," he said.

Two months later, the two outermost air chambers of the prototype had started to bend out of shape and underwater footage showed that shackles connecting the barrier to the permanent mooring system were failing.

Since then, the engineering team has been busy looking into different 20 connections to the mooring system as well as to the barrier — so busy, indeed, that they would not discuss details. "We are evaluating what changes we may make to the barrier design for long-term durability. We now expect a redesigned version of the prototype will be back in the water early next year," a spokesman says.

The priority is to make sure that the pilot system works properly, he adds. "This way we ensure we are testing specifically those aspects on the prototype that we need to understand and master for a successful pilot and ocean deployment."

Early in 2016, a study of ocean plastic movements by Dr. Erik van Sebille and Peter Sherman from Imperial College London cast doubt on whether placing plastic collectors in the North Pacific gyre made sense, suggesting that coasts, particularly around China and the Indonesian islands, would be better sites.

Their computer simulations of a 10-year project between 2015 and 2025 showed that coastal collectors would remove 31 per cent of microplastics (particles under 5mm), whereas collectors in the Pacific Garbage patch gyre would remove only 17 per cent. The report was published in Environmental Research Letters.

Could TOC's calculations be wrong? TOC says: "From its start, TOC has decided to focus its work on the gyres. First, because we had (and still have) a plan, and the idea of van Sebille and Sherman would require a different system and new engineering again. For us this would be an add-on, or a spin-off, but not a simple replication of the work we have been doing, and investing our funders' money in.

"Of the five major concentrations of "garbage-soup" in the world's oceans, the Pacific Garbage Patch is the largest (estimates range from twice the size of Britain to as big as Texas)."

"The van Sebille and Sherman proposal would not solve the entire problem because the gyres account for the largest concentration of plastic in the world and are the only places ... where plastic actually accumulates.

"Preliminary results from our expeditions show there are several tens of millions of pieces of plastic per km^2 in the garbage patches, while Law et al. showed in 2014 that concentration outside the gyres is zero. If this accumulated plastic is not removed, it will slowly degrade into much more dangerous microplastics.

"The time to act is now."

Persistent Plastic

The qualities that started our love affair with plastics in the 1950s (lightness, cheapness, durability) are also why it persists in the sea.

"Once plastic enters the sea, currents move it around, it might be thrown back on to a beach, it might be eaten by animals, or it might stay afloat moving into one of the infamous garbage patches," explains

Richard Thompson, professor of Marine Biology and head of the International Marine Litter Research Unit at Plymouth University.

"In the environment, mechanical action from the waves and UV light 30 from the sun can cause the break-up {of?} the plastic into smaller and smaller pieces. A Styrofoam cup might end up in thousands of microscopic pellets. Yet the rate of degradation is highly variable depending on the surrounding environmental conditions. It is very difficult to put any real timescale on how quickly these processes happen," he adds.

At least one million seabirds and hundreds of thousands of marine mammals die each year due to plastic pollution, according to The Ocean Clean-Up. They get entangled in larger debris and mistake smaller fragments for food. When marine animals eat plastic, harmful chemicals move up the food chain.

A University of California, Davis study in *Science Advances* (November 2016) showed that seabirds, particularly petrels and albatross, eat marine plastic because some debris smells of a sulfurous compound they have relied on for thousands of years to tell them where to find food.

Slat's ability to raise money and support is remarkable. Collu says it suggests that the general public is more interested in engineering research than we may imagine—certainly in the more emotive types of research. Crowdfunding, he speculates, may well be the only mechanism for solving some global, interdisciplinary problems. "Who makes money from cleaning the ocean? Economically, it doesn't make sense to most investors or companies. It's not a direct monetary return, it is an environmental return," he says.

Cleaning up the seas is a monumental task. "We've had 60 years in training for the throwaway society, so it's not going to happen overnight," says Thompson. We need a range of approaches from novel clean-up schemes to rethinking the entire plastics economy. As individuals, directing some of our passion for the oceans back to the land (and our rubbish bins) would be a start.

Marine Litter Plastic Initiatives

In 2011, plastics organizations from around the world joined to 35 announce the Declaration of the Global Plastics Associations for Solutions on Marine Litter.

Since then, 60 plastics organizations in 34 countries have signed and more than 260 marine litter solutions projects have been planned, put into action, or completed.

Projects include Operation Clean Sweep, to prevent the escape of plastic pellets used in manufacturing, and the Marine Litter Action Network, a knowledge-sharing initiative funded by the trade body PlasticsEurope through the Marine Conservation Society.

Understanding the Text

1. How large is the Pacific garbage patch? To what does the author compare it? Is that comparison effective?

2. How does the TOC plan to remove half of the garbage? What are the limitations to their plan?

3. What does "turning off the tap" mean? Is this an important part of the cleanup?

Reflection and Response

4. The article talks about the importance of crowdfunding to support any project that focuses on cleaning up the garbage. Would you donate money to a project like this, even if your contribution was small? Why or why not?

5. What could you do to ensure that the plastic you use does not end up in the ocean?

6. Does the author effectively explain the causes and effects of the Great Pacific Garbage Patch? What does she do well and what could be improved for better clarity?

Making Connections

7. Research The Ocean Cleanup. What are they currently working on? What are their current crowdfunding numbers?

8. Look up the effect that plastic can have on sea animals. Are there any organizations that are dedicated to treating animals harmed by trash? What are they and how do they get their funding?

9. What are the connections between this article and Amy Westervelt's article, "Can Recycling Be Bad for the Environment?" What do the arguments in these two articles portray about the use and manufacturing of plastic?

Five Years after Fukushima, Japan's Nuclear Debate Is Heating Up

Mark Hay

Mark Hay is a freelance journalist and editor based in Brooklyn, New York. His work has appeared in publications such as *New Yorker Online*, *Slate*, and *VICE Magazine*. Much of his writing focuses on subcultures and identity, as well as culture and politics.

"Five Years after Fukushima" touches on the devastating impact of Japan's nuclear power-plant disaster five years after it occurred. Specifically, the article discusses how Japan will rebuild and restructure their nuclear power program and how the decision to do so has been divisive among Japan's citizens.

Last Thursday, Japanese Prime Minister Shinzo Abe threw his weight behind the redevelopment of his nation's nuclear energy plants. It was a bold stance, made bolder because he voiced it on the eve of the fifth anniversary of the earthquake-tsunami in northeastern Japan that left 18,500 dead or missing and precipitated the Fukushima nuclear disaster — the world's worst since Chernobyl and the reason for the eventual shutdown of the nation's 54 nuclear facilities.

Abe's case for nuclear redevelopment is strong, simple, and already accepted by many in the nation: "Our resource-poor country cannot do without nuclear power to secure the stability of energy supply while considering what makes economic sense and the issue of climate change," Abe said at a press conference last week. Post-Fukushima regulations, the prime minister argues, make nuclear power safer than ever, as do major advances in reactor technology. This belief has led the nation to greenlight the reopening of a few reactors, starting with two in Kagoshima in August 2015, with seemingly minimal pushback.

But Abe's narrative isn't the only way of looking at this. Others, like Naoto Kan, who was prime minister during the Fukushima disaster, have argued that the nation doesn't need nuclear power at all. Instead, they say, renewable energy sources are the future of Japan. They may look more expensive and less feasible than restoring the nation's massive nuclear capacity. But that may be an illusion. It can be hard from a layman's perspective to sort out who's right about Japan's nuclear future, Abe or Kan. But a number of studies and pilot projects suggest that Kan's correct when he says Japan could thrive without ever-troublesome nuclear power — although the country's political powers seem stacked against that viable future.

Those who agree with Abe see nuclear power as vital, given what's happened to Japan without it. As of 2011, Japan had the third-greatest nuclear

A wave approaches Miyako City, Japan, after an earthquake struck on March 11, 2011. The powerful earthquake, combined with the massive tsunami, killed more than 15,800, devastated many eastern coastline communities, and triggered a nuclear catastrophe at the Fukushima Daiichi nuclear power station.

Mainchi Shimbun/Reuters

capacity among the world's nations, behind only France and the United States, with reactors providing 30 percent of the country's energy. Some hoped to hit 60 percent reliance by 2100. But since shutting off the reactors, Japan has been forced to rely on imported, costlier fuels, rapidly becoming the world's largest gas importer, second-largest coal importer, and third-largest crude importer to feed its massive energy needs. Even with global oil prices in a tailspin, Japan's 84 percent reliance on these materials has sent utility prices through the roof and spurred the worrying creation of dozens of new coal plants, which produce some of the smoggiest energy out there.

Looking at the numbers, Abe's followers argue that the nation needs 5 to derive at least 22 percent of its energy from nuclear power by 2030 to thrive—which is to say that 30 to 37 reactors must be online by then. That figure seems to accord with the government's 2015 15-year energy plan, which aims to boost renewable energy contributions to between 22 and 24 percent of the grid, alongside nuclear revivals.

But these predictions shortchange Japan's renewable potential. Sure, outside of hydropower, renewables account for just about 3 percent of Japan's grid right now, and the sector has grown miserably slowly since the beginning of the new millennium. But that's at least in part because, from 2002 to 2011, Japan was nuclear-obsessive.

"As of 2011, Japan had the third-greatest nuclear capacity among the world's nations, behind only France and the United States, with reactors providing 30 percent of the country's energy." Some companies are eager to invest in Japan's untapped solar potential. Even if they could just complete existing proposals (like offshore arrays), some think they could fill 8 percent of Japan's energy needs, all without affecting otherwise productive land. In a 2011 report, the country's Ministry of the Environment backed the power of wind, arguing that installing arrays of turbines along unused wind hotspots—even if they only ran a quarter of the time—could provide energy equivalent to 40 nuclear reactors. And a slew of companies are exploring the nation's geothermal potential (the world's third greatest), which may be able to provide up to a third of the nation's power needs—essentially doing the same thing as nuclear energy but with much less risk.

"To import a very complex and difficult technology to boil water in the world's most seismically active country when there is such vast geothermal potential strikes me as madness," Canadian renewables expert David Suzuki told the *Japan Times* in 2013.

Critics argue that perhaps Japan does have great renewables potential, but it's obviously not moving quickly enough, even with post-Fukushima incentives, to offset traditional fuels. Meanwhile, up to 40 nuclear reactors could come back online in the blink of an eye.

But this account misses the fact that renewables' slow development 10 isn't proof that they suck. (Although, admittedly, Japanese solar technology is lagging and it does take a good amount of time and money to develop renewable energy facilities.) Renewables are mainly bogged down by entrenched interests, from groups like the nation's geothermal spa association, which fears (it seems baselessly) that drilling for such power could rob them of their hot springs, to monopolistic utility companies that are allied with nuclear power interests and reluctant to reform their grids.

It also misses the fact that just because Japan has nuclear reactors it can restart doesn't necessarily make nuclear power a cheap answer, economically or socially. Although officials and industry experts have made the case that panic about nuclear disasters is overblown and shortsighted and insist that they can create foolproof security systems, the public still has its doubts. Inspired in part by the long, fraught process of cleaning up Fukushima, and in part by concerns among experts and local residents that new safety regimes may not be as perfect as advertised, antinuclear sentiment remains high in the nation.

The courts recently bolstered popular skepticism as well: Just before Abe's big pro-nuclear declaration, a district judge ordered the closure of a recently reopened nuclear reactor in Takahama—the second reopened since the moratorium. The courts ruled in favor of a local interest group, which argued that the new plants hadn't factored in a number of major security concerns, cutting corners to speed toward reactivation—a view likely strengthened by the closure of one of the plant's reactors soon after restarting because of technical failures.

And it's not like Japan can just flip back on nuclear power plants. Especially with new security concerns, it'll cost millions upon millions just to reactivate a single facility, and it will then take an unknown amount of time to resolve legal challenges and the concerns of an understandably shaken public. These factors could arguably put the cost of a new nuclear facility on par with the development of some renewable energy facilities.

If that's the case, then Abe and company are wrong. The future of Japan is not tied to the thorny issue of nuclear power. Not only could they match and exceed its potential with renewables, but they could do so without reactors' murky safety and social baggage. Sure, a big push against vested interests and toward new major projects would be needed to get renewables revved up. But Japan managed that sort of paradigm shift in the 1960s with its first nuclear plant. It should be even easier to achieve with geothermal, solar, and wind facilities, especially with so much popular desire for a nuclear alternative. Perhaps Abe's right in a way and Japan does need nuclear power to get back on economic track *for now*—but even if that is the case, it should just be a temporary step on the road to building out infrastructure for a renewable future.

Understanding the Text

1. Why does the Japanese prime minister want to redevelop the country's nuclear power supply plants?
2. What do those who oppose the redevelop have to say about nuclear power?
3. What does the article say about the financial aspect of redeveloping the nuclear power plants?

Reflection and Response

4. Given the various facts and opinions presented by the article, do you believe that Japan should or should not redevelop their nuclear power supply plants? Why or why not?
5. Find an opinion or position in the article that you disagree with and create an argument to support your position.

Making Connections

6. Research other nuclear power disasters. How were those disasters handled?
7. Look up the statistics surrounding the environmental impacts of nuclear power. Do the financial benefits of nuclear power outweigh the environmental impact? Explain your answer.

Challenges to Sustainability in Africa

Patricia Kameri-Mbote

Patricia Kameri-Mbote holds a PhD in property rights and environmental law from Stanford University. Kameri-Mbote is a professor of law and dean at the School of Law at the University of Nairobi. The World Conservation Union has acknowledged Kameri-Mbote as a renowned thinker in the environmental and sustainability field. Kameri-Mbote is on the board of several environmental organizations, such as the Kenya Land Conservation Trust, the Global Council of Water and Sanitation Program, and the Advocates Coalition for Development and Environment in Uganda.

This article was published in the journal for the Society for International Development, a network of individuals and organizations promoting sustainable development in global communities. "Challenges to Sustainability in Africa" outlines the issues and obstacles surrounding sustainable development in African communities from various perspectives. The article also provides a possible solution, noting that for sustainable development to be achievable in Africa, it needs to be viewed as an intersectional issue. As you read the article, think about the unique issues surrounding sustainability in Africa as well as the issues that are common to other continents, countries, and communities discussed in this book.

Introduction

Sustainability as defined in the Report of the World Commission on Environment and Development (1987) denotes development that meets the needs of current generations without compromising the ability of future generations to meet their needs. It has elements of equity among current generations and across successive generations (Brown Weiss, 1989). The challenges to sustainability in African states are multifaceted, cross-sectoral and multidisciplinary in nature. These challenges range from social, economic, political and environmental challenges. They cut across the different sectors in the countries with a few of them being unique to a specific sector.

Pointers to Sustainability in Africa

There are some encouraging pointers to sustainability in Africa today. These include the following:

- More children in school with countries adopting the universal primary education policy.

- Remarkable improvements in malaria, HIV and AIDS control, and measles immunization.
- Concern for environmental sustainability with about 43 countries promulgating framework environmental laws and a good number enshrining the right to a healthy environment in their constitution.
- Increased use of improved water sources.
- Greater use of technology with the expansion of mobile telephony use in Africa for communication, data exchange and money transfer increasing rapidly.
- Political, legal and judicial sector reforms to promote the rule of law.
- Land reform embraced as a key agenda in many countries and as a regional initiative.
- Proliferation of regional and sub-regional economic and development bodies in different parts of the continent.

Indeed, various African countries have in the recent past shown potential expansion in a number of their critical industries thus creating growth opportunities. Others have improved local investment conditions and thus attracted new players in their local economies.

Challenges to Sustainability

There are, however, some threats to sustainability, which, if not attended to, can negate the gains that have been made over the years. These include the following:

- Inequalities on the basis of class, age and gender.
- Claims for sub-national or ethnic citizenship that threaten national unity.
- Poor governance and non-adherence to the rule of law.
- Preponderance of intra-state conflict.
- Environmental degradation.
- High disease burden and absence of accessible health care.
- Emphasis on primary goods (agricultural and environmental) in an age of technology and information goods.

The State of Africa

A recent research carried out in Egypt and Kenya on employment and 5
entrepreneurial opportunities for women in export-processing zones
revealed that the major challenges to sustainability include:

- weak enforcement of labor law;
- underdeveloped environmental standards policies and regulations;
- lower labor standards in Kenya;
- risk of migrant labor abuse;
- and low status of women.

Businesses and enterprises also face various challenges. In a study carried out by Africa Practice Ltd. African Business and Sustainable Development, the companies were required to come up with a list of challenges
they faced in the quest to achieve sustainability in their businesses. The
survey generated the following challenges:

- Shortages of clean water.
- Environmental challenges such as climate change evidenced by
  extreme weather events; loss of biodiversity; air water and waste
  pollution.
- Poverty.
- Food insecurity and undernutrition.
- Economic instability. Political instability. {separate bullet?}
- High disease burden.

In this study, poverty was the most commonly cited challenge followed by disease and climate change and loss of biodiversity coming
in at joint third. According to the World Bank, in sub-Saharan Africa,
the US$1.25 a day poverty rate has shown no sustained decline between
1981 and 2005, at around 50 percent. In absolute terms, the number
of poor people has nearly doubled, from 200 million in 1981 to 380
million in 2005. The average life expectancy in the region is 54 years
(2008 figures) with the leading cause of death being HIV/AIDS, followed
closely by malaria.

African countries are well endowed with numerous mineral resources,
which have the potential of promoting economic growth of these countries if those minerals are properly harnessed. However, the mining
industry faces challenges such as corruption, environmental degradation
as well as unscrupulous and destructive mining activities leading to considerable environmental problems. Such problems include chronic soil

degradation, chemical contamination and air pollution. The entry of actors such as China in the mining and oil exploration sectors in African countries has implications for sustainability given that environmental standards in such countries are not stringent.

Environmental Degradation

Environmental degradation is also a major setback to Africa's sustainability. Climate change resulting from negative environmental trends poses a great threat to the continent's sustainability and its food supplies, even though Africa has contributed little to the global greenhouse gas emissions. Global warming will act as a threat multiplier for many African countries.

> "Climate change resulting from negative environmental trends poses a great threat to the continent's sustainability and its food supplies, even though Africa has contributed little to the global greenhouse gas emissions."

For instance, there is evidence that climate variability has significant economic costs in Kenya with aggregate models indicating that additional net economic costs could be equivalent to a loss of almost 3 percent of GDP each year by 2030 and estimating immediate needs for addressing current climate and preparing for the future as US$500 million/year for the year 2012 (Government of Kenya, 2010). It is also estimated that the cost of adaptation by 2030 is likely to increase to the range of $1-2 billion (Government of Kenya, 2010). This is likely impact on the availability and allocation of resources for other pressing needs such as health, education, infrastructure development, and maintenance and overall development of the country.

Related to environmental degradation is the issue of land grabs. The 10 *Financial Times Weekend* (2009) highlighted a growing trend in sub-Saharan Africa in which land concessions are negotiated between foreign investors and African Governments or private African companies that are often closely tied to African Government leaders. Countries cited in the report are Madagascar and Sudan but there are other examples across the continent such as Angola, Ethiopia, Ghana, Kenya, Mozambique, Nigeria, Togo, United Republic of Tanzania and Zambia. The land is leased for the production of food stuff mainly for export as well as to generate biofuels and feedstocks (cane sugar, jatropha, palm oil and soybeans). These leases must be considered with the context of land tenure insecurity for many small holder farmers in the countries involved as well as the need for food security.

Economic Instability

Economic instability is also a significant challenge to sustainability in Africa. Like the rest of the world, Africa has had to deal with effects of the global economic crisis. Many African countries have western countries as the markets for their products and the reduced buying power in these countries affects their exports. The generally weaker state of African countries' economies affects their capacity to withstand economic and ecological crises.

Governance

Governance and adherence to the rule of law are other challenges to sustainability. Governance is undergirded by the rule of law, which is critical for the economy and for prudent ecological stewardship.

The rule of law provides the necessary predictability and order thus guaranteeing social rights and government accountability. More specifically, it ensures that there is freedom from arbitrary governmental actions in the management of national affairs and resources; sets the rules of the game in investments, property, contracts and dispute resolution and makes governments transparent and accountable. The rule of law can stem grand corruption in development projects; patronage in the allocation of project contracts; privatization of public resources by those in power and abuse of human rights to stem opposition.

While many countries in Africa have laws that are clear and written, the major problem is that these laws are not obeyed by all and in some cases official action is not consistent with the declared rules. The issue of some persons operating above the law is common in many countries and has led to revolts in some countries with the people demanding the end of impunity.

Way Forward

To fully address challenges to sustainability in Africa, we must address 15 the economic, social, political, economic, cultural, legal conceptions of that development and grant to all as is due to them. The right to development needs to be realized by not only states but also groups and individuals. We must revisit the concept of sustainable development as not just growth however obtained, but growth tempered with indicators that ensure that it is realized for all in the present and does not diminish the prospects for future generations. We must remove sources of "unfreedom" (Sen, 1999) by targeting the poor, marginalized and underprivileged in society since inequity can erode development gains. Different actors, structures and institutions need to be brought together to ensure that development is sustainable. For instance, political leadership, legislatures and law enforcement agencies need to work together to ensure that declared rules are implemented. In addition, there is need to enlist cooperation from traditional governance institutions that are closer to the people while ensuring that the norms they carry do not result in further marginalization of the youth and women.

References

1. Brown Weiss, Edith (1989). "In Fairness to Future Generations: International law, common patrimony, and intergenerational equity." Innovation in International Law.

2. *Financial Times Weekend* 10–11 January 2009, p. 1.

3. Government of Kenya. "National Climate Change Response Strategy." April 2010.

4. Sen, Amartya. Development as Freedom, Oxford: Oxford University Press, 1999.

5. World Commission on Environment and Development. "Our Common Future: From One Earth to One World." 1987.

6. Yeager, Racheal. "Growth Potential and Sustainability Challenges in Africa." 2010. http://blog.bsr.org/2010/06/ growth-potential-and-sustainability.html, accessed 2 September 2010.

Understanding the Text

1. Name three of the challenges of sustainability in Africa and why they pose a particular threat.

2. What are "land grabs" and how do they relate to environmental degradation?

3. What does the author say about obedience to laws related to sustainability and the environment?

Reflection and Response

4. How is poverty connected to sustainability?

5. In what ways is sustainability related to human rights?

6. What parallels do you see in sustainability initiatives in Africa and in North America? How are the challenges and opportunities similar or different?

Making Connections

7. The author discusses challenges to sustainability as they pertain to African women. What are the connections between this article and JR Thorpe's "What Exactly Is Ecofeminism?" in Chapter 2?

8. The Report of the World Commission on Environment and Development (Brundtland report) is referenced in this article. How does Kameri-Mbote's argument reinforce or reflect the ideas discussed in the Brundtland report?

9. Research air pollution in one of Africa's cities. How does it compare to a city of your choosing from the United States?

How Much Is Left? The Limits of Earth's Resources

Michael Moyer and Carina Storrs

Michael Moyer is a technology editor for *Scientific American*. In addition, he writes about digital culture, energy, and environmental issues, and he has appeared on CNN Headline News, Discovery Channel, and National Geographic Channel. Carina Storrs is a freelance writer based in New York City. She studied environmental reporting at New York University and later received her PhD in microbiology from Columbia University. She has written and edited for Health.com, *Scientific American*, *Popular Science*, and ScienceLine.org.

This article outlines the limits to resources on the planet. It also provides a list of potential environmental events and corresponding dates (for example, the peak of oil and species extinction). As you read, think about the ways in which limited resources affect our quality of life and how this pattern could continue in the future.

If the twentieth century was an expansive era seemingly without boundaries—a time of jet planes, space travel and the Internet—the early years of the twenty-first have showed us the limits of our small world. Regional blackouts remind us that the flow of energy we used to take for granted may be in tight supply. The once mighty Colorado River, tapped by thirsty metropolises of the desert West, no longer reaches the ocean. Oil is so hard to find that new wells extend many kilometers underneath the seafloor. The boundless atmosphere is now reeling from two centuries' worth of greenhouse gas emissions. Even life itself seems to be running out, as biologists warn that we are in the midst of a global extinction event comparable to the last throes of the dinosaurs.

The constraints on our resources and environment—compounded by the rise of the middle class in nations such as China and India—will shape the rest of this century and beyond. Here is a visual accounting of what we have left to work with, a map of our resources plotted against time.

1976–2005: Glacier Melt Accelerates

Glaciers have been losing their mass at an accelerating rate in recent decades. In some regions such as Europe and the Americas, glaciers now lose more than half a meter each year.

2014: The Peak of Oil

The most common answer to "how much oil is left" is "depends on how hard you want to look." As easy-to-reach fields run dry, new technologies allow oil companies to tap harder-to-reach places (such as 5,500 meters under the Gulf of Mexico). Traditional statistical models of oil supply do not account for these advances, but a new approach to production forecasting explicitly incorporates multiple waves of technological improvement. Though still controversial, this multicyclic approach predicts that global oil production is set to peak in four years and that by the 2050s we will have pulled all but 10 percent of the world's oil from the ground.

"If the twentieth century was an expansive era seemingly without boundaries — a time of jet planes, space travel and the Internet — the early years of the twenty-first have showed us the limits of our small world."

2025: Battle over Water

In many parts of the world, one major river supplies water to multiple 5 countries. Climate change, pollution and population growth are putting a significant strain on supplies. In some areas renewable water reserves are in danger of dropping below the 500 cubic meters per person per year considered a minimum for a functioning society.

Potential Hot Spots

Egypt: A coalition of countries led by Ethiopia is challenging old agreements that allow Egypt to use more than 50 percent of the Nile's flow. Without the river, all of Egypt would be desert.

Eastern Europe: Decades of pollution have fouled the Danube, leaving downstream countries, such as Hungary and the Republic of Moldova, scrambling to find new sources of water.

Middle East: The Jordan River, racked by drought and diverted by Israeli, Syrian and Jordanian dams, has lost 95 percent of its former flow.

Former Soviet Union: The Aral Sea, at one time the world's fourth-largest inland sea, has lost 75 percent of its water because of agricultural diversion programs begun in the 1960s.

2028: Indium

Indium is a [soft, silvery metal that sits between cadmium and tin on the periodic table]. Indium tin oxide is a thin-film conductor used in flat-panel televisions. At current production levels, known indium reserves contain an 18-year world supply.

2029: Silver

Because silver naturally kills microbes, it is increasingly used in bandages and as coatings for consumer products. At current production levels, about 19 years' worth of silver remains in the ground, but recycling should extend that supply by decades.

2030: Gold

The global financial crisis has boosted demand for gold, which is seen by many as a tangible (and therefore lower-risk) investment. According to Julian Phillips, editor of the Gold Forecaster newsletter, probably about 20 years are left of gold that can be easily mined.

Fewer Fish

Fish are our last truly wild food, but the rise in demand for seafood has pushed many species to the brink of extinction. Here are five of the most vulnerable.

Hammerhead sharks have declined by 89 percent since 1986. The animals are sought for their fins, which are a delicacy in soup.

Russian sturgeon have lost spawning grounds because of exploitation for caviar. Numbers are down 90 percent since 1965.

Yellowmouth grouper may exist only in pockets of its former range, from Florida to Brazil.

European eel populations have declined by 80 percent since 1968; because the fish reproduces late in life, recovery could take 200 years.

Orange roughy off the coast of New Zealand have declined by 80 percent since the 1970s because of overfishing by huge bottom trawlers.

Our Mass Extinction

Biologists warn that we are living in the midst of a mass extinction on 10 par with the other five great events in Earth's history, including the Permian-Triassic extinction (also known as the Great Dying; it knocked out up to 96 percent of all life on Earth) and the Cretaceous-Tertiary extinction that killed the dinosaurs. The cause of our troubles? Us. Human mastery over the planet has pushed many species out of their native habitats; others have succumbed to hunting or environmental pollutants. If trends continue — and unfortunately, species loss is accelerating — the world will soon be a far less diverse place.

2044: Copper

Copper is in just about everything in infrastructure, from pipes to electrical equipment. Known reserves currently stand at 540 million metric tons, but recent geologic work in South America indicates there may be an additional 1.3 billion metric tons of copper hidden in the Andes Mountains.

2050: Feeding a Warming World

Researchers have recently started to untangle the complex ways rising temperatures will affect global agriculture. They expect climate change to lead to longer growing seasons in some countries; in others the heat will increase the frequency of extreme weather events or the prevalence of pests. In the United States, productivity is expected to rise in the Plains states but fall further in the already struggling Southwest. Russia and China will gain; India and Mexico will lose. In general, developing nations will take the biggest hits. By 2050 counteracting the ill effects of climate change on nutrition will cost more than $7 billion a year.

Mortal Threats

As the total number of species declines, some have fared worse than others. Here are five life-forms, the estimated percentage of species thought to be endangered, and an example of the threats they face.

Mammals

18 percent endangered

The Iberian lynx feeds on rabbits, a prey in short supply in the lynx's habitat ever since a pediatrician introduced the disease myxomatosis from Australia to France in 1952 to kill the rabbits in his garden.

Plants

8 percent endangered

The St. Helena redwood is native to the island in the South Atlantic where Napoleon lived his last years. Its excellent timber led to exploitation; by the 20th century only one remained in the wild.

Lizards

20 percent endangered

The blue spiny lizard must retreat from the sun before it overheats; higher temperatures have cut down on the time it can forage for food.

Birds

10 percent endangered

The black-necked crane suffers from habitat loss in the wetlands of the Tibetan plateau.

Amphibians

30 percent endangered

Archey's frog has been devastated by a fungal disease in its native New Zealand.

2060: Changing the Course of a River

Climate change will shift weather patterns, leading to big changes in the amount of rain that falls in any given region, as well as the amount of water flowing through streams and rivers. Scientists at the U.S. Geological Survey averaged the results of twelve climate models to predict how streamflow will alter over the next fifty years. While East Africa, Argentina and other regions benefit from more water, southern Europe and the western United States will suffer.

2070: Himalayan Ice

Snow melt from the Himalayas is a prime source of water for Asia's major river valleys, including the Yellow, Yangtze, Mekong and Ganges. By 2070 ice-covered landmass in the Himalayas could decrease by 43 percent.

2072: Limits of Coal

Unlike oil, coal is widely thought to be virtually inexhaustible. Not so, says David Rutledge of the California Institute of Technology. Governments routinely overestimate their reserves by a factor of four or more on the assumption that hard-to-reach seams will one day open up to new technology. Mature coal mines show that this has not been the case. The U.K. — the birthplace of coal mining — offers an example. Production grew through the 19th and early 20th centuries, then fell as supplies were depleted. Cumulative production curves in the U.K. and other mature regions have followed a predictable S shape. By extrapolating to the rest of the world's coal fields, Rutledge concludes that the world will extract 90 percent of available coal by 2072.

2100: The Alps

Parts of the Alps are warming so quickly that the Rhone Glacier is expected to have disappeared by the end of the century.

2560: Lithium

Because lithium is an essential component of the batteries in electric cars, many industry analysts have worried publicly that supplies won't keep up with growing demand for the metal. Still, known lithium reserves are big enough to keep us supplied for more than five centuries, even ignoring the vast supply of lithium in seawater.

Understanding the Text

1. How long do the authors think it will take for the world to run out of oil?
2. Which countries could be most severely impacted by a water shortage?
3. Which species of fish are at the greatest risk of endangerment?

Reflection and Response

4. Do you agree that our "mass extinction" is imminent? Why or why not?
5. How do you react to the information in this article? How does it make you think about your future?
6. Which of the limits addressed in this article do you believe to have the most impact on you, your family, or your region?

Making Connections

7. Choose one event on this timeline that interests you and write about it. Do you think that event is likely to occur? Why or why not?
8. The authors write that if weather patterns shift because of climate change, rainfall will be affected. Do some research to find out what else could be affected by changing weather patterns.

6

How Are Tourism and Recreation Connected to Sustainability?

You may think that sustainability is serious business — and it is. Sustainability involves difficult decisions and complex thinking in business, political, and social spheres. However, sustainability is also connected to the things we do in our free time. Most of us are lucky enough to have some time to travel, to attend and participate in leisure activities, and to enjoy various forms of recreation. These activities are serious business in themselves, and they have a significant impact on sustainability. The travel, recreation, and sports industries are trillion-dollar businesses, and they are also responsible for massive usages of resources like fuel, raw materials, and space. However, many people are drawn to sustainability out of a desire to protect and preserve resources that they use for recreation — most travelers, adventurers, and sports enthusiasts recognize the need for sustainability to ensure that their favorite activities can continue. The industries surrounding travel, leisure, and tourism have begun to notice the public interest in sustainability, and many have adopted more sustainable practices and policies in response to public demand.

This chapter examines the role of tourism, leisure activities, and recreation in creating and engaging with a more sustainably minded public. The chapter begins with a focus on sustainable tourism and ecotourism, which involves low-impact, education-based travel to natural areas. Williams's article explains what sustainable tourism should look like by referencing the three pillars of sustainability. Geerts's article extends this focus further, looking at the challenges to sustainability created by overtourism. The excerpt from O'Brien's book explains the importance of natural parks as sites for sustainable tourism, proposing solutions for more sustainable management of protected natural sites in the future. Hanna's article takes up the debate regarding the positive and negative outcomes of zoos and aquariums, and their collective role in environmental sustainability. Robyn Migliorini's essay draws on her own experiences as a hunter to ask whether wildlife hunting can persist into the future without harming "wilderness" itself. The final essay in the chapter and in the book, by Patagonia CEO Yvon Chouinard, explains how and why Chouinard transformed his outdoor clothing company to more sustainable practices, thereby raising important questions about whether business and the natural environment can ever be truly symbiotic.

As you read this final chapter, consider the ways in which recreational activities relate to sustainability. Do the articles in this chapter make you reconsider the impact of tourism and recreation on our shared resources? Do you engage in sustainable recreation, or do you plan to change your recreational activities to become more sustainable? In what ways are tourism and leisure activities both detrimental and beneficial to sustainability?

Why Sustainable Tourism Should Matter to You

Amanda Williams

Amanda Williams is the author of the travel blog "A Dangerous Business," named after a quote from the *Lord of the Rings* series. Williams received a bachelor's degree in journalism at Ohio Northern University and a master's degree in Hospitality and Tourism Management at Kent State University. She created her blog in February 2010 and has since written many articles about travel and tourism.

In this article, Amanda Williams begins by defining and explaining the difference between truly sustainable tourism and greenwashing, an unethical strategy sometimes used by travel companies to entice environmentally responsible people. Williams discusses the three pillars of sustainable tourism — environmental, economic, and sociocultural — and how all three pillars need to be present in order for a place or travel plan to be deemed "eco-friendly." As you read, think about the travelling you have done and whether or not it could be considered sustainable.

The words "sustainable" and "responsible" have become buzzwords in tourism in recent years, right up there with "eco-friendly" as the newest thing to strive for for many tour companies and travel businesses.

But *sustainable tourism*. What is it, really? And why should the average tourist like you or I care about it?

When buzzwords like these come up, it's a natural reaction, I think, to tune out. To assume that glazed-eye look and let your mind wander a bit because clearly these sorts of things are for executives and experts to worry about, right?

Well, you'd actually be wrong.

Sure, tourism boards and tour companies can pledge to more sus- 5 tainable practices in their businesses. But until we as tourists care about sustainability and responsible travel, the efforts of those executives and experts will only go so far.

Before I can answer the question of why sustainable tourism should matter to you, though, I first need to explain what "sustainable tourism" actually means.

What Is Sustainable Tourism?

To most people, "sustainable" is synonymous with "eco-friendly." They think of geothermal-powered hotels, conservation efforts, and companies concerned with their carbon footprints.

And it's true that being environmentally conscious *is* a big part of being sustainable. But it's not the only thing to consider. An attraction or destination can be as "green" as green can be, and still not be sustainable.

When it comes to sustainability, there are actually three main parts which we can look at as "pillars." These pillars are environmental, economic, and sociocultural. They all are equally important, just as all four walls are important to holding up the roof of a house. Tourism has to be sustainable in all three areas to truly be considered "sustainable tourism."

Environmental Sustainability

The environment is obviously important to tourism—without the place, tourism would not exist. Both the natural environment (such as beaches, forests, and waterways) and the built environment (such as historic buildings and ruins) must be preserved for an area to be environmentally sustainable.

Environmental sustainability means making sure resources in an area (whatever they may be) can be preserved for use by future generations of both locals and tourists. And it's much more than just reusing towels in a hotel and calling it being "green." It means being aware of the impact that lots of visitors can have on a destination and finding ways to make that impact as positive as possible.

Sociocultural Sustainability

When an area starts being visited by tourists, there are bound to be some social and cultural impacts of those tourists on the host community. Locals may see increased congestion and overcrowding in towns and cities, the introduction of new languages and values, and perhaps even an influx of migrant workers to be employed in the tourist industry. Some destinations may even see an increase in instances of petty crime.

Sociocultural sustainability, then, means minimizing these negative impacts and focusing on more positive ones, such as promoting cultural exchange and preserving local traditions. This can usually be achieved by getting the locals involved in the tourism industry. This could be as simple as encouraging the sharing of interesting local customs (like artwork or dancing), or as involved as making it easier for locals to start or own new businesses to serve tourists.

Having the community involved will not only offer visitors a more genuine experience, but the locals will be more likely to see tourism in a positive light because they will feel a sense of ownership and pride in it.

Economic Sustainability

The last pillar of sustainability revolves around perhaps the most 15 important part: the money. Many people don't take into account economics when thinking about sustainability, but it's really the key to making a tourism venture sustainable.

In not-so-interesting technical terms, economic sustainability means building linkages and reducing leakages. In simpler terms, this essentially means *keeping the money local.* A hotel or company owned and operated by a foreigner or huge international brand is not likely to contribute much to the local economy—the money will likely "leak" overseas instead. This is not sustainable in the long run because it means the destination will not see any of those tourism dollars, and may begin to question the tourism industry altogether.

Not only should the community be *involved* in tourism, but they should also all share in the financial benefits gleaned from it in order to encourage them to care about the other pillars just as much.

Why Does Sustainable Tourism Matter?

So why does all of this matter? Clearly tourism has survived up until now without such a huge discussion about sustainable, responsible travel.

But here's the thing we have to remember: it's only in the last couple of decades that tourism has truly exploded. More people around the world have disposable income and an interest in travel today than ever before. This is putting a strain on the tourism industry as a whole—and especially on the most popular destinations.

For this reason, sustainable tourism is incredibly important right now. 20

I remember the first time I saw Angkor Wat in Cambodia. I was so incredibly excited to see those iconic towers and lily-littered moat. It's a UNESCO World Heritage Site, after all, and one of the largest religious monuments in the world.

But as soon as I arrived, I knew immediately that something was wrong.

First, I was paying $40 for a 3-day pass to all the Angkor temples in a country where many people don't even make that much income in a month. (I later learned that the company that manages Angkor isn't even based in the country.) Second, the site was incredibly crowded with both tourists in short shorts and hawkers selling cheap souvenirs.

I didn't feel like I was at a temple, and I certainly didn't feel good about spending my money there.

I've written about my thoughts on Cambodia before, but basically what I saw at Angkor Wat was unsustainable tourism personified. Tourism where making money is the prime objective and the preservation of the site is secondary. Tourism where visitors aren't interacting with locals in any meaningful way and where the locals aren't benefitting a whole lot financially.

I've said it before, but I'll say it again: I'm scared to see what Angkor Wat will look like 20 years from now.

Because that's the thing about sustainable tourism and why we really should care: **sustainable tourism helps preserve sites like Angkor Wat for future generations.** If we only think short-term (i.e., just about our own travels), who knows how much longer some of these historical, cultural, and natural sites will be around.

> "Because that's the thing about sustainable tourism and why we really should care: sustainable tourism helps preserve sites like Angkor Wat for future generations."

25

Tourism for Tomorrow

So now that you have a better grasp of what sustainable tourism is and why it matters, how can you ensure that *you're* traveling responsibly?

The next time you're torn between two attractions or destinations or hotels or tour companies, consider these questions:

- Which one is locally owned? 30
- Which one employs local people?
- Which one contributes the most to the local economy?
- Which one is more sensitive to its impacts on the host community?
- Which one is better for the environment?

Basically, which one is more sustainable? 35

Things that are red flags when it comes to sustainability include:

- **Companies the promote "local" tours but only employ non-local guides.** Remember those "leakages" we talked about, and how important it is for locals to get involved in tourism in order to feel ownership in it? Companies who hire exclusively non-local guides or drivers are not really sustainable since much of the money tourists spend with them is not staying in the destination.

- **Attractions that exploit people or animals.** Don't engage in orphanage tourism. Don't ride elephants. Don't go to tiger temples. Basically, don't participate in tourism that forces people or animals to perform demeaning or painful tasks just for the sake of entertaining you.

- **Places that are over-touristed instead of preserved.** Angkor Wat, for example, is not really being properly maintained or preserved, and the main temples can be way too crowded. I'm not saying you shouldn't go to places like this—just do your research and see if there are any alternatives you can visit instead, or perhaps a less crowded time of year to go.

- **Companies that promote "eco-friendly" travel but can't back it up.** "Greenwashing" is a big problem in tourism. If a company is truly dedicated to being environmentally friendly, you should be able to tell by their actions and initiatives. Look for companies that offset their carbon footprint, participate in recycling, support reforestation, and legitimately take steps to ensure that they are leaving a positive footprint on the environment.   40

In the end, it's up to US as travelers to do a better job of supporting sustainable tourism (demanding it, even) so that we can ensure better tourism for the future.

Understanding the Text

1. How does the author define the three pillars of sustainable tourism and how are they related? How does this align with the description of sustainability in the Introduction to this book?
2. According to the author, why is sustainable tourism important?
3. What are the red flags regarding travel that are discussed in this article?

Reflection and Response

4. Have your travel experiences been sustainable? If so, what did you do that would qualify it as sustainable? If not, how might you make your future travel plans more sustainable?
5. Do you agree with the author about the importance of sustainable travel? Why or why not?

Making Connections

6. Do some research on tourist destinations. How do they describe themselves in terms of their environmental awareness/sustainability efforts? Evaluate their statements using the questions the author offers for consideration when planning a trip.
7. Disney's resorts and amusement parks claim they have done extensive research on sustainability and have designed their parks to be "environmentally friendly." Read up on their efforts and decide whether they could be deemed a sustainable tourist destination. Create an argument to support your opinion.

Overtourism and the Struggle for Sustainable Tourism Development

Wouter Geerts

Wouter Geerts is a senior travel analyst at Euromonitor International, a global and independent market research organization. Geerts earned his PhD in business travel, with a special interest in environmentalism and sustainability in industries, at Royal Holloway University in London. Geerts is a frequent contributor to Euromonitor International's blog, where he writes about the travel and tourism industry.

"Overtourism and the Struggle for Sustainable Tourism Development," originally published on Skift.com, a platform providing news, ideas, and market research on all facets of the travel industry, explores the toll tourism can take on destinations like Barcelona, Machu Picchu, and Zion National Park. The article defines sustainable tourism while discussing proposed solutions and challenges the travel industry faces in becoming more sustainable. As you read, think about how your role as a tourist might impact the destinations you visit.

With 2017 being the United Nations' International Year of Sustainable Tourism for Development, now is as good a time as ever to take stock of the opportunities and challenges faced by tourism providers trying to ensure the long-term sustainability of the industry.

While tourism is important to many local and national economies, overcrowding is changing the perception of the benefits of mass tourism. Spain is a prime example of a country struggling with its popularity.

Barcelona's relationship with tourism has been shaky for a number of years now. Already in 2014, the documentary "Bye Bye Barcelona" highlighted the negative impact of mass tourism on the city. Locals fear that they will be priced out of the housing market, eventually resulting in Barcelona losing population diversity and character. The local government has stopped issuing licenses for new hotels and has banned change-of-use permits required for holiday lets.

And Barcelona is not alone. As of 2017, Santorini is limiting the number of cruise visitors to 8,000 per day. Local activists in Venice have asked government to ban cruise ships stopping in its harbor, as cruise visitors have quintupled in the past 15 years. Cinque Terre on the Italian coast is capping the number of visitors to 1.5 million per year. Popular attractions including Machu Picchu and Mount Everest are capping the number of visitors and require visitors to be accompanied by a recognized guide, and Zion National Park is looking at proposals to limit visitors through a reservation system.

Capping tourists is a drastic measure, and surely not something desti- 5
nations would like to do. It is often seen as a last resort, and the fact that
more and more tourist destinations see no other way to remain sustainable and competitive is telling of the apparent failure of other initiatives.

Defining Sustainable Tourism

Sustainable tourism development is not a new phenomenon. Already
in 1992 the International Hotels Environment Initiative was launched.
And since then the drive by organizations in the tourism industry to
implement the concept of sustainability has led to the growth of many
alternative formats of tourism. From eco-friendly to ethical, the objective
of sustainable tourism is to retain the economic and social advantages
of tourism development, while reducing or mitigating any undesirable
impacts on the natural, historic, cultural or social environment.

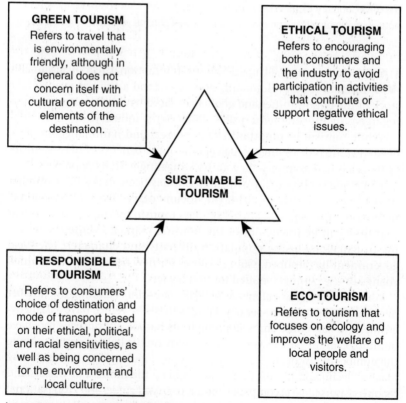

GREEN TOURISM
Refers to travel that
is environmentally
friendly, although in
general does not
concern itself with
cultural or economic
elements of the
destination.

ETHICAL TOURISM
Refers to encouraging
both consumers and
the industry to avoid
participation in activities
that contribute or
support negative ethical
issues.

**SUSTAINABLE
TOURISM**

**RESPONISIBLE
TOURISM**
Refers to consumers'
choice of destination and
mode of transport based
on their ethical, political,
and racial sensitivities, as
well as being concerned
for the environment and
local culture.

ECO-TOURISM
Refers to tourism that
focuses on ecology and
improves the welfare of
local people and
visitors.

Infographic on Sustainable Tourism

Governments, Businesses, and Individuals All Must Take Responsibility

The problem with sustainable tourism development, as most of the key issues of our time, is that it requires the informed participation of all relevant stakeholders, as well as strong political leadership to ensure wide participation and consensus building. As Trump's recent insinuation that climate change is a hoax created by the Chinese shows, this participation and commitment is not always easy to find. Achieving sustainable tourism is a continuous process, and it requires constant monitoring of impacts, introducing the necessary preventive and corrective measures whenever necessary.

Sustainable tourism development can only be achieved if governments, businesses and individuals take responsibility for improving their (and others') behavior. While understanding of behavior is improving, taking responsibility is often lacking.

The Business Case for Sustainable Development Falls Short

Hotel companies provide a good example of what can be achieved through commitment, but also what is still unachievable if efforts are not concerted and far-reaching enough.

The business case for corporate social responsibility (CSR) is one of 10 the strongest arguments in favor of sustainable development in the hotel industry, with many hotels implementing CSR practices to increase their profitability. Most major hotel chains have their own set of targets to reduce the negative impact on the natural environment and provide benefits for the local community. Concerted efforts such as the International Tourism Partnership (ITP) see hotel chains collaborate to increase their influence and to share best practices.

However, hotels implementing sustainability practices to reduce money can only take us so far. The same goes for airlines who are seemingly focusing solely on technological innovations to improve their environmental performances. To achieve genuinely sustainable tourism development, companies will need to go beyond the business case and use truly innovative thinking around traveler expectations, and use sustainability practices to shape and improve experiences.

The Attitude-Behavior Gap Provides Challenges

One glaring issue here is that there is persistently conflicting data on what travelers really want. While surveys show that individuals feel increasingly responsible about their impact on the environment, this does not necessarily translate into action, a phenomenon that has in the past been referred to as the 30:3 syndrome. While 30% of respondents to a survey claimed to be ethical consumers, only 3% actually bought ethical products.

This provides a difficult situation for tourism players. On the one hand, providing sustainable products and services can be pushed as an entry-level way for people to interact with ideas around sustainable development and their personal impact. On the other hand, it promotes increased consumption, while in the long run reducing consumption might be the key to combating climate issues. Luxury hotels, in particular, have struggled with asking its guests to reduce their consumption after they have paid large amounts to stay in the hotel.

It Starts with Information

Change is in the air, however, and it all starts with information. One thing is beyond doubt: in order to get guests to change their behavior, companies need to start providing better information. Without providing information, individuals cannot be expected to know why and how to change their current behavior.

"One thing is beyond doubt: in order to get guests to change their behavior, companies need to start providing better information."

Take the following example: local produce has seen a strong rise in popularity in the past decade, and supermarkets and hospitality establishments are increasingly offering a wide range of locally sourced foods. When considering the environmental impact of food consumption, however, it is often far from clear whether it is better to, for example, buy tomatoes which are produced locally in an artificially heated greenhouse, or whether to opt for the naturally ripened, and subsequently flown in, tomatoes from a country with a warmer climate. This means that for consumers it is often hard to decide whether a product is truly more ethical than alternatives, or whether a company is "greenwashing." The result is consumers mistrusting information provided by companies, and companies subsequently providing less CSR information, spiraling into a vicious cycle.

The Environmental Certification Landscape Reduces Clarity

One way to combat the fear of greenwashing, is by licensing good behavior. Environmental certification schemes provide travelers with more accurate information about the environmental performance of destinations and hotels, and offer management a save way of promoting their achievements.

Again, however, there are issues here. The sheer number of certification schemes offered, and the way they are monitored, is a point of concern. There are over 100 sustainability certification schemes for tourism and hospitality organizations. The large number of schemes means that they become less recognizable and less trusted by travelers, especially since each geographical region has its own certification scheme. The proliferation of different certification schemes, and other programs and standards, has the opposite effect to what it tries to achieve. Instead of providing clarity regarding which hotels are the frontrunners, the sheer number of different programs only clouds the market.

How to Move Forward

The terms "responsible tourism" and "sustainable tourism" indicate that this is only a part of all tourism, and today this reasoning runs true. However, at the current trajectory, in 10 years, all tourism will have to be responsible and sustainable. As Fabian Cousteau said at the WTTC Global Summit 2016: "I look forward to the day when there is no sustainable tourism. Just tourism." This shift results in travelers increasingly expecting their airlines, accommodation providers, tour guides and attractions to be environmentally and socially responsible.

In the past decades, tourism has gone from being sidelined to being one of the key industries to achieve the Sustainable Development Goals. The tourism industry needs to own up to its responsibility and see sustainable development as an opportunity to improve the longevity of the very product the industry relies on. Working together with all stakeholders, including local communities, regulators, employees, guests and competitors, will be key to the success of the tourism industry in the long run.

Today, the overwhelming reason for tourism businesses to implement 20 environmental practices is to reduce costs. This "light-green" approach to sustainable tourism development falls short, and it is likely that practices which save costs will become the norm. Hotels will need to try and stand out through truly innovative thinking around guest expectations and using sustainability practices to improve experiences. Running a successful business will mean involving employees, local communities, and guests in equal measures in the decision-making process.

Understanding the Text

1. According to Geerts, what is the objective of sustainable tourism? What is the central problem of sustainable tourism development?

2. How is the 30:3 rule related to sustainable tourism development, and why does it pose a significant dilemma?

3. Geerts states that "the overwhelming reason for tourism businesses to implement environmental practices is to reduce costs." Why does he believe that is problematic?

Reflection and Response

4. What could you do to make sure your travel choices are sustainable?

5. Have you ever considered tourism as being environmentally invasive or a danger to the environment?

6. Now that you have read this article, how do you imagine locals might feel about their home being a tourist destination?

Making Connections

7. What are the connections between this article and the previous article in the chapter, "Why Sustainable Tourism Should Matter to You"?

8. Research a hotel in your dream travel destination. Do they have any sustainability practices? How do they market those practices and how does it influence your choice to stay there?

9. Imagine you have been hired as a sustainable tourism consultant, and develop a list of ten strategies or guidelines for creating a sustainable destination.

Our National Parks and the Search for Sustainability

Bob O'Brien

Bob O'Brien was a professor of geography at San Diego State University. He taught courses on national parks, outdoor recreation, and ecotourism. An avid traveler, Bob explored all seven continents and twice completed the 222-mile John Muir Trail.

This excerpt from O'Brien's book *Our National Parks and the Search for Sustainability* examines the history of national parks and explains their importance to society. In the book, O'Brien suggests that national parks are good for environmental preservation and simultaneously provide enjoyment for visitors. He also proposes some solutions for how national parks could be preserved. As you read, think about the importance of national parks. What role do they play in our culture?

When we complain about lack of political concern with the environment we should think back 125 years, to the time when the first national park was established, and be thankful for what we have. Then, there were no environmental legislation, no environmental organizations, and almost no ecological concern. There were of course far fewer people in the United States, only about 40 million in 1872, but they were capable of immense destruction with no environmental laws or ethics to stop them. Most of the big game animals in America, such as bison, elk, and antelope, were in danger of becoming extinct, and landscapes from forests to grasslands were losing their productivity. The entire natural landscape had little value for most people, and without the environmental consciousness that came with the national parks movement, the nation would be far bleaker than it is today.

I consider the establishment of Yellowstone National Park° one of the real miracles of American history. In the midst of one of the most rapacious eras in our history, we quietly set aside an area the size of one of the original states to be preserved in perpetuity. The establishment of national parks has probably been the most copied of American institutions, emulated by over a hundred nations today.

President Grant° signed the Yellowstone National Park Act on March 1, 1872. The key words in this act of only six hundred words

---

Yellowstone National Park: a national park located primarily in Wyoming. It was established in 1872 as the first U.S. national park and has many geothermal features, including the popular Old Faithful Geyser.

President Grant: Ulysses S. Grant (1822–1885), the eighteenth president of the United States (1869–77).

were: "[Yellowstone Park] . . . is hereby reserved and withdrawn from settlement, occupancy, or sale under the laws of the United States, and dedicated and set apart as a public park or pleasuring-ground for the benefit and enjoyment of the people . . . [and] such regulations shall provide for the preservation from injury or spoliation of all timber, mineral deposits, natural curiosities, or wonders within said park, and their retention in their natural condition."

Here we have an act that breaks new ground in two major fields: it gave to the *people* of the United States—not individuals, not states—a large parcel of land to enjoy as a park, and it called for the preservation of that landscape in its natural state, in perpetuity. We have then the forerunner of thousands of areas throughout the world preserved as parks, wilderness areas, game refuges, and other areas for the enjoyment of the people. We also have, in reality, one of the first attempts at a sustainable use of a landscape.

Sustainability is the key word for environmentalists today, or for that matter anyone who cares about the future of this planet. At one time it may have been possible to live off the capital of the land, to leave the world a little less able to support those who came afterwards; now we *have* to find a sustainable lifestyle to have any hope at all for the future. Yet, with so many people of the world living in grinding poverty, sustainability becomes an almost impossible dream. The rainforest and its priceless contribution to world biodiversity° and climatic stability count for less than the few years' survival it can promise to those who slash and burn. On a different level, even in the United States and Canada it is hard to preserve the small amount of ancient forest left when jobs in lumbering are at stake. Here, and through much of the world where remnants of the natural landscape exist, ecotourism offers almost the only hope of saving those landscapes.

Ecotourism is a form of tourism that offers economic support to attractive tourist destinations that would otherwise be exploited for timber, minerals, agriculture, or water resources. Classic ecotourism locations—Costa Rica, Nepal, Africa—are relatively poor areas where the influx of foreign travel dollars offers the alternative to cutting the rainforest, farming steep hillsides, or killing elephants. The same principles, however, can be applied to raft trips through the Grand Canyon, which helped keep dams out of the canyon, or making a tourist destination out of a historic village where a shopping center is planned.

The basic idea of national parks, from the beginning, was to preserve the parks for the people's enjoyment. It became obvious, however, that

biodiversity: diversity among and within plant and animal species in an environment.

if a person's enjoyment consisted of breaking off pieces of one of Yellowstone's geyser cones for souvenirs or catching hundreds of trout in an afternoon, this brand of ecotourism was not going to work. The use must be sustainable. Protecting the parks meant preserving the park from commercial exploitation, *and* preserving it from the tourists. The first goal was the most important in the early years of the national parks, while the second has been the most important in recent years.

The national parks have been highly successful in achieving their earliest goals: to preserve the parks from commercial exploitation and to make easily accessible the most scenic portions of the United States. The preservation question is the subject of this book, but let's look at the geographic question: are the most scenic portions of the United States in the National Park System? One has only to flip through any travel brochure or picture book of the United States to answer in the affirmative, but listing superlatives also hints at the attractiveness of the national parks. Here are a few: tallest mountain in North America and one of tallest in the world from base to top (Mount McKinley in Denali National Park); most active volcanic area in United States (Hawaii Volcanoes National Park); most recent volcano in the conterminous United States (Mount Saint Helens Volcanic National Monument, run by the U.S. Forest Service); largest canyon in the world (Grand Canyon); tallest waterfalls in the United States (Yosemite); deepest lake in the United States (Crater Lake); tallest, largest, and oldest trees in the world (Redwood, Sequoia, and Great Basin National Parks); highest temperature in the United States (Death Valley); and. greatest annual snowfall in the world (Mount Rainier).

> "We must be proud of our wisdom in setting aside national parks."

Focusing on the unique and spectacular might cause us to ignore what ultimately will be the most important factor in park management: preserving habitat and ecosystems. The value of park areas has climbed sharply in the last few decades as the acreage of natural areas in the United States has been reduced. Rocky Mountain National Park was probably not the most beautiful section of the Colorado Rocky Mountains that could have been preserved in a park, but as the years go by it is becoming increasingly unique as ski resorts and backcountry vehicles scar the rest of the Colorado backcountry. It is becoming evident that we should have paid more attention to the "ordinary" landscapes such as prairie, coastal lagoons, marshlands, and hardwood forests, which might be ecologically more important than spectacular landscapes like mountains.

Other benefits seemed even more obscure when the national parks 10 were first established. Wildlife, for example, was not particularly abundant in Yellowstone National Park compared to areas outside the park in the 1870s. Animals, like humans, prefer rich, warm lowlands to high, cold plateaus. The animals will live, however, where they need to live to survive, and in the days when game laws were virtually nonexistent they found safety inside park boundaries. Because it was protected, Yellowstone National Park became the home of the last wild buffalo herd in the United States, some of the last elk, and some of the last trumpeter swans. National parks gave breathing room to many species in the days before game laws had a chance to protect wildlife.

Watershed protection is an added bonus in having national parks. Many rivers, such as the Snake, Yellowstone, and Missouri, flow out of our parks pure and naturally regulated by uncut vegetation and undisturbed soil that absorbs the often copious rainfall. How many dams and water treatment plants would be necessary to replace what we get for free in the parks? The sight of a free-flowing stream, undammed and unpolluted, is a sight rare enough to thrill many park visitors.

Wilderness travel has become a major form of outdoor recreation. More and more people are discovering the ultimate delight in the out-of-doors, where the landscape is unmarred by roads, buildings, and the crush of people. In the national parks, wilderness begins just beyond the shoulder of the road and can be enjoyed by visitors the minute they enter park boundaries. Outside the national parks, roads invariably mean development, whether cutover forests, mined hillsides, or dammed streams. To the park motorist, roads seem numerous, but by far the greatest acreage in most national parks is roadless. Of course, the best wilderness experience comes when you leave roads far behind, and set out on foot to discover land affected only by nature.

Most visitors want only to escape the urban environment, and even the most crowded areas of the parks can fill that need. Visitors are apt to feel they are back in the city in the area surrounding Old Faithful, where thousands of people mingle for food, lodging, and parking. Then they catch a glimpse of a buffalo in the distance and can look miles beyond into pristine wilderness.

The first attention given to outdoor recreation by the federal government centered on the national parks, although it was not intended as a primary purpose of the parks. Recreational travel by car, bicycle, or on foot; recreational living in tent, trailer, cabin, or resort; boating, swimming, fishing, nature study, cross-country skiing, and mountaineering can reach their qualitative peak in the national parks. The escalation of these pursuits has worried many who feel that they could take place just as easily outside the parks, but most of the pursuits mentioned above can, with care, continue to be enjoyed at their present level, and some, like hiking, can be much expanded.

In a situation that makes local chambers of commerce happy and 15
fills environmentalists with foreboding, the National Park System has
become one of the top tourist attractions in the world. It would be hard
to think of a way to extract a greater monetary benefit from developing
the resources of any park than the tourist dollars that flow into it now.
Even cutting back development within the parks would not stem the flow
of tourist income into the surrounding areas, because the more beautiful
the parks become, the more people are going to want to see them.

Finally, the educational value of the national parks is immense. People
come to the Grand Canyon primarily to see one of the great natural wonders in the world. Many of them will also just look awhile, take a picture,
and leave. But most will wonder how the canyon was formed and stand
in awe at the unimaginable duration represented by one of the greatest
exposures of geologic time in the world. They might also wonder how
the area is being preserved by the National Park Service (NPS) for future
generations and what is being done about current problems such as the
noise from overflights and overcrowding. The answers are available there
from rangers, in visitor centers, and in an extensive literature on the canyon and the park, although lack of funds has reduced the educational
potential of this and other national parks.

We must be proud of our wisdom in setting aside national parks.
We all sometimes look at our past and think of ourselves as heartless
exploiters of the country's natural wealth. Thanks to the national parks,
however, and other forms of preservation that have followed, we have
probably saved more of the country's outstanding scenic, historic, and
scientific areas than we have lost. Furthermore, there is every expectation
that the national parks might someday represent one of the largest areas
of sustainable use in the world.

Understanding the Text

1. Which national park does O'Brien consider "one of the real miracles of
   American history"? Why was its establishment important?
2. What are some benefits of national parks as described in this article? How
   do economics and education factor in to these benefits?

Reflection and Response

3. How do you think environmentalism has changed over the past century?
4. Why do you think national parks are important?
5. What is the danger in focusing only on the "unique and spectacular" in
   national parks? Why should we have more "ordinary" places preserved?

Making Connections

6. Have you ever visited a national park? Describe the experience. If you haven't, research the nearest one and describe it.

7. This article also discusses sustainable tourism. How does O'Brien's opinion compare to the previous articles by Williams and Geerts?

8. John Muir's article in Chapter 1 of this book (page 39) addresses a similar topic and location. Imagine a conversation between O'Brien and Muir. What would they have to say to each other? Would Muir agree with (or be surprised by) the things that O'Brien mentions?

What Zoo Critics Don't Understand

Jack Hanna

Zookeeper Jack Hanna is widely recognized for his appearances on television programs, including *Jack Hanna's Wild Countdown* and *Jack Hanna's Into the Wild*, where he performs animal demonstrations and speaks on animal welfare. Hanna served as the director of the Columbus Zoo and Aquarium in Ohio for fourteen years, during which time he increased the zoo's annual attendance by over 400 percent. He currently serves as the zoo's director emeritus, continuing to appear on television and travel to discuss the importance of zoos.

This article was published in *Time* magazine in 2015, amid harsh criticisms aimed at zoos and programs like SeaWorld. The article encourages dialogue between zoos and zoo critics, while also defending zoos by pointing out the safety and support they provide for endangered species. As you read, consider your position on zoos and what you might ask a zookeeper if given the chance.

D r. Jane Goodall recently made two statements critical of zoos and aquariums. She said two elephants in a zoo in Seattle should be released to a sanctuary and that SeaWorld should be shut down. After the Woodland Park Zoo in Seattle invited her to learn more about the zoo's decisions regarding elephants, she took them up on their invitation. I admire Dr. Goodall for her willingness to learn more and re-evaluate her initial comments. I hope Dr. Goodall will also engage in a conversation with SeaWorld about her concerns.

I encourage other zoo critics to do the same thing—engage in a meaningful dialogue so that together we can do the best thing for animals. I'm growing weary of the us-versus-them mentality. Although zoo critics and zoo champions have some differing philosophies, we all have the same priorities—animal welfare, conservation, and education. I am confident we can co-exist and be more productive if we work side-by-side.

Visiting zoos and aquariums is the largest recreational activity in the United States. More than 175 million people visit zoos and aquariums accredited by the Association of Zoos and Aquariums (AZA) each year. Zoos and aquariums play a critical role in the survival of endangered species and allow people from all walks of life to experience and learn about the animal world. Animals in zoos are ambassadors to their cousins in the wild—they educate people about the importance of wildlife. After a visit to the zoo—listening, seeing, smelling—people often leave with a newfound understanding and compassion for wildlife.

AZA accreditation requires excellence in animal care and welfare, conservation, education and scientific studies. There are more than 200 accredited institutions, and in 2013, they donated nearly $160 million to support about 2,450 conservation projects in more than 120 countries. Species such as the black-footed ferret, California condor, Mexican wolf, scimitar-horned oryx, and Przewalski's horses have overcome near-extinction in part because of zoos' commitment to conservation.

Critics say the only place animals belong is in the wild, but those   5
boundaries are shrinking each day. Having traveled the world, the only places I consider truly "wild" are Antarctica, parts of the Amazon and some places in Africa. Even in Africa, the "wild" places tend to be national parks with guarded boundaries. Animals face many challenges, including habitat loss, poaching, severe weather, and war. The "wild" is not necessarily the idyllic place people imagine. Poaching has decimated the northern white rhino population—the last known male has his own personal 24-hour security to ensure he isn't poached for his horn.

I've loved animals since I was a young boy and have dedicated my life to improving zoos and educating people about wildlife. In my more than 40-year career, I've taken an active role in modernizing zoological

Zoologist Jack Hanna with the author, Christian Weisser.
Courtesy Christian Weisser

parks to provide top-notch habitats, veterinary care, and enrichment, and meaningful educational opportunities for guests. During my tenure at the Columbus Zoo and Aquarium and the Wilds, I've had the pleasure of working with dozens of zoos, including SeaWorld Parks and Entertainment.

I can tell you firsthand that the animals in SeaWorld's parks receive world-class care. Their zoological team shares my commitment to protecting and preserving species; educating young people about the risks that animals face in the natural world; and inspiring the next generation of conservationists, marine biologists, scientists, and animal enthusiasts. The animal care teams at SeaWorld understand the value of studying animals in zoological settings in order to save future generations.

Furthermore, this spring I witnessed SeaWorld's rescue teams in full swing. More than 25,000 animals owe their lives to SeaWorld animal rescue teams. Just this year, they have saved more than 500 sea lions on the West Coast. The SeaWorld team has worked around the clock to rehabilitate these animals, all with the goal of returning them to the wild. The team at SeaWorld San Diego even built two new pools to accommodate them, and closed its Sea Lion and Otter Show so that its staff could dedicate more time to nursing the pups back to health.

Every aquarium and zoo I work with believes its mission includes raising awareness about the challenges faced by animals around the world. We know animals have the power to touch our hearts, and when this happens, it opens the door to education that can inspire people to participate in protecting animals and conserving their environments. As worldwide animal populations continue to decline and children have less face-to-face experiences with animals, it's my hope that all animal advocates—zoos, researchers, scientists, activists, philanthropists, the media, and animal lovers everywhere—will join forces to make a difference.

> "We know animals have the power to touch our hearts, and when this happens, it opens the door to education that can inspire people to participate in protecting animals and conserving their environments."

Understanding the Text

1. What is the "critical role" that zoos play, according to the author?
2. How does the author challenge the argument that all animals belong in the wild?
3. What is AZA accreditation and how does it relate to zoos?

Reflection and Response

4. Do you find Jack Hanna's personal attestment effective in supporting his general argument?
5. What is your personal opinion on zoos and aquariums? Do you believe they are ethical? Why or why not?
6. Have you visited a zoo recently? If so, what sort of treatment and environment did you see being provided for the animals?

Making Connections

7. How does this article connect to Elizabeth Kolbert's "The Sixth Extinction" in Chapter 3? Do you believe Kolbert would be a supporter or critic of zoos?
8. Research a zoo in your state, or a nearby state. Do they address the concerns of zoo critics anywhere on their website? How so?

Is Hunting Sustainable?

Robyn Migliorini

Robyn Migliorini holds a PhD in Clinical Psychology from San Diego State University. She is a self-taught hunter who had never touched a gun or bow before the age of 23. Her website, Modern Hunters, was born out of this experience. Her articles and blog postings frequently focus on eco-friendly hunting practices and the connection between humans and nature.

"Is Hunting Sustainable?" was originally published on the Modern Hunters website. The article discusses the importance of hunters working with nature to ensure that the natural life cycle of animals isn't disrupted. Migliorini describes how state and federal legislatures manage and regulate hunting, ensuring that species are not over-harvested. As you read, consider some of the benefits and criticisms of hunting, as well as any personal experiences you might have with wild animals.

> Oh, give me a home where the buffalo roam,
> Where the deer and the antelope play
>
> —BREWSTER HIGLEY, "HOME ON THE RANGE" (1872)

Thirty years after "Home on the Range" was written, only 500 buffalo remained in the United States. In Kansas—Higley's home state—deer were gone and antelope practically nonexistent. Their habitats largely destroyed by human development, these iconic game animals were hunted out of existence.

In an era where "eco-friendly" is the hip phrase of the day, new hunters and the hunting curious are more frequently asking if hunting is sustainable. Could I take up hunting, they wonder, as an environmentally-conscious means to eat? Is hunting better for the earth than buying meat at the grocery store? Should we all just revert back to a hunter-gatherer lifestyle to "save the planet"?

The phrase "sustainability" conjures myriad associations, from serious environmentalism to halfhearted greenwashing. We often label things as sustainable when they're simply better than the environmentally destructive status quo. But in the strictest sense, sustainability refers to the ability to be continued indefinitely without detriment to environmental integrity.

Can Hunting Sustain Itself?

Hunting is a practice that relies on the health of the wild. When I consider the sustainability of hunting, I ask—can hunting persist into the foreseeable future without harming the very wild upon which it depends?

In his book *Bloodties*, Ted Kerasote writes, "As a farmer you reap what 5
you have sown; as a hunter-gatherer you reap what the land provides from her pagan solicitude." The essence of Kerasote's point is well taken, but what wild land provides boils down to much more than pagan solicitude. While hunters don't usually reap what we individually sow, hunters do reap what we collectively sow. The degree to which we, as a group, conserve and harvest now helps determine the populations of wild plants and animals in the future.

My ability to find and kill wild animals for food depends on natural cycles far greater and richer than I am able to enumerate. With reproduction, growth, death, and decay the earth recycles itself. When I take a mule deer buck or a pair of jackrabbits from my local desert, I influence that cycle.

Left unmanaged, hunting would be—and was—unsustainable. In the 1800s, wild animals seemed like a limitless resource to many hunters.

Robyn Migliorini on a desert hunt.
Courtesy Robyn Migliorini

But by the early 1900s, before the advent of hunting regulations, things had changed. Habitat loss, mostly from clearing forest to create farms, and over-hunting had left most game populations in a sorry state. Wild turkeys were nearly wiped out. Duck numbers plummeted. Whitetail deer were uncommon in places like Connecticut and extirpated in Kansas. As Mark Schlegel writes, "We were plucking America bare."

Thankfully—after pushing many species to or over the brink of extinction—hunters lobbied for restrictions on hunting. Eventually federal Wildlife Restoration acts, new state fish and game agencies, and taxes on weapons and ammunition helped protect remaining wild animals. With regulations, money, and political willpower, many states went to great lengths to restore decimated animal populations. Turkey in Missouri, sage grouse in North Dakota, and elk in Tennessee tell the American restoration and conservation success story. Many hunters have cherished sustainability and practiced ecological stewardship for decades.

Hunting, fishing, and trapping are now professionally managed. Wildlife biologists monitor populations and set quotas for the number of animals to be harvested in a given season. The money paid for hunting licenses, tags, and stamps is fed back into the conservation system. Taxes on firearms and ammunition provide hundreds of millions of dollars for wild lands each year. And while illegal hunting (poaching) still exists, by and large the regulatory system seems to be working. Hunting can sustain itself. And assuming the number of hunters remains stable and current trends of land protection, habitat restoration, and population management continue, hunting will be sustainable into the future.

Hunting for Sustainable Food

Is hunted venison more environmentally friendly than beef from the   10
supermarket? Is wild quail a more ecologically responsible culinary choice than factory-farmed chicken? Almost certainly. Industrial meat production is riddled with environmental ills, from high levels of carbon emissions to air and water pollution.

By contrast, no extra energy is used to raise wild animals. We don't have to grow grains with pesticides to feed and fatten them. Forests and sagebrush do not need to be cleared. Their waste nourishes, rather than taints, the earth and water. Wild game isn't treated with antibiotics and comes fully unprocessed. As long as wild animals haven't been eating from a contaminated environment, they are truly "organic" meat. Compared to their industrially raised counterparts, elk and quail have a relatively small environmental footprint.

Does that mean hunting is the future of sustainable meat? Should everyone start hunting?

The simple truth about responsible wildlife management is that not everyone can hunt and harvest animals. In the United States we have too many people and not nearly enough wild animals to feed everyone. If all Americans tried to replace their current industrial meat consumption with wild game, they would quickly realize the impossibility of their quest. Demand would far overwhelm supply. Most people would not be able to acquire big game tags due to limits set by biologists. Daily bag limits would need to be cut. Season lengths would need to be reduced.

Unless we want to overturn massive portions of developed land back to the wilderness, only some people will be able to hunt for their food. If we want to preserve wild animals for perpetuity and feed all of America, universal hunting is not the answer. Hunting as a sustainable practice is simply not scalable.

"Hunting as a sustainable practice is simply not scalable."

There are other do-it-yourself sustainable alternatives to the industrial meat industry that are much more feasible. For example, everyone in America with a backyard could raise chickens or ducks. Sure, some cities and homeowners associations would have to change their rules, but it would be fairly easy to implement and scale. Realistically, small-scale conscientious local farming and ranching will play the biggest role in the quest for widely available sustainable meat.

This doesn't mean hunting can't be a part of the sustainable food movement. And it doesn't mean there's no room for new hunters. For every newcomer who learns to hunt, dollars are fed into the U.S. wildlife conservation system. Each new hunter can contribute another voice to groups of sportsmen and women advocating for our wild lands. How much hunting can grow will ultimately be determined by the health and productivity of our forests, plains, and streams. I don't think hunting has reached the limit of its growth yet.

The Eco-Friendly Hunter

For new hunters looking to minimize negative impact on the environment, take heed. There are more and less eco-friendly ways to go about harvesting wild animals.

In line with the locavore food movement, one way to reduce your environmental impact is to hunt close to home. Long-distance car travel requires burning fossil fuel. Plane travel requires burning far more of it. Unfortunately, for many hunters, pursuing local animals is difficult or impossible. Private land and city regulations can close off nearby opportunities. If you're new to hunting, I recommend spending some time researching huntable land in your county or state. Our article "Where Can I Go Hunting?" may be of some assistance.

Hunting can also be fairly gear-intensive. From an environmental standpoint, the production of that gear requires a lot of energy and other natural resources. If you'd like to go a more sustainable route, take a more minimalist perspective to hunting gear. Buy good quality to start, buy only what you need, and resist the urge to always have the latest-and-greatest. Used gear is a great option, too. Many online outdoor and hunting forums have "classifieds" where users can buy or sell gear. Nick and I have acquired a fair chunk of our gear this way, which has saved us a lot of money over the years.

Lead bullets are a contentious topic, but the truth is that excess 20 amounts of lead are not great for ecosystem health. There are non-lead options that are less toxic, but even those aren't perfect. Check out Nick's review of non-lead bullet options, if you're interested.

Finally, you may consider choosing your quarry based upon local environmental needs. Do you live in an area where overabundant deer are eating too much of the local plant life? You could prioritize hunting deer. With natural predators wiped out in the eastern and Midwestern U.S., hunting is a very important and cost-effective method to keep whitetail deer under control. Does your state have a serious wild pig problem? Maybe now is a good time to learn to hunt pigs. The more your hunting goals align with game management plans, the better for environmental health and sustainability.

Conclusion

So is hunting sustainable? It is in some, but not all ways. As a source of food, wild game has a relatively low environmental footprint compared to industrial meat production. But unfortunately, universal hunting and gathering as a primary means to eat in modern America is simply not feasible. Hunting will likely be only a small part of America's local and sustainable food movement.

The wild is a precious and limited resource. Animal populations can be maintained for future generations thanks to decades of regulatory and conservation efforts from sportsmen and women. As a new hunter, you can be a part of this important stewardship. Hunting can sustain itself through our continued efforts.

Understanding the Text

1. What was the result of hunting in the early 1900s?

2. Why does the author claim that hunted meat is healthier than meat bought at a supermarket?

3. What are the author's suggestions for eco-friendly hunting?

Reflection and Response

4. Do you believe that hunting is helpful or harmful to the environment? Explain your opinion.

5. Would you consider hunting for your own meat?

6. Does the author's experience with hunting effectively support her argument?

Making Connections

7. Research the hunting laws in your state. What are the specific regulations? Can you find the current population of an animal that is regularly hunted? How has their population changed over the past couple of years and what does this suggest about the sustainability of hunting?

8. How does this article connect to Jack Hanna's "What Zoo Critics Don't Understand"?

9. How does this article connect with Aldo Leopold's "Thinking like a Mountain," which appears in Chapter 1?

10. Compare and contrast this article with an article or blog posting that is critical of hunting. Which piece makes the better argument, and why?

Let My People Go Surfing

Yvon Chouinard

Yvon Chouinard, born in 1938 in Lewiston, Maine, is considered by *Fortune* to be the most successful outdoor industry businessman in history. Growing up in Maine and Southern California, Chouinard became an avid rock climber, surfer, environmentalist, and businessman. He is the founder and owner of Patagonia, an international clothing and outdoor gear company.

This article begins with personal anecdotes from Chouinard as he explains the purpose of his company, Patagonia. He describes his transition from outdoor athlete to businessman. He then explains how Patagonia worked to become a more sustainable company. As you read, think about the things Patagonia did to become more sustainable, including recycling and reducing pollution.

I had always avoided thinking of myself as a businessman. I was a climber, a surfer, a kayaker, a skier and a blacksmith. We simply enjoyed making good tools and functional clothes that we, and our friends, wanted. My wife, Malinda, and I owned only a beat-up Ford van and a heavily mort-gaged, soon-to-be-condemned cabin on the beach. And now, in 1975, we had a heavily leveraged company with employees with families of their own, all depending on us.

After pondering our responsibilities and financial liabilities, it dawned on me one day that I was a businessman, and would probably continue to be one for a long time. It was clear that in order to survive at this game we had to get serious. But I also knew that I would never be happy play-ing by the normal rules of business. If I had to be a businessman, I was going to do it on my terms.

Work had to be enjoyable on a daily basis. We all had to come to work on the balls of our feet, going up the stairs two steps at a time. We needed to be surrounded by friends who could dress whatever way they wanted, even barefoot. We needed to have flex time to surf the waves when they were good, or ski the powder after a big snowstorm, or stay home and take care of a sick child. We needed to blur that distinction between work and play and family.

From the mid-1980s to 1990, sales at Patagonia° grew from $20 million to $100 million. Malinda and I were not personally any wealthier,

---

Patagonia: a Ventura, California–based clothing company, focusing mainly on high-end outdoor clothing. The company, founded by Yvon Chouinard in 1972, is a member of several environmental movements.

Yvon Chouinard (seated), Patagonia's founder, at his home in Ventura, California. The company's flex-time policy allows for surfing when the waves are good.
Courtesy of Tierney Gearon

as we kept the profits in the company. In many ways the growth was exciting. We were never bored. New employees, including those in the lowest-paid positions in retail stores or the warehouse, could rise rapidly to better-paying jobs. For a few positions we conducted searches — and we could claim our pick of the litter within both the apparel and outdoor industries. But most of the new employees we hired came through a well-rooted and fast-growing grapevine.

Despite our own growth at Patagonia, we were able, in many ways, to   5 keep alive our cultural values. We still came to work on the balls of our feet. People ran or surfed at lunch, or played volleyball in the sandpit at the back of the building.

In growing the business, however, we had nearly outgrown our natural niche, the specialty outdoor market. By the late 1980s the company was expanding at a rate that, if sustained, would have made us a billion-dollar company in a decade.

Can you have it all? The question haunted me as Patagonia evolved. Another problem would come to haunt me more — the deterioration of the natural world. I saw that deterioration first with my own eyes, when I returned to climb or surf or fish in places I knew, like Nepal, Africa or

Polynesia, and saw what had happened in the few years since I'd last been there.

In Africa, forests and grassland were disappearing as the population grew. Global warming was melting glaciers that had been part of the continent's climbing history. The emergence of AIDS and Ebola coincided with the clear-cutting of forests and the wholesale pursuit of bush meat, such as infected chimpanzees.

On a kayaking trip to the Russian Far East, before the collapse of the old Soviet Union, I found that the Russians had destroyed much of their country trying to keep up with the U.S. in their arms race.

Closer to home, I saw the relentless paving over of Southern   10 California's remaining coastline and hillsides. In Wyoming, where I spent summers for 30 years, I saw fewer wild animals each year, caught smaller fish, and suffered through weeks of debilitating, record-setting 90-degree heat. But most environmental devastation the eye doesn't see. I learned more by reading about the rapid loss of topsoil and groundwater, about the clear-cutting of tropical forests and the growing list of endangered plant and animal and bird species, and of people in the once pristine Arctic who are now being warned not to eat the local mammals and fish because of toxins from industrial nations.

At the same time, at Patagonia, we slowly became aware that uphill battles fought by small, dedicated groups of people to save patches of habitat could yield significant results. We began to make regular donations to smaller groups working to save or restore habitat, rather than giving the money to large NGOs° with big staffs, overheads and corporate connections. In 1986, we committed to donate 10 percent of profits each year to these groups. We later upped the ante to 1 percent of sales, or 10 percent of pre-tax profits, whichever was greater. We have kept to that commitment every year, boom or bust.

We also realized that in addition to addressing these external crises, we had to look within the company and reduce our own role as a corporate polluter. We began recycling paper waste in 1984 and conducted an intensive search for a source of paper with a higher percentage of recycled content for our catalog. In 1990, we were the first catalog in the U.S. to use recycled paper. In that first year, switching to recycled paper saved 3,500,000 kilowatt hours of electricity, 6,000,000 gallons of water, kept 52,000 pounds of pollutants out of the air and 1,560 cubic yards of solid waste out of landfills, and it prevented 14,500 trees from being felled. We also researched and pioneered the use of recycled, reused and less toxic

NGOs: nongovernmental organizations.

materials in our construction and remodeling projects. We worked with Wellman and Malden Mills to develop recycled polyester for use in our PCP® Synchilla fleece.

All the while we continued to grow. We experienced so much success on so many fronts during the late 1980s that we began to believe the expansion would never end. And we planned to just keep going.

Then, in 1991, after all those years of 30 percent to 50 percent compound annual growth and trying to have it all, Patagonia hit the wall. The United States had entered a recession, and the growth we had always planned on, and bought inventory for, stopped.

The crisis soon deepened. Our primary lender was itself in financial 15 trouble, and it sharply reduced our credit line. To bring our borrowing within the new limits we had to drastically reduce spending.

Our own company had exceeded its resources and limitations; we had become dependent, like the world economy, on growth we could not sustain. But as a small company, we couldn't ignore the problem and wish it away. We were forced to rethink our priorities and institute new practices. We had to start breaking the rules.

"You have to know your strengths and limitations and live within your means. The same is true for a business."

I took a dozen of our top managers to Argentina, to the windswept mountains of the real Patagonia, for a walkabout. In the course of roaming around those wild lands, we asked ourselves why we were in business and what kind of business we wanted Patagonia to be. A billion-dollar company? Okay, but not if it meant we had to make products we couldn't be proud of. And we discussed what we could do to help stem the environmental harm we caused as a company. We talked about the values we had in common, and the shared culture that had brought everyone to Patagonia, Inc., and not another company.

We knew that uncontrolled growth put at risk the values that had made the company succeed so far. Those values couldn't be expressed in a how-to operations manual offering pat answers. We needed philosophical and inspirational guides to make sure we always asked the right questions and found the right answers.

While our managers debated what steps to take to address the sales and cash-flow crisis, I began to lead week-long employee seminars in what we called Philosophies. We'd take a busload at a time to places like Yosemite or the Marin Headlands above San Francisco, camp out, and gather under the trees to talk. The goal was to teach every employee in the company our business and environmental ethics and values.

I realize now that what I was trying to do was to instill in my company, 20
at a critical time, lessons that I had already learned as an individual—and
as a climber, surfer, kayaker and fly fisherman. I had always tried to live
my life fairly simply and by 1991, knowing what I knew about the state
of the environment, I had begun to eat lower on the food chain and
reduce my consumption of material goods. Doing risk sports had taught
me another important lesson: never exceed your limits. You push the
envelope and you live for those moments when you're right on the edge,
but you don't go over. You have to be true to yourself; you have to know
your strengths and limitations and live within your means. The same is
true for a business. The sooner a company tries to be what it is not, the
sooner it tries to "have it all," the sooner it will die.

Understanding the Text

1. Who is Chouinard and how did he develop his business?
2. What did Patagonia do to help the environment?
3. What happened to the company when the country went into recession?

Reflection and Response

4. What are some ways Patagonia could continue to keep its business sustainable?
5. What are some things Chouinard learned from his life experiences? How did his experiences as an outdoorsman and athlete inform his business philosophy?
6. Why would it be financially savvy for an outdoor clothing and equipment company (such as Patagonia) to devote so much attention to sustainability? Is the company's philosophy good business, good ethics, or both?

Making Connections

7. Spend some time browsing Patagonia's website, particularly those sections addressing the company's sustainability and environmental impact. What current efforts toward sustainability are they undertaking?
8. Research another company that makes outdoor clothing or equipment. What could that company learn about sustainability from Patagonia? Conversely, what could Patagonia learn from that company?

Sentence Guides for Academic Writers

Being a college student means being a college writer. No matter what field you are studying, your instructors will ask you to make sense of what you are learning through writing. When you work on writing assignments in college, you are, in most cases, being asked to write for an academic audience.

Writing academically means thinking academically — asking a lot of questions, digging into the ideas of others, and entering into scholarly debates and academic conversations. As a college writer, you will be asked to read different kinds of texts; understand and evaluate authors' ideas, arguments, and methods; and contribute your own ideas. In this way, you present yourself as a participant in an academic conversation.

What does it mean to be part of an *academic conversation*? Well, think of it this way: You and your friends may have an ongoing debate about the best film trilogy of all time. During your conversations with one another, you analyze the details of the films, introduce points you want your friends to consider, listen to their ideas, and perhaps cite what the critics have said about a particular trilogy. This kind of conversation is not unlike what happens among scholars in academic writing — except they could be debating the best public policy for a social problem or the most promising new theory in treating disease.

If you are uncertain about what academic writing *sounds like* or if you're not sure you're any good at it, this booklet offers guidance for you at the sentence level. It helps answer questions such as these:

How can I present the ideas of others in a way that demonstrates my understanding of the debate?

How can I agree with someone, but add a new idea?

How can I disagree with a scholar without seeming, well, rude?

How can I make clear in my writing which ideas are mine and which ideas are someone else's?

The following sections offer sentence guides for you to use and adapt to your own writing situations. As in all writing that you do, you will have to think about your purpose (reason for writing) and your audience (readers) before knowing which guides will be most appropriate for a particular piece of writing or for a certain part of your essay.

The guides are organized to help you present background information, the views and claims of others, and your own views and claims — all in the context of your purpose and audience.

Academic Writers Present Information and Others' Views

When you write in academic situations, you may be asked to spend some time giving background information for or setting a context for your main idea or argument. This often requires you to present or summarize what is known or what has already been said in relation to the question you are asking in your writing.

SG1   Presenting What Is Known or Assumed

When you write, you will find that you occasionally need to present something that is known, such as a specific fact or a statistic. The following structures are useful when you are providing background information.

As we know from history, _____ .

X has shown that _____ .

Research by X and Y suggests that _____ .

According to X, _____ percent of _____ are/favor _____ .

In other situations, you may have the need to present information that is assumed or that is conventional wisdom.

People often believe that _____ .

Conventional wisdom leads us to believe _____ .

Many Americans share the idea that _____ .

_____ is a widely held belief.

In order to challenge an assumption or a widely held belief, you have to acknowledge it first. Doing so lets your readers believe that you are placing your ideas in an appropriate context.

Although many people are led to believe X, there is significant benefit to considering the merits of Y.

College students tend to believe that _____ when, in fact, the opposite is much more likely the case.

SG2   Presenting Others' Views

As a writer, you build your own *ethos*, or credibility, by being able to fairly and accurately represent the views of others. As an academic writer, you will be expected to demonstrate your understanding of a text by summarizing the views or arguments of its author(s). To do so, you will use language such as the following.

X argues that _____ .

X emphasizes the need for _____ .

In this important article, X and Y claim _____ .

X endorses _____ because _____ .

X and Y have recently criticized the idea that _____.

_____, according to X, is the most critical cause of _____.

Although you will create your own variations of these sentences as you draft and revise, the guides can be useful tools for thinking through how best to present another writer's claim or finding clearly and concisely.

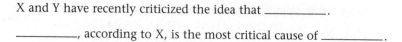 Presenting Direct Quotations

When the exact words of a source are important for accuracy, authority, emphasis, or flavor, you will want to use a direct quotation. Ordinarily, you will present direct quotations with language of your own that suggests how you are using the source.

X characterizes the problem this way: ". . ."

According to X, _____ is defined as ". . ."

". . . ," explains X.

X argues strongly in favor of the policy, pointing out that ". . ."

Note: You will generally cite direct quotations according to the documentation style your readers expect. MLA style, often used in English and in other humanities courses, recommends using the author name paired with a page number, if there is one. APA style, used in most social sciences, requires the year of publication generally after the mention of the source, with page numbers after the quoted material. In *Chicago* style, used in history and in some humanities courses, writers use superscript numbers (like this[6]) to refer readers to footnotes or endnotes. In-text citations, like the ones shown below, refer readers to entries in the works cited or reference list.

MLA Lazarín argues that our overreliance on testing in K-12 schools "does not put students first" (20).

APA Lazarín (2014) argues that our overreliance on testing in K-12 schools "does not put students first." (p. 20)

Chicago Lazarín argues that our overreliance on testing in K-12 schools "does not put students first."[6]

Many writers use direct quotations to advance an argument of their own:

> Standardized testing makes it easier for administrators to measure student performance, but it may not be the best way to measure it. Too much testing wears students out and communicates the idea that recall is the most important skill we want them to develop. Even education policy advisor Melissa Lazarín argues that our overreliance on testing in K-12 schools "does not put students first" (20).

Student writer's idea

Source's idea

SG4   Presenting Alternative Views

Most debates, whether they are scholarly or popular, are complex—often with more than two sides to an issue. Sometimes you will have to synthesize the views of multiple participants in the debate before you introduce your own ideas.

On the one hand, X reports that _____, but on the other hand, Y insists that _____.

Even though X endorses the policy, Y refers to it as "..."

X, however, isn't convinced and instead argues _____.

X and Y have supported the theory in the past, but new research by Z suggests that _____.

Academic Writers Present Their Own Views

When you write for an academic audience, you will indeed have to demonstrate that you are familiar with the views of others who are asking the same kinds of questions as you are. Much writing that is done for academic purposes asks you to put your arguments in the context of existing arguments—in a way asking you to connect the known to the new.

When you are asked to write a summary or an informative text, your own views and arguments are generally not called for. However, much of the writing you will be assigned to do in college asks you to take a persuasive stance and present a reasoned argument—at times in response to a single text, and at other times in response to multiple texts.

SG5 Presenting Your Own Views: Agreement and Extension

Sometimes you agree with the author of a source.

X's argument is convincing because _____.

Because X's approach is so _____, it is the best way to _____.

X makes an important point when she says _____.

Other times you find you agree with the author of a source, but you want to extend the point or go a bit deeper in your own investigation. In a way, you acknowledge the source for getting you so far in the conversation, but then you move the conversation along with a related comment or finding.

X's proposal for _____ is indeed worth considering. Going one step further, _____.

X makes the claim that _____. By extension, isn't it also true, then, that _____?

_____ has been adequately explained by X. Now, let's move beyond that idea and ask whether _____.

SG6 Presenting Your Own Views: Queries and Skepticism

You may be intimidated when you're asked to talk back to a source, especially if the source is a well-known scholar or expert or even just a frequent voice in a particular debate. College-level writing asks you to be skeptical, however, and approach academic questions with the mind of an investigator. It is OK to doubt, to question, to challenge—because the end result is often new knowledge or new understanding about a subject.

Couldn't it also be argued that _____?

But is everyone willing to agree that this is the case?

While X insists that _____ is so, he is perhaps asking the wrong question to begin with.

The claims that X and Y have made, while intelligent and well-meaning, leave many unconvinced because they have failed to consider _____.

A Note about Using First Person "I"

Some disciplines look favorably upon the use of the first person "I" in academic writing. Others do not and instead stick to using third person. If you are given a writing assignment for a class, you are better off asking your instructor what he or she prefers or reading through any samples given than *guessing* what might be expected.

First person (*I, me, my, we, us, our*)

I question Heddinger's methods and small sample size.

Harnessing children's technology obsession in the classroom is, I believe, the key to improving learning.

Lanza's interpretation focuses on circle imagery as symbolic of the family; my analysis leads me in a different direction entirely.

We would, in fact, benefit from looser laws about farming on our personal property.

Third person (names and other nouns)

Heddinger's methods and small sample size are questionable.

Harnessing children's technology obsession in the classroom is the key to improving learning.

Lanza's interpretation focuses on circle imagery as symbolic of the family; other readers' analyses may point in a different direction entirely.

Many Americans would, in fact, benefit from looser laws about farming on personal property.

You may feel as if not being able to use "I" in an essay in which you present your ideas about a topic is unfair or will lead to weaker statements. Know that you can make a strong argument even if you write in the third person. Third person writing allows you to sound more assertive, credible, and academic.

 Presenting Your Own Views: Disagreement or Correction

You may find that at times the only response you have to a text or to an author is complete disagreement.

X's claims about _____ are completely misguided.

X presents a long metaphor comparing _____ to _____; in the end, the comparison is unconvincing because _____.

It can be tempting to disregard a source completely if you detect a piece of information that strikes you as false or that you know to be untrue.

Although X reports that _____, recent studies indicate that is not the case.

While X and Y insist that is _____ so, an examination of their figures shows that they have made an important miscalculation.

SG8   Presenting and Countering Objections to Your Argument

Effective college writers know that their arguments are stronger when they can anticipate objections that others might make.

Some will object to this proposal on the grounds that _____.

Not everyone will embrace _____; they may argue instead that _____.

Countering, or responding to, opposing voices fairly and respectfully strengthens your writing and your *ethos*, or credibility.

X and Y might contend that this interpretation is faulty; however, _____.

Most _____ believe that there is too much risk in this approach. But what they have failed to take into consideration is _____.

Academic Writers Persuade by Putting It All Together

Readers of academic writing often want to know what's at stake in a particular debate or text. Aside from crafting individual sentences, you must, of course, keep the bigger picture in mind as you attempt to persuade, inform, evaluate, or review.

SG9   Presenting Stakeholders

When you write, you may be doing so as a member of a group affected by the research conversation you have entered. For example, you may be among the thousands of students in your state whose level of debt may change as a result of new laws about financing a college education. In this case, you are a *stakeholder* in the matter. In other words, you have an interest in the matter as a person who could be impacted by the outcome of a decision. On the other hand, you may be writing as an investigator of a topic that interests you but that you aren't directly connected with. You may be persuading your audience on behalf of a group of interested stakeholders—a group of which you yourself are not a member.

You can give your writing some teeth if you make it clear who is being affected by the discussion of the issue and the decisions that have or will be made about the issue. The groups of stakeholders are highlighted in the following sentences.

> Viewers of Kurosawa's films may not agree with X that _____.

> The research will come as a surprise to parents of children with Type 1 diabetes.

> X's claims have the power to offend potentially every low-wage earner in the state.

> Marathoners might want to reconsider their training regimen if stories such as those told by X and Y are validated by the medical community.

SG10   Presenting the "So What"

For readers to be motivated to read your writing, they have to feel as if you're either addressing something that matters to them or addressing something that matters very much to you or that should matter to us all. Good academic writing often hooks readers with a sense of urgency—a serious response to a reader's "So what?"

> Having a frank discussion about _____ now will put us in a far better position to deal with _____ in the future. If we are unwilling or unable to do so, we risk _____.

> Such a breakthrough will affect _____ in three significant ways.

It is easy to believe that the stakes aren't high enough to be alarming; in fact, _____ will be affected by _____.

Widespread disapproval of and censorship of such fiction/films/art will mean _____ for us in the future. Culture should represent _____.

_____ could bring about unprecedented opportunities for _____ to participate in _____, something never seen before.

New experimentation in _____ could allow scientists to investigate _____ in ways they couldn't have imagined _____ years ago.

SG11 Presenting the Players and Positions in a Debate

Some disciplines ask writers to compose a review of the literature as a part of a larger project—or sometimes as a freestanding assignment. In a review of the literature, the writer sets forth a research question, summarizes the key sources that have addressed the question, puts the current research in the context of other voices in the research conversation, and identifies any gaps in the research.

Writing that presents a debate, its players, and their positions can often be lengthy. What follows, however, can give you the sense of the flow of ideas and turns in such a piece of writing.

_____ affects more than 30% of children in America, and signs point to a worsening situation in years to come because of A, B, and C. Solutions to the problem have eluded even the sharpest policy minds and brightest researchers. In an important 2003 study, W found that _____, which pointed to more problems than solutions. [. . .] Research by X and Y made strides in our understanding of _____ but still didn't offer specific strategies for children and families struggling to _____. [. . .] When Z rejected both the methods and the findings of X and Y, arguing that _____, policy makers and health-care experts were optimistic. [. . .] Too much discussion of _____, however, and too little discussion of _____, may lead us to solutions that are ultimately too expensive to sustain.

Student writer states the problem.

Student writer summarizes the views of others on the topic.

Student writer presents her view in the context of current research.

Appendix: Verbs Matter

Using a variety of verbs in your sentences can add strength and clarity as you present others' views and your own views.

When you want to present a view fairly neutrally

acknowledges	observes
adds	points out
admits	reports
comments	suggest
contends	writes
notes	

X points out that the plan had unintended outcomes.

When you want to present a stronger view

argues	emphasizes
asserts	insists
declares	

Y argues in favor of a ban on _____; but Z insists the plan is misguided.

When you want to show agreement

agrees
confirms
endorses

An endorsement of X's position is smart for a number of reasons.

When you want to show contrast or disagreement

compares	refutes
denies	rejects
disputes	

The town must come together and reject X's claims that _____ is in the best interest of the citizens.

When you want to anticipate an objection

admits
acknowledges
concedes

Y admits that closer study of _____, with a much larger sample, is necessary for _____.

Acknowledgments *(continued from page iv)*

Index of Authors and Titles